Foundations of Human Resource Development

Richard A. Swanson
Elwood F. Holton III

Volume 1 of 2

16

EasyRead Large

Copyright Page from the Original Book

Foundations of Human Resource Development

Berrett-Koehler Publishers, Inc.
235 Montgomery Street, Suite 650
San Francisco, California 94104-2916
Tel: (415) 288-0260, Fax: (415) 362-2512
www.bkconnection.com

BK

Ordering information for print editions
Quantity sales. Special discounts are available on quantity purchases by corporations, associations, and others. For details, contact the "Special Sales Department" at the Berrett-Koehler
address above.
Individual sales. Berrett-Koehler publications are available through most bookstores. They can
also be ordered directly from Berrett-Koehler: Tel: (800) 929-2929; Fax: (802) 864-7626;
www.bkconnection.com
Orders for college textbook/course adoption use. Please contact Berrett-Koehler: Tel: (800)
929-2929; Fax: (802) 864-7626.
Orders by U.S. trade bookstores and wholesalers. Please contact Ingram Publisher Services,
Tel: (800) 509-4887; Fax: (800) 838-1149; E-mail: customer.service@ingrampublisher
services.com; or visit www.ingrampublisherservices.com/Ordering for details about electronic
ordering.

Berrett-Koehler and the BK logo are registered trademarks of Berrett-Koehler Publishers, Inc.

Second Edition
Hardcover print edition ISBN 978-1-57675-496-2
PDF e-book ISBN 978-1-57675-803-8

2009-1

Book production management: Michael Bass Associates
Cover design: Richard Adelson

ReadHowYouWant partners with publishers to provide books for ALL Kinds of Readers. For more information about Becoming A **RHYW** Registered Reader and to find more titles in your preferred format, visit:

www.readhowyouwant.com

TABLE OF CONTENTS

A publication in the Berrett-Koehler Organizational Performance Series

Richard A. Swanson and Barbara L. Swanson, Series Editors

Note: Instructors and readers are encouraged to go to http://textbookresources.net and http://richardswanson.com to access resources for this and other books in this series.

Dedicated to the vision of leading the human resource development profession through research.

List of Figures

Preface

Human resource development (HRD) is a very large field of practice and a relatively young academic discipline. Furthermore, HRD is deeply concerned with developing and unleashing expertise and with the dynamic issues of individual and organizational change. Such a profession requires a complete and thoughtful foundational text. That is the purpose of this book.

This book is intended to serve the needs of both practitioners and academics by adding clarity to their professional journeys. While the authors and contributors have personal preferences as to the purpose and primary means of doing HRD work, the attempt has been to provide a fair review of the range of major views that exist in the profession.

This is not a manual of practices book. Many books in HRD outline their version of "best practices" but do not probe the foundations of practice. This book does the opposite. For the most part, it defines the fundamentals while providing an overview of practice. Readers who seek a deeper understanding of theory and models that support best practice; who seek to understand the history and philosophies of HRD; who want to think more deeply about learning, performance, and change; and who prefer to be reflective about their practice rather than blindly following the latest formulas will find this book a refreshing and thoughtful explication of the field.

Because the discipline of HRD is young, there has been relatively little work to define the foundations of the field. The authors have struggled with this book to draw boundaries without building walls. Thus, this book continues the conversation about foundations. In a discipline as young as HRD, anything close to a consensus about its foundations will be a work in progress for many years.

This book is directed toward several audiences. First, it is designed for university courses in HRD. I argue that every HRD academic program needs a course that teaches field foundations. Second, HRD researchers will find the book a thought-provoking and useful guide to core research issues. Third, it is written for reflective practitioners who actively seek to lead the field as it grows and matures. Finally, almost every practitioner will find parts of the book that will add depth to their practice.

The book's twenty-one chapters are organized into seven parts. The first part, "Introduction to Human Resource Development," establishes a basic understanding of HRD; the general HRD model and the process it relies on to do its work; and the history of HRD. Part

Two, "Theory and Philosophy in Human Resource Development," provides the critical theoretical and philosophical foundations of HRD. Both of these perspectives have generally been missing among HRD professionals and are believed to be essential for understanding and advancing the field. Part Three, "Perspectives of Human Resource Development," explores the learning and performance paradigms of HRD and associated models within each. This section attempts to clarify the learning-performance perspectives and their logical connection.

Part Four, "Developing Expertise through Training and Development," captures the essence of the training and development component of HRD as well as the nature of expertise. Illustrations of training and development practice employed in host organizations are presented along with variations in core thinking, processes, interventions, and tools. Part Five, "Unleashing Expertise through Organization Development," describes the essence of the organization development component of HRD as well as the nature of the change process. This section also presents examples of organization development as well as variations in core thinking, processes, interventions, and tools.

Part Six, "Advancing Human Resource Development," focuses on HRD's role in the high-level organizational and system-level issues of strategy, accountability, and HRD policy and planning. Part Seven, "Human Resource Development into the Future," addresses such contemporary issues as globalization, technology, and the identification of the challenges to HRD.

My sincere thanks go to the many HRD scholars throughout the world and their good work. They have made this book possible. While I am responsible for the updates in this second edition, a large number of the excellent ideas and writing contributions by Elwood F. Holton III have been carried forward from the first edition. Ed is known by all in the profession as a first-class HRD scholar and a person who has given much to the discipline.

In addition, I want to thank several HRD colleagues for providing in this second edition contributions related to their specializations: Alexandre Ardichvili, Theo J. Bastiaens, Thomas J. Chermack, Richard W. Herling, K. Peter Kuchinke, Sharon S. Naquin, Wendy E.A. Ruona, Richard J. Torraco, Greg G. Wang, and Karen E. Watkins. Their perspectives and voices add an important dimension to the book. Four outstanding scholars—Kenneth R. Bartlett, Susan A. Lynham, Walter R. Nord, and Barbara L. Swanson—provided important critical and constructive reviews of the book.

Finally, I would like to acknowledge the organizational partners that provided support for this second edition. I am grateful for the support I received from Berrett-Koehler Publishers and the University of Texas at Tyler.

Richard A. Swanson
http://richardswanson.com

PART ONE

Introduction to Human Resource Development

This first section provides an overview of Human Resource Development as a field of practice, the basics it relies on to do its work, and the history of the discipline.

CHAPTERS

1 Human Resource Development as a Professional Field of Practice
2 Basics of Human Resource Development
3 History of Human Resource Development

CHAPTER1

Human Resource Development as a Professional Field of Practice

CHAPTER OUTLINE

Introduction
Purpose of HRD
Definition of HRD
- Training and Development for New Technology
- Organization Development for a Growing Company

Origins of HRD
HRD Context
HRD Core Beliefs
HRD as a Discipline and a Professional Field of Practice
Conclusion
Reflection Questions

INTRODUCTION

Human resource development (HRD) is a relatively young academic discipline but an old and well-established field of practice. The idea of human beings purposefully developing themselves in order to improve the conditions in which they live seems almost part of human nature. HRD theory and practice are deeply rooted in this developing and advancing perspective.

This first chapter serves to highlight the purpose, definition, origins, context, and core beliefs of HRD. These highlights provide an initial understanding of HRD and functions as an advanced organizer for the book. The chapters that follow fully explore the depth and range of thinking within the theory and practice of HRD.

PURPOSE OF HRD

HRD is about adult human beings functioning in productive systems. The purpose of HRD is to focus on the resource that humans bring to the success equation—both personal success and organizational system success. The two core threads of HRD are (1) individual and organizational learning, and (2) individual and organizational performance (Ruona, 2000; Swanson, 1996a; Watkins and Marsick, 1996).

Although some view learning and performance as alternatives or rivals, most see them as partners in a formula for success. Thus, assessment of HRD successes or results can be categorized into the broad domains of learning and performance. In all cases, the intent is improvement.

DEFINITION OF HRD

Figure 1.1 Human Resource Development: Definitions, Components, Applications, and Contexts Source: Swanson, 2008.

HRD has numerous definitions. Throughout the book, we continually reflect on alternative views of HRD to expose readers to the range of thinking in the profession. The definition put forth is this book is as follows:

HRD is a process of developing and unleashing expertise for the purpose of improving individual, team, work process, and organizational system performance.

HRD efforts typically take place under the additional banners of "training and development" and "organization development" as well as numerous other titles. Figure 1.1 illustrates the definition and scope of HRD in such realms as performance improvement, organizational learning, career development, and management and leadership development (Swanson, 2008).

The alternative definitions of HRD that have been presented over the years mark the boundaries of the profession. Figure 1.2 (adapted from Weinberger, 1998) provides a historical report of the range of HRD definitions found in the literature.

You can think of HRD in more than one way. Our preferred definition describes HRD as a process. Using the process perspective, HRD can be thought of as both a system and a journey. This perspective does not inform us as to who does HRD or where it resides in the organization. At the definitional level, it is useful to think about HRD as a process open to engaging different people at different times and located in different places inside and outside the host organization.

Another way to talk about HRD is to refer to it as a department, function, and job. It can be thought of as an HRD department or division in a particular organization with people working as HRD managers, specialists, and so forth.

Furthermore, these people work in spaces called HRD centers, training rooms, retreat centers, and corporate universities. HRD can also be identified in terms of the context and content it supports—for example, training and organization development in insurance sales. Even under these department, function, job, and physical space titles, HRD can also be defined as a process.

Two major realms of practice take place within HRD. One is organization development (OD); the other is training and development (T&D). As their names imply, OD focuses at the organization level and connects with individuals, while T&D focuses on individuals and connects with the organization. The HRD literature regularly presents a wide variety of case studies from practice. The following are examples of T&D and OD practice.

Training and Development for New Technology

Plant modernization and technology implementation are strategies corporations use for productivity and quality improvement. Such efforts typically have parallel T&D efforts in planning and carrying out such change. Midwest Steel Corporation, for example, utilized systematically developed structured training instead of an abbreviated vendor-provided overview presentation. The consequences were too great for Midwest Steel to be so casual about the installation of the new steelmaking technology. The T&D staff carried out a detailed analysis of the expertise required to operate the new ladle preheaters. This analysis served as the basis for the training program development, delivery, and evaluation of operator expertise. Furthermore, following the implementation of the T&D program, a cost-benefit analysis that compared production gains to training costs demonstrated a short-term 135 percent return on investment. Continued use of the structured training program resulted in even higher financial returns for the corporation (Martelli, 1998).

Figure 1.2 Human Resource Development Definitions over Time

AUTHOR	DEFINITION	KEY COMPONENTS	UNDERLYING THEORIES
Harbison and Myers (1964)	Human resource development is the process of increasing the knowledge, the skills, and the capacities of all the people in the society (p.2).	High-level manpower and its full utilization	Development economics

AUTHOR	DEFINITION	KEY COMPO-NENTS	UNDERLYING THEORIES
Nadler (1970)	HRD is a series of organized activities conducted within a specified time and designed to produce behavioral change (p.3).	Behavioral change; adult learning	Psychology
Jones (1981)	HRD is a systematic expansion of people's work-related abilities, focused on the attainment of both organization and personal goals (p.188).	Performance, organizational, and personal goals	Philosophical; systems; psychology; economics
Chalofsky and Lincoln, (1983)	Discipline of HRD is the study of how individuals and groups in organizations change through learning.	Adult learning	Psychology

AUTHOR	DEFINITION	KEY COMPONENTS	UNDERLYING THEORIES
Swanson (1987)	HRD is a process of improving an organization's performance through the capabilities of its personnel. HRD includes activities dealing with work design, aptitude, expertise and motivation.	Organizational performance	Economics; psychology; systems
Smith, R. (1988)	HRD consists of programs and activities, direct and indirect, instructional and/or individual that positively affect the development of the individual and the productivity and profit of the organization (p.1).	Training and development; organizational performance	Economics; systems; psychology

AUTHOR	DEFINITION	KEY COMPONENTS	UNDERLYING THEORIES
Watkins (1989)	HRD is the field of study and practice responsible for the fostering of a long-term, work-related learning capacity at the individual, group, and organizational level of organizations. As such, it includes—but is not limited to—training, career development, and organizational development (p.427).	Learning capacity; training and development; career development; organizational development	Psychology; systems; economics; performance improvement
McLagan (1989)	HRD is the integrated use of training and development, career development and organizational development to improve individual and organizational effectiveness (p.7).	Training and development; career development; organizational development	Psychology; systems; economics

AUTHOR	DEFINITION	KEY COMPONENTS	UNDERLYING THEORIES
Gilley and England (1989)	HRD is organized learning activities arranged within an organization to improve performance and/or personal growth for the purpose of improving the job, the individual, and/or the organization (p.5).	Learning activities; performance improvement	Psychology; systems; economics; performance improvement
Nadler and Nadler (1970)	HRD is organized learning experiences provided by employees within a specified period of time to bring about the possibility of performance improvement and/or personal growth (p.6).	Learning and performance improvement	Performance improvement; psychology

AUTHOR	DEFINITION	KEY COMPONENTS	UNDERLYING THEORIES
Smith (1990)	HRD is the process of determining the optimum methods of developing and improving the human resources of an organization and the systematic improvement of the performance and productivity of employees through training, education and development and leadership for the mutual attainment of organizational and personal goals (p.16).	Performance improvement	Performance improvement; systems; psychology; economics

AUTHOR	DEFINITION	KEY COMPONENTS	UNDERLYING THEORIES
Chalofsky (1992)	HRD is the study and practice of increasing the learning capacity of individuals, groups, collectives and organizations through the development and application of learning-based interventions for the purpose of optimizing human and organizational growth and effectiveness (p.179).	Learning capacity; performance improvement	Systems; psychology; human performance

AUTHOR	DEFINITION	KEY COMPONENTS	UNDERLYING THEORIES
Marsick and Watkins (1994)	HRD as a combination of training, career development, and organizational development offers the theoretical integration needed to envision a learning organization, but it must also be positioned to act strategically throughout the organization (p.355).	Training and development; career development; organizational development; learning organization	Human performance; organizational performance; systems; economics; psychology
Swanson (1995)	HRD is a process of developing and unleashing human expertise through organization development and personnel training and development for the purpose of improving performance (p.208).	Training and development; organization development; performance improvement at the organization, work process, and individual levels	Systems; economics; psychology

AUTHOR	DEFINITION	KEY COMPO-NENTS	UNDERLYING THEORIES
McLean and McLean (2001)	HRD is any process or activity that, either initially or over the long term, has the potential to develop adults' work-based knowledge, expertise, productivity, and satisfaction, whether for personal or group/team gain, or for the benefit of an organization, community, nation, or, ultimately, the whole of humanity (p.313).		Development economics; psychology

AUTHOR	DEFINITION	KEY COMPONENTS	UNDERLYING THEORIES
Swanson (2009)	HRD is a process of developing and unleashing expertise for the purpose of improving organizational system, work process, team, and individual performance. HRD efforts in organizations often take place under the additional banners of training and development, organization development, performance improvement, organizational learning, career management, leadership development, etc.	Developing expertise; unleashing expertise; performance improvement	Systems; economics; psychology

Organization Development for a Growing Company

A young and quickly growing company found itself working with systems and expertise inadequate for its present volume of business. The problems of creating and improving work systems were tackled head-on with the use of an organization development consultant. The consultant engaged employee groups in the following five-phase process: (1) building a new foundation, (2) high-involvement strategic planning, (3) assessment of people systems and technical systems, (4) implementing the new organization design, and (5) reflection, assessment, and next steps. The combination of learning, team planning and decision making, and employee involvement in implementing changes proved successful in advancing the company and creating a sense of employee ownership (Hardt, 1998).

ORIGINS OF HRD

It is easy to logically connect the origins of HRD to the history of humankind and the training required to survive or advance. While HRD is a relatively new term, training—the largest component of HRD—can be tracked back through the evolution of the human race. Chapter 3, on HRD's history, provides a long-range view of the profession. For now, it is important to recognize that contemporary HRD originated in the massive development effort that took place in the United States during

World War II. Under the name of the "Training within Industry" project (Dooley, 1945), this massive development effort gave birth to (1) systematic performance-based training, (2) improvement of work processes, and (3) the improvement of human relations in the workplace—or contemporary HRD, as it began being called in the 1970s.

HRD CONTEXT

HRD almost always functions within the context of a host organization. The organization can be a corporation, business, industry, government agency, or nonprofit organization—large or small. The host organization is a system with mission-driven goals and outputs. In an international context, the host organization for HRD can be a nation. Strategic investment in HRD at this level can range from maintaining high-level national workforce competitiveness to fundamentally elevating a nation out of poverty and disarray.

The host organization may also be a multinational or global organization with operations in many continents and many nations. Such complex organizations can both affect the structure of HRD and be the focus of HRD work. HRD has traditionally been sensitive to culture within an organization and between organizations. Thus, making the transition to global issues has been relatively easy for HRD.

HRD can be thought of as a subsystem that functions within the larger host system for the purpose of advancing, supporting, harmonizing, and at times leading the host system. Take, for example, a company that produces and sells cars. Responsible HRD would be ever vigilant to this primary focus of the company and see itself as supporting, shaping, or leading the various elements of the complex automobile organizational system in which it functions. Much more will be said about this contextual reality of HRD in the following chapters. For now, it is important to think about the great variations in how HRD fits into any one organization, as well as the many varieties of organizations that exist in society. This complexity is compounded by the cultural variations in which HRD functions from region to region and nation to nation. While some find the milieu baffling, for others it is an interesting and exciting profession! For those who find HRD baffling and for those new to the profession, acquiring a solid orientation to the theory and practice of HRD as presented in this book will prove a sound investment.

HRD CORE BELIEFS

HRD professionals, functioning as individuals or work groups, rarely reveal their core beliefs. This is not to say that they do not have core beliefs. The reality is that most HRD professionals are busy, action-oriented people who have not taken the time to articulate their beliefs. Yet almost all decisions and actions on the part of HRD professionals are fundamentally influenced by subconscious core beliefs.

The idea of core beliefs is discussed in a number of places throughout this book. To describe what motivates and frames the HRD profession, we reveal for now one set of HRD core beliefs and a brief interpretation of each.

1. *Organizations are human-made entities that rely on human expertise to establish and achieve their goals.* This belief acknowledges that organizations are changeable and vulnerable. Organizations have been created by humankind and can soar or crumble, and HRD is intricately connected to the fate of any organization

2. *Human expertise is developed and maximized through HRD processes and should be applied for the mutual long-term and/or short-term benefits of the sponsoring organization and the individuals involved.* HRD professionals have powerful tools available

to get others to think, accept, and act. The ethical concern is that these tools can be used for negative, harmful, or exploitative purposes. As a profession, HRD seeks positive ends and fair outcomes.

3.   *HRD professionals are advocates of individual/group, work process, and organizational integrity.* HRD professionals typically have a very privileged position of accessing information that transcends the boundaries and levels of individuals, groups, work processes, and the organization. Access to rich information and the ability to see things that others may not also carries a responsibility. At times harmony is required, while at other times the blunt truth is required.

Gilley and Maycunich have set forth a set of principles to guide the profession. These principles can also be interpreted as a set of core beliefs. They contend that effective HRD practice

1.   integrates eclectic theoretical disciplines;
2.   is based on satisfying stakeholder needs and expectations;
3.   is responsive but responsible;
4.   uses evaluation as a continuous improvement process;
5.   is designed to improve organization effectiveness;

6. relies on relationship mapping to enhance operational efficiency;
7. is linked to the organization's strategic business goals and objectives;
8. is based on partnerships;
9. is results oriented;
10. assumes credibility as essential;
11. utilizes strategic planning to help the organization integrate vision, mission, strategy, and practice;
12. relies on the analysis process to identify priorities;
13. is based on purposeful and meaningful measurement; and
14. promotes diversity and equity in the workplace (Gilley and Maycunich, 2000, pp.79–99).

Most sets of principles are based on core beliefs that may or may not be made explicit. The pressures for stating principles of practice are greater than for stating overarching beliefs. Both have a place, however, and deserve serious attention by the profession.

HRD AS A DISCIPLINE AND A PROFESSIONAL FIELD OF PRACTICE

The HRD profession and its components are large and widely recognized. As with any applied field that exists in a large number and variety of organizations, HRD can take on a variety of names and roles. This can be confusing to those outside the profession and sometimes confusing to those within the profession. We take the position that this variation is not always bad. We see this book, and HRD, as embracing the thinking that underlies

- training,
- training and development,
- employee development,
- technical training,
- management development,
- executive and leadership development,
- human performance technology,
- performance improvement,
- organization development,
- career development,
- scenario planning,
- organizational learning,
- change management, and
- coaching.

We also see this book, and HRD, as overlapping with the theory and practice underlying other closely linked domains, including the following:

- Workforce planning
- Organizational and process effectiveness
- Quality improvement
- Strategic organizational planning

- Human resource management (HRM)
- Human resources (HR)

Probably the most apparent connection is with the organizational use of the term "human resources" (HR). HR can be conceived as having two major components—HRD and HRM. As an umbrella term, HR is often confused with HRM goals and activities such as hiring, compensation, and compliance issues. Even when HRD and HRM are managed under the HR title, their relative foci tend to be fairly discrete and keyed to the terms "development" versus "management."

CONCLUSION

The practice of HRD is dominated by positive intentions for improving the expertise of individuals, teams, work processes, and the overall organization. Most observers suggest that HRD evokes common-sense thinking and actions. This perspective has both positive and negative consequences. One positive consequence is the ease with which people are willing to contribute and participate in HRD processes. One negative consequence is that many people working in the field—both short-term and long-term—have little more than common sense to rely on. Having said this, we are reminded of the adage that "there is nothing common about common sense" (Deming, 1993). Common sense is the superficial assessment called face validity in the measurement and assessment profession. Something can appear to be valid but be dead wrong, while something can appear invalid and yet be right. For excellence in HRD, common sense is not enough.

The ultimate goal of this book is to reveal the underlying thinking and evidence supporting the HRD profession and its processes and tools, allowing HRD professionals to confidently accept and apply theories and tools that actually work, while at the same time ridding themselves of frivolous and invalid theories and practices. Foundational HRD theory and practice are the focus of this book.

REFLECTION QUESTIONS

1. Identify a definition of HRD presented in this chapter (see Figure 1.2) that makes the *most* sense to you and explain why.
2. Identify a definition of HRD presented in this chapter (see Figure 1.2) that makes the *least* sense to you and explain why.
3. Of the three HRD core beliefs presented in this chapter, which one is closest to your beliefs and why?
4. Based on the ideas presented in this chapter, what is it about HRD that interests you the most?

CHAPTER 2

Introduction to Human Resource Development Models and Processes

CHAPTER OUTLINE

Introduction
Points of Agreement
- Belief in Human Potential
- Goal of Improvement
- Problem-Solving Orientation
- Systems Thinking
HRD Worldviews
- HRD and Its environment
- The Learner Perspective
- The Organizational Perspective
- Global Context
HRD Process
- Process Phases of HRD
- Interplay between the Phases of the HRD Process
Threats to Excellent Practice
- Turning the HRD Process into an Event
- The Rate of Change
- Characteristics of the Key Players

Ethics and Integrity Standards
- Standards
Conclusion
Reflection Questions

INTRODUCTION

There is no single way to view Human Resource Development (HRD) or to go about the work of it. This chapter presents some of the basic underpinnings of HRD as a further orientation to its basic framework. The selection of HRD basics in this chapter is intended to illustrate and is not exhaustive. You should be prepared to expand on the ideas offered in this chapter as you progress through the book. These basics serve to orient readers who are new to HRD and also refresh the thinking of those already familiar with the profession.

POINTS OF AGREEMENT

As with any field of theory and practice, there are rival views and intense debates. This is especially true among scholars. One characterization of scholars holds that they spend 80 percent of their time debating about the 20 percent of a subject on which they disagree. Pointing out these differences is important, and this will take place throughout the book. Even more important is the need to point out areas of agreement, for it is here that the solid core of HRD theory and practice can be found. In contrast, areas of disagreement create the tension required for serious reflection and inquiry by scholars and reflective practitioners, ultimately yielding renewal and advancement.

HRD is an evolving discipline, which makes for exciting debates within the profession. It is important for those engaging in and listening to these debates not to lose sight of their points of agreement. Four overriding points of agreement include belief in human potential, the goal of improvement, a problem-solving orientation, and systems thinking.

Belief in Human Potential

"Some Humans ain't Human" is a song written and performed by John Prine (2005). While Prine explores the dark side of some of humanity through song, HRD professionals try to head off problems in organizations and explore the positive side. Pragmatically, not ideologically, HRD professionals advocate for human potential, human development opportunities, and fairness. HRD professionals are proud of their humanity and talk about humans and humaneness in ways that few other business professionals do (Chalofsky, 2000). Human resource *development* professionals are unique in this respect, even when compared to their human resource *management* counterparts.

Goal of Improvement

The idea of improvement overarches almost all HRD definitions, models, and practices. To improve means "to raise to a better quality or condition; make better" (Agnes, 2006, p.718). The improvement ideas of positive change, attaining expertise, developing excellent quality, and making things better is central to HRD. This core goal of *improvement* is possibly the single most important idea in the profession and the core motivator of HRD professionals.

The HRD profession focuses on making things better and creating an improved future state. Examples include everything from helping individuals learn new content to helping organizational systems determine their strategic direction. There has been a core debate among HRD professionals as to the purpose of HRD being either learning or performance. For example, Krempl and Pace (2001) contend that HRD "goals should clearly link to business outcomes" (p.55), while Bierema (1996) states that "valuing development only if it contributes to productivity is a point of view that has perpetuated the mechanistic model of the past three hundred years" (p.24). It is interesting to listen more closely to each side and to discover that learning is seen as an avenue to performance and that performance requires learning (Ruona, 2000). In both cases there is the overarching concern for improvement.

Problem-Solving Orientation

HRD is oriented to solutions—to solving problems. A problem can be thought of as "a question, matter, situation, or person that is perplexing or difficult" (Agnes, 2006, p.1144). It is these perplexing or difficult situations, matters, and people that most often justify HRD and ignite the HRD process. Insofar as HRD professionals see themselves as constructive and positive agents, some do not want to talk about their work in the language of problems. Essentially, their view is that there is a present state and a future desirable state and the gap between is the *opportunity* (or problem to be solved).

At times HRD professionals know more about the present state than the desired future state, and at other times they know more about the desired future state than the actual present state. HRD critics often say that HRD practitioners know more about what needs to be done than they know about either the present or desired states. Other critics might say that many HRD people are more interested in their programs and activities than in the requirements of their host organization. These criticisms can be summarized as "having a solution in search of a problem" and "a program with no evidence of results."

With all the various models and tools reported in the HRD literature, each with its own jargon, it is useful to think generally about HRD as a problem-defining and problem-solving process. HRD professionals have numerous strategies for defining the problem and even more strategies for going about solving the problem (techniques for making things better). A core idea within HRD is to think of it being focused on solving problems for the purpose of improvement. (More positive terms to use would be *opportunities* or *requirements*—improvement opportunities or improvement requirements.)

Systems Thinking

HRD professionals talk about systems views and systems thinking. They think this way about themselves and the systems they serve. Systems thinking is basic to HRD theory and practice. Systems thinking is described as "a conceptual framework, a body of knowledge and tools that have been developed over the past fifty years, to make full patterns clearer, and to help us see how to change them effectively" (Senge, 1990, p.7). Systems thinking is an outgrowth of systems theory. General systems theory was first described by Boulding (1956) and Bertalanffy (1962) with a clear *antimechanistic* view of the world and the full acknowledgment that all systems are ultimately *open systems*—not closed systems.

The basic systems theory model includes inputs, processes, and outputs of a system as well as a feedback loop. Furthermore, basic systems theory acknowledges that the system is influenced by its larger surrounding system or environment (see Figure 2.1), and overall systems are not to be thought of as linear.

This informed view is referred to as an *open system* or a system that is capable of being influenced by forces external to the system under focus. These ideas provide the basis for many practical HRD tools for viewing improvement problems (opportunities) and for taking action.

Systems thinking allows HRD to view itself as a system and to view its host, or sponsoring organization, as a system. When HRD professionals speak of HRD as a system, they generally think of HRD as being a subsystem within a larger organizational system. Analysis experts sometimes refer to subsystems as *processes.* Thus, HRD is more often discussed as a process than a system. This is not meant to be confusing—most people simply acknowledge that a systems view and a process view are almost the same. It can be said, however, that when people talk about a systems view, they are usually thinking more broadly and more generally than when they are talking about a process view. There is a point when the system and process views overlap.

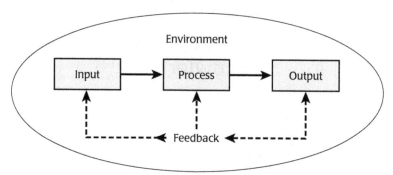

Figure 2.1 Basic Systems Model

Basic systems theory—the root of systems thinking—informs us that there are initial and fundamental requirements for engaging in systems thinking and analysis about systems (and processes). Quite frankly, just being able to answer and gain consensus on the following three questions is enough systems thinking for most HRD practitioners.

1. *What is the name and purpose of the system?* What systems are called, and what their purposes may be, are often points of great departure from one person to another. By naming the system, people can first agree as to what system they are talking about. It is very interesting to have intelligent and experienced people in a room begin to talk about a situation only to find

out that the unnamed system some are talking about differs from the system others are talking about. Furthermore, differing perspectives on the purpose of the system are almost always under contention until made explicit.

2. *What are the parts or elements of the system?* This question throws another elementary but essential challenge to a systems thinker. We find that people with a singular or limited worldview only see the world through that lens. Examples we have seen include production people not seeing the customer, sales people not seeing production, new technology people only seeing technology itself as the system rather than the larger system of people, processes and outputs, and legal people seeing the system as conflictive by nature rather than harmonious. With these limited views, individuals will be drawn to varying perceptions of the parts or elements of the system that may not match reality.

3. *What are the relationships between the parts?* Here is the real magic of systems theory—analyzing the relationships between the parts and the impact of those relationships. Even HRD experts wonder if they ever get it complete. Indeed, good analysts are the first to admit their own shortcom-

ings. Yet, their belief is that in the struggle to understand a system, an analyst ends up with a better and more complete understanding of that system. Studying the relationship between parts forces analysts to dive deeper into understanding and explaining a system—why it works and why it is not working. A simple example to illustrate this point is when enormous pressure is put on an employee only to find out if he or she can, in fact, perform a task. If the person can then perform the task, expertise is not the missing piece. Thus, the idea that people are not performing tasks well, and therefore training is needed, is unacceptable until more is known. Workers may know how to perform the task well but are unable to, or choose not to, for many reasons. You probably could name several from your own experience. There are numerous reasons in any system why things happen and do not happen. Figuring these out requires more than superficial analysis or metaphoric analogies. Systems theory is basic.

HRD WORLDVIEWS

The good news is that HRD professionals almost always have a worldview. The bad news is that they rarely articulate it and systematically operationalize it for themselves, their colleagues, and their clients. Years ago, Zemke and Kerlinger (1982, pp.17–25) implored HRD professionals to have general mental models for the purpose of being able to figure out the complexity and context surrounding HRD work.

HRD and Its Environment

Figure 2.2 contains a worldview generally useful to the purpose and context of HRD. This contextual model positions HRD as a five-phase system or process paralleling and connecting with the other processes in the system or organization. The organizational system and the processes within each have their inputs, work processes, and output. The environment in which the organizational system functions is also identified and illustrated. The organizational system is seen to have its unique mission and strategy, organization structure, technology, and human resources. Its economic, political, and cultural forces characterize the larger environment. As expected, this is an open system where influence of any component can slide up and down the levels of this model. For example, powerful global economy influences can push down the need and nature of an executive development program sponsored by a particular HRD department in a specific company.

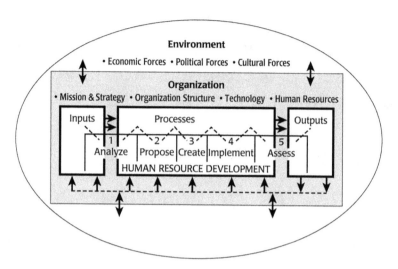

Figure 2.2 Human Resource Development in Context of the Organization and Environment Source: Swanson, 2001, p.305.

The Learner Perspective

Other worldviews that gain support in HRD include a view of the organizational systems as productive enterprises involving individuals as leaders, learners, and contributors. Figure 2.3 stems from the original work of Malcolm Knowles, considered in the United States to be the father of adult learning or *andragogy.* The perspective of andragogy in practice places adult learning principles into the context of adult life through the perspectives of (1) the goals and purposes for learning, and (2) individual and situational differences. In Figure 2.3 you see the six adult learning principles enveloped by the contextual purpose and situational issues that impact learning and development. The HRD worldview related to the adult learner is concerned with the learning process as it takes place within the context of the learning purpose and situation (Knowles, Holton, and Swanson, 2005).

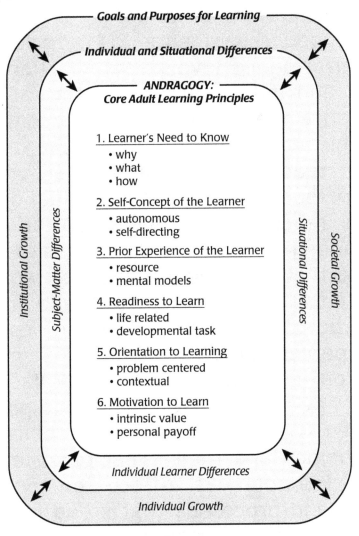

Figure 2.3 Andragogy in Practice Source: Knowles, Swanson, and Holton, 2005, p.4.

The Organizational Perspective

The organizational worldview perspective is presented here by the work of Rummler and Brache (1995). They offer one perspective on the organizational variables that explains organizational performance. In their matrix of Nine Performance Variables, the dominance of the organization and its need to perform is acknowledged (see Figure 2.4). Included are three performance levels—organization, work process, and individual contributor—and three performance needs: goals, design, and management. This worldview argues for the organization that reaches to the individual, while the learner perspective has the individual dominating and reaching to the organization. The organization performance view takes the general stance that good people may be working in bad systems. For example, the quality improvement expert, W. Edwards Deming, estimated that 90 percent of the problems that might be blamed on individuals in the workplace are a result of having them working in bad processes or systems. He fundamentally believed in human beings and their capacity to learn and perform. His goal was to focus on the system structure and processes that stood in the way of learning and performance.

Global Context

Adam Smith, a Scottish philosopher and political economist, was the author of a 1776 book titled, *An Inquiry into the Nature and Causes of the Wealth of Nations.* His treatise spurs continuing interpretations of the socio-technical-economic systems that provoke scholars and decision-makers even to the present day. His commitment was to capitalistic free markets and how rational self-interest and competition can lead to common well-being.

| | THE THREE PERFORMANCE NEEDS | | |
	Goals	Design	Management
Organization Level	Organization Goals	Organization Design	Organization Management
Process Level	Process Goals	Process Design	Process Management
Job/Performer Level	Job Goals	Job Design	Job Management

THE THREE LEVELS OF PERFORMANCE

Figure 2.4 Nine Performance Variables Source: Rummler and Brache, 2005, p.8. Used with permission.

In stark contrast, *Capital: A Critique of Political Economy* (1887), the work of Karl Marx, Prussian philosopher and political economist, also continues to provoke scholars and decision makers. Marx argued that capitalism leads to class struggles that will result in destruction and the ultimate rise of communism.

The context in which Smith and Marx advanced their theories has fundamentally changed, but most would argue that the motivation of human beings has not changed. Global political, economic, and cultural forces have radically shifted in the twenty-first century and will continue to change. In the past, these factors that were on the outer rim of concerns for most HRD professionals—those things that happened in faraway nations—are now a part of standard organizational considerations. To its credit, HRD has had a long tradition of cultural sensitivity as it has worked from region to region nationally and from one work group to another. Easing into multinational people interaction issues has been relatively painless for the HRD profession, and there has been high demand for HRD expertise in aiding individuals to function in the globalization process.

McLean and McLean (2001) have hypothesized that HRD is an important factor in the inevitable move to globalization. They note that while globalization is not new, its present demands are so intense that it fundamentally changes the way and rate at which change occurs. Globalization "enables the world to reach into individuals, corporations, and nation-states farther, faster, deeper, and cheaper than ever before" (Friedman, 2000, p.9). One framework for HRD to use in dealing with day-to-day issues related to globalization is to adopt the following new mindsets (Rhinesmith, 1995):

- Gather global trends on learning related technology, training, and organization development to improve the competitive edge.
- Think and work through contradictory needs resulting from paradoxes and confrontations in a complex global world.
- View the organization as a process rather than a structure.
- Increase ability to work with people having various abilities, experiences, and cultures.
- Manage continuous change and uncertainty.
- Seek lifelong learning and organizational improvement on numerous fronts.

It is important to note that these mindsets are less than adequate in resolving the larger social-economic-political struggle between political economies—Smith, Marx, and those in between—when thinking about fundamental humaneness, system viability, and meaningful participation in rival systems.

Our overall message in presenting these several worldviews is that every HRD professional should have a worldview that allows him or her to think through situations time and time again. Conceptual worldview models help HRD professionals gain clarity from the complex situations they face.

Thus far we have discussed core ideas that influence HRD. Each of these basic ideas assists in understanding the challenges HRD faces and the strategies it takes in facing those challenges. The ideas include:

- belief in human potential,
- improvement as a goal,
- problem-solving orientation,
- systems thinking,
- worldviews, and
- global context.

HRD PROCESS

Based on the ideas in the prior sections, it is rational to think of HRD as a purposeful process or system. Thus, the general consensus regards HRD as a process. In addition to being thought of as a process, HRD is viewed as a function, a department, and a job.

Our position is that the dominant view of HRD should be that of a process. Moreover, the views of HRD as a function, department, and job are less important contextual variations.

When HRD is viewed as a process and is thought of in terms of input, process, output, and feedback within a dynamic environment, then potential contributors and partners are not excluded. Within HRD there are specialized terms for these elements. In that HRD needs to engage others in the organizational system to support and carry out portions of HRD work, it is best to have the process view as the dominant view.

Most often HRD is talked about as a process and not a system. Furthermore, the process elements are most commonly called *phases* instead of elements or steps.

Process Phases of HRD

We have defined HRD as a five-phase process that is essentially a problem-defining and problem-solving method. HRD and its two primary components—training and development (T&D) and organization development (OD)—are each five-phase processes. Variations in the wording for the HRD, T&D, and OD process phases have a common thread with varying terminology. Here are all three variations:

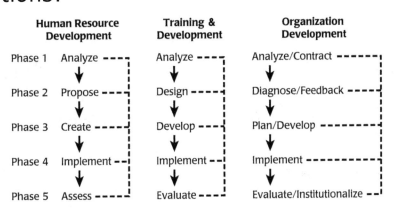

	Human Resource Development	Training & Development	Organization Development
Phase 1	Analyze	Analyze	Analyze/Contract
Phase 2	Propose	Design	Diagnose/Feedback
Phase 3	Create	Develop	Plan/Develop
Phase 4	Implement	Implement	Implement
Phase 5	Assess	Evaluate	Evaluate/Institutionalize

Interplay between the Phases of the HRD Process

The process phase view suggests that they are major stages in the HRD process and that each phase has an important relationship crucial to achieving the desired outcomes. One of the biggest professional problems facing HRD practitioners is in honoring all phases. Studies of HRD practice reveal shortcomings at the analysis and assessment/evaluation phases. These are the two most strategic phases of the HRD process. The disturbing shortcomings are compounded because relationships between the phases rely on the analysis phase for direction and substance. Furthermore, organizational commitment to HRD is dependent on positive performance results reported at the assessment/evaluation phase (Kusy, 1984; Mattson, 2001).

THREATS TO EXCELLENT PRACTICE

Davis and Davis (1998) tell us that "The HRD movement, on its way to becoming a serious profession, can no longer afford an atheoretical approach" (p.41). Even so, there are serious threats to theoretically sound and systematic HRD. Three of those threats are discussed here briefly.

Turning the HRD Process into an Event

This is an ever-present threat to a systematic approach to HRD. The actual time that people get together within the HRD process can become the focal point, with the real reason for getting together being lost. Obsessions with fun-filled events and hearing everyone's full opinion on a matter can become an end unto itself rather than a means to an end. An irrational concern for participant satisfaction can also fuel the possibility of undermining the process.

The Rate of Change

The familiar saying, "The faster I go, the behinder I get," haunts most HRD practitioners. The intensity of the rate of change requires more from HRD, which then can serve to undermine a systematic HRD process. Not enough time? It is very tempting to eliminate the assessment or cut back on the up-front analysis and go with the off-the-top-of-your-head analysis or to bypass the final assessment phase. The demand for speedy interventions is always a challenge and threat to high quality HRD.

Characteristics of the Key Players

Sleezer (1991) informs us of the strengths and liabilities of three critically important characteristics of key players in impacting HRD: (1) the HRD professional/analyst, (2) the client/decision maker, and (3) the host organization. Examples include: an analyst overly focused on human relationships may ignore hard organizational system level performance data; a client/decision maker can be guilty of not being able to see the forest because of the trees; and host organizations can have such deeply imbedded norms and values that they interfere with opportunities for change. When the characteristics of the key players are ignored and not managed properly, the integrity of the HRD process will likely erode. Responsibly engaging multiple stakeholders and multiple sources of data in the HRD process is essential to good practice and requires careful attention. These characteristics influence the thoroughness and integrity of the overall process. When they are ignored, the integrity of the process can seriously erode.

ETHICS AND INTEGRITY STANDARDS

Human Resource Development (HRD) as a profession and a discipline is focused on training and development and organization development programs, along with career development, quality improvement, change efforts, and complimentary human resource management practices to advance the performance of individuals, teams, work processes, organizations, communities, and society.

HRD professionals are engaged in HRD-related practice, research, consulting, and instruction/facilitation/teaching. They strive to create a body of research-based knowledge and to apply that knowledge to HRD in various organizational, community, and societal settings, functioning as professors, researchers, organization development consultants, administrators, trainers, managers, and leaders. HRD and its host organizations are concerned about ethical practices (Krause and Voss, 2007).

The Academy of Human Resource Development (AHRD) has produced *Standards on Ethics and Integrity* (AHRD, 1999) to provide guidance for HRD professionals engaged in practice, research, consulting, and instruction/facilitation/teaching. Although these principles are aspiring in nature, they provide standards of conduct and set forth a common set of values. Adherence to these standards furthers HRD as a profession. The primary goal of the AHRD standards is to manage more clearly the ethics of balancing among individuals, groups, organizations, communities, and societies whenever conflicting needs arise. Case studies connected to the ethics and integrity standards have also been produced to assist in the interpretation of the standards (Aragon and Hatcher, 2001).

To ensure this balance, these standards identify a common set of values upon which HRD professionals build their professional and research work. In addition, the standards clarify both the general principles and the decision rules that cover most situations encountered by HRD professionals. They have as their primary goal the welfare and protection of the individuals, groups, and organizations with whom HRD professionals work.

Adherence to a dynamic set of standards for a professional's work-related conduct requires a personal commitment to the lifelong effort to act ethically; to encourage ethical behavior by students, supervisors, employees, and colleagues as appropriate; and to consult with others, as needed, concerning ethical problems. It is the individual responsibility of each professional to aspire to the highest possible standards of conduct. Such professionals respect and protect human and civil rights and do not knowingly participate in or condone unfair discriminatory practices.

In providing both the universal principles and limited decision rules to cover the many situations encountered by HRD professionals, this document is intended to be generic and is not intended to be a comprehensive, problem-solving, or procedural document. Each professional's personal experience as well as his or her individual and cultural values should be used to interpret, apply, and supplement the principles and rules set forth.

Standards

The contents outline for the standards follow. A full standards document is available on the AHRD Web site (www.ahrd.org).

TABLE OF CONTENTS FOR THE AHRD STANDARDS ON ETHICS AND INTEGRITY

Preface
Purpose
General Principles
Competence,Integrity,ProfessionalResponsibility

Respect for People's Rights and Dignity
Concern for Others' Welfare
Social Responsibility
Standards
General Standards
Boundaries of Competence; Maintenance of Expertise; Basis for Research and Professional Judgments; Description of HRD Professionals' Work; Respecting Others; Nondiscrimination; Exploitative Relationships; Misuse of HRD Professionals' Work; Multiple Relationships; Consultations and Referrals; Third Party Request for Services; Delegation to and Supervision of Subordinates; Documentation of Professional and Research Work; Records and Data; Fees and Financial Arrangements; Accuracy in Reports to Payers and Funding Sources; Referrals and Fees
Research and Evaluation
Research and Evaluation in Professional Context; Data Collection Responsibility; Compliance with Law and Standards; Institutional Approval; Informed Consent; Incentives to Participants; Deception in Research; Interpretation and Explanation of Research and Evaluation Results.
Advertising and Other Public Statements

CONCLUSION

To be effective over time, it is essential to have a worldview model for thinking about how HRD fits into the milieu of an organization and society. It is also essential to have a process view of how HRD works and connects with other processes. Taking the five-phase process view of HRD, the HRD profession has traditionally been stronger in the middle creation and implementation phases and has been working hard to master the analysis and assessment phases at each end of the process. In pursuit of problems, improvements, and systematic practice, HRD professionals struggle to maintain high standards of excellence, ethics, and integrity.

REFLECTION QUESTIONS

1. Is there a relationship between the improvement goal, problem-solving orientation, and systems thinking "agreements" within the HRD profession? Explain.
2. What about systems thinking in this chapter attracts you? What repels you?
3. What, if any, is the logical connection between the three graphic models in this chapter?
4. How does your general worldview fit with the HRD worldview (Figure 2.2)?

CHAPTER 3

History of Human Resource Development

CHAPTER OUTLINE

Introduction
The Beginnings: Survival through Labor and Learning
- Use of Tools and Mutual Cooperation
  100 B.C.–A.D. 300: The Influence of the Greeks and Romans
- Greek Disdain for Menial Work
  - Pragmatic View of the Romans
  300–1300: The Middle Ages
- Monastic School Influence
- Apprenticeship Method
- Organization of Merchant and Craft Guilds
  1400–1800: The Renaissance
- Secular Education for Girls and Boys
- Sensory Learning
- Experience, the Best Teacher
- Manual Training
  Apprenticeship in Colonial America
- European Influence
- Early Leaders
  Industrial Era in America

- Decline of Apprenticeship
- Training and Corporation Schools
- Public Education and Training
- Chautauqua Movement
- Role of Government in Training
  Twentieth-Century Influences in America
- Early 1900s
- World Wars
  Evolution of the Organization Development
Component of HRD
- Shift to the Human Resources School of Thought
- Laboratory Training
  - Survey Research and Feedback
- Action Research (Problem-Solving) Techniques
- Tavistock Sociotechnical Systems and Quality of Work Life
- Strategic Change
- Transformation of Contemporary Work Organizations
- Evolving Nature of Work
  Management and Leadership Development in the United States
- Setting the Stage: American Business in the 1800s
- The Struggle for Professionalization of Management: 1900–1928
- Depression Era: 1929–1939
- Management Development Boom: 1940–1953

- Management Reform Movement: 1953–1970
- Modern Management Era: 1970–2000
  Emergence of the HRD Research Community
- Early University Programs
- Academy of Human Resource Development
  HRD History Time Line
  Reflection Questions

INTRODUCTION

The history of human resource development reveals that education, training, and organization development of all sorts are largely the products of social and economic conditions. Scott's (1914) early characterization of education is still meaningful: "education is the attempt of a civilization to perpetuate what it believes to be most vital in itself" (p.73).

Training and development has a unique role in the history of the human resource development (HRD) profession. As you will read in this chapter, training—in the form of parent – child, or master – apprentice workplace learning models—has existed throughout all recorded history. The history of HRD helps the reader understand (1) the origins of the HRD profession, (2) the major developments and events, and (3) the reason why the profession is as it now exists.

THE BEGINNINGS: SURVIVAL THROUGH LABOR AND LEARNING

Human experience and the nature of human resource development have passed through many stages since the beginning of the human journey. Training in its most simple form was found among our most primitive ancestors. The development of humans was driven exclusively by the need to survive. When learning first involved the making of simple tools from wood, stone, and fibers, primitive humans knew nothing about the productive use of fire and of metals. Harnessing these elements became critical to further development of the human race.

The context of primitive education was limited to the family or tribe, and education was a science, such, as they were known at the time, informal, and often-chaotic activity. It occurred through unconscious imitation of the head of a family or group, usually the father. Even as recently as the early twentieth century, Monroe (1907) points out, "the father, then, becomes the one who trains the younger generation in the formal conduct of life—in the proper way of doing things" (p.8). Yet despite its informality, an essential feature of education was apparent even in this most primitive form—"the fitting of the child to his physical and social environment through the appropriation of the experience of previous generations" (Monroe, 1907, p.1).

Use of Tools and Mutual Cooperation

Eventually humans gained the ability to control fire for the cooking of food, the smelting of metals, and the making of simple mechanical and agricultural tools. This allowed people to engage in crafts and undertake domestic activities previously impossible without basic tools. It also led to a true division of labor where some pursued weaving, others became carpenters, still others stone masons, and so on.

For the first time, people began to rely on tools and on each other to meet their needs. Indeed, humankind's progress through the ages has been inextricably linked to the development of practical tools and securing the bonds of mutual cooperation necessary for survival. With these developments came a new form of education—one characterized by conscious imitation rather than the unconscious imitation of earlier education (Bennett, 1926). The transfer of skill from one person to another now became a conscious process. Learning occurred through deliberate imitation of examples provided by one who had achieved mastery of a particular skill. Yet, education followed no theory or system and had not yet become a rational process. Those seeking a skill simply copied a model over and over until it could be precisely reproduced. Despite some advancement, the training of one person by another was still a quite primitive process.

Especially during humankind's early history, modest intellectual development came almost exclusively through efforts to adapt to a harsh physical and social environment. As Davidson (1900) states, "Human culture advances in proportion as men husband their powers by the use of implements, and by union for mutual help. Such husbandry requires higher and higher education" (p.25). The education and training needed for human progress was painfully slow to develop.

100 B.C.–A.D. 300: THE INFLUENCEOF THE GREEKS AND ROMANS

The key Roman legacy was their ingenuity in creating the institutions needed to carry out political and social agendas. Although Roman education did not have the persistent influence of Greek contributions, the Roman educational infrastructure and organization of schools continued to persist well after the conquest and fall of the Roman Empire

Greek Disdain for Menial Work

The legacy of "the golden age of Greece" has been a philosophy of education that, unlike any culture since that of ancient Greece, is most consistent with the present notion of a liberal education. Indeed, the Greeks were the first to see education as providing an opportunity for individual development (Moore, 1936).

The Greek conception of education included many dimensions vital to individual development that are still valued today. Human inquiry into all phases of life—nature, man, the supernatural—was an important dimension of Greek education that is today often considered the pursuit of knowledge for its own sake. The moral dimension of education, which emphasized the ethical rights and responsibilities of individuals, first found expression during the Greek era. In addition, aesthetic education and education's role as an agent of culturation and citizenship were first proposed by the Greeks. Above all, the Greeks viewed education as a vehicle for individual development and personal achievement. Through education, the Greeks sought to gain the capabilities of using and even profiting by their talents.

Despite this perspective, the Greeks did not hold the same generous view of training in the trades and mechanical arts (Bennett, 1926). They felt disdain toward what were seen as menial occupations such as farming, cattle raising, shoemaking, smithing, and tool making. Socrates is the source of some reasons for this contempt for handwork. He wrote of these trades as ruining the bodies of those who work at them, having gloomy and distasteful working conditions, allowing little time for leisure, and providing no development of the mind or soul (Moore, 1936). With this attitude toward manual work, it is not surprising that training in manual arts had no place in the education of upper class Greek youth. Yet training in manual arts was not completely shunned by the Greeks, for it was through an enduring system of apprenticeship among the lower classes that skills were developed in construction, manufacturing, agriculture, and other areas that were instrumental in the historic accomplishments of Greek civilization. Although not held in high esteem by the Greek upper classes, apprenticeship training clearly had an important role in the development of ancient Greece.

It is difficult to overstate the influence of the Greek era on the subsequent development of the philosophy and methods of education. It is remarkable that the present notion of education as a means for personal and intellectual development had its roots so long ago.

In light of this rich legacy, it seems almost trivial to note that the Greeks could not develop the infrastructure or institutions to allow a majority of their citizens to become educated. Most ancient Greeks did not have their freedom, and only the small minority of Greeks who were free could participate in education. Ironically, a belief in the importance of education and personal development coexisted with the reality of slavery.

Pragmatic View of the Romans

The Romans adopted Greek ideals but went further by integrating them into Roman life through the establishment of laws and institutions. Unlike the standards of excellence and harmony held by the Greeks, the Romans were a more practical people whose judgments were based on usefulness and effectiveness. Although their influence on education was not nearly as profound as that of the Greeks, the Romans provide an example of how laws and political infrastructure can be used to achieve long-term social, economic, and cultural change.

The great Roman achievements in public works, architecture, and the construction of roads and aqueducts is well known, and yet there is little evidence that the handwork and mechanical arts required for these accomplishments were valued by the Romans. Like the Greeks, the Romans relied on laborers and tradesmen to develop the infrastructure of their empire, despite the fact that manual skills were never held in high esteem. Romans acquired these skills through family apprenticeship. An important duty of Roman fathers was the development of practical skills and trades in their children.

The Roman Empire, like others that reached a period of great success, eventually began to decline. Roman life became more corrupt as lethargy and materialism replaced the virility and strength of character associated with early Rome. Roman education became artificial and drained of the vitality it once had. Even before the invasion of Rome by barbarians from the north, education provided by the early Christian Church was gradually replacing Roman education in both substance and spirit. The influence of Christianity on the purposes and methods of education would continue to grow throughout the Middle Ages.

300–1300: THE MIDDLE AGES

The goals and methods of training continued to be influenced by the many developments that occurred during an extended period in history known as the Middle Ages. Barlow (1967) characterizes the period spanned by the Middle Ages in the following way:

> The so-called Middle Ages account for approximately a thousand years of history between ancient and modern. Beginning in the early 300s and extending into the early 1300s, the period is divided into two nearly equal parts. The turning point between the early and later Middle Ages is marked at 800, when Charlemagne was crowned Holy Roman Emperor. (p.18)

The influence of Christianity permeated medieval life. Although successive imperial decrees during the fourth century made Christianity the official religion of the Roman Empire, for all practical purposes institutional control of the people had already passed to the Church. In the wake of the decadent Romans and barbarous Goths and Vandals, there was a great need for the structure and moral discipline that Christianity offered. The Church also embraced the lower classes, which had been neglected by the pagan society of Rome and the elitist culture of Greece.

Greco-Roman culture and education were methodically displaced by the training and rituals of Christianity. Training in Church dogma and spiritual consciousness replaced Greek aesthetic and intellectual ideals, and rigid moral training and discipline were substituted for Roman materialism. Under the dominance of Christianity, the education of that era received a completely new character.

Monastic School Influence

An important element of Christian discipline and teaching is the spiritual value of one's own labor. This was exemplified by the fervor and discipline of early Christian monastic life. As the intellectual landscape became more barren in the Middle Ages, the burden of academic learning and preserving the classics fell almost completely to Christian monasteries.

The Christian value of labor and the role of the monastery as guardian of academic learning combined to provide an environment conducive to the advancement of manual labor and training in manual and mechanical arts. As monasteries were intended to be separate from the secular world and as self-sufficient as possible, they operated many small-scale agricultural and industrial functions needed to maintain an independent existence such as gardens, mills, bakeries, and various shops for construction and maintenance. Monks and prelates skilled in these trades directed monastery operations and provided the necessary training in agriculture, practical arts and crafts, and various building and mechanical skills (Bennett, 1926). Practical learning, such as it was at that time, was a central part of monastic life.

Monasteries were also the center of intellectual life, preserving literature and art throughout the Middle Ages. All who participated in monastic life were taught basic reading and writing skills. In addition, monks worked tirelessly at writing manuscripts, producing and preserving books, and developing their skills in the arts of painting, music, and sculpture. As the skills of writing and bookmaking were held in high esteem, academic and artistic training were also an important part of monastic life.

Outside the monasteries participation in skilled labor was also the principal means of learning new skills and improving one's economic position. As crafts and trades became more differentiated and specialized, apprenticeship continued to emerge as the dominant mode of transmitting practical and technical expertise from one person to another.

Apprenticeship Method

Apprenticeship has been a basic and persistent influence on the development of workplace and is probably the most important nonschool institution around which training has grown. With roots in the very beginning of recorded history, apprenticeship training from parent to child and master to apprentice has been the most enduring of all methods for transferring knowledge and skill. Bennett (1926) observes that until the nineteenth century a great majority of people, even those from the more progressive nations, received no formal schooling, and what education they acquired was through some form of apprenticeship. This also included the professions such as law and medicine.

Davis (1978) characterizes apprenticeship as a system for preparing the young to become expert workers. The three stages of apprenticeship—apprentice, journeyman, and master—varied in length and in sophistication of expertise developed. One began training as an apprentice for a period of about seven years under direction of a master, one who had achieved the highest level of expertise at a particular vocation. The master was expected to provide apprentices not only with occupational training but also with the same moral, religious, and civic instruction that he would give his own child. The master gradually would impart all of the "mysteries" of his craft—the generally not-so-mysterious rules, recipes, and methods of applying basic arts and sciences to the craft—to apprentices over the course of their apprenticeship. As a journeyman who had achieved the basic skills and understandings of his craft, one could begin working as a day laborer, start to earn a fixed wage, and if mutually agreeable, work with other masters of the craft. After another period of several years developing his skills as a journeyman, one may have mastered the competencies expected of the craft or present a masterpiece to demonstrate his skills and achieve the level of master. A master craftsman could set up his own business, take on apprentices, and provide instruction in the vocation.

Organization of Merchant and Craft Guilds

One of the most characteristic features of medieval life in the later half of the Middle Ages was the organization of merchant and craft guilds. These associations were formed among those with common interests for mutual protection and benefit. Craftsmen and artisans organized themselves by occupation to protect themselves from substandard workmanship and low wages and selling prices. Working hours were strictly regulated, and quality standards for products and workmanship were established. Some guilds even prescribed the tools and methods a guild member must use to perform their trade.

By the fourteenth century, most guilds had begun offering education to members and their children in addition to the apprenticeships by which one initially earned membership in the guild. Guild-sponsored educational activities were of two kinds: elementary education provided by clergymen for the children of guild members, and an apprenticeship indenture system for the sons of guild journeymen. These were provided both as benefits to members and to further the interests and influence of the guilds. The first craft guild found in written records was the Candlemakers' Guild of Paris in 1061 (Barlow, 1967).

As guilds maintained strict standards for the skills needed to gain membership, they were forerunners of the craft unions of today that still require a prescribed level of competence for membership. Like the guilds, today's craft unions also regulate the quantity and quality of work, restrict the number of new apprentices, and closely monitor wages and prices.

By the close of the thirteenth century, a restless individualism was awakening the intellectual dormancy of the Middle Ages. The unity of medieval thought was broken by rebellion against medieval discipline, the revival of classical learning, and the revolt against the Catholic Church known as the Protestant Reformation. In addition, two developments facilitated the intellectual revival of the Renaissance and eventually brought education within the reach of more than just the rich: the use of the vernacular in writing and the invention of printing. Latin had long been the dominant language of learning and religion, even though the great masses of people did not understand it. Even minor progress in bringing reading and writing skills to more people could not take place until this language barrier had been penetrated. In the fourteenth century, books such as Dante's *The Divine Comedy* and Bocaccio's *Decameron* began to appear in languages more people could understand. Shortly thereafter, in about 1450, the printing of books from type was invented. Prior to this invention, books had to be meticulously copied by hand from manuscripts, a process that inhibited the widespread availability of books and other printed materials. Despite these advances, the Renaissance remained a great revival of learning limited to the few with wealth and education. It would still be centuries before more people could begin to enjoy the benefits of education and personal development. The most common type of training at this time continued in roughly the same form it had always been—the father – son or master – apprentice system.

1400–1800: THE RENAISSANCE

The Renaissance heralded a new era of scientific and philosophical thinking. A continuous stream of social, political, and scientific advances began to appear as great minds struggled with the practical and philosophical problems of the day. Several figures had a profound impact on historical developments, including advancements in education and training, during and after the Renaissance. Four such influential figures were Martin Luther, John Locke, Jean-Jacques Rousseau, and Johan Pestalozzi. The influences of these men are examined in this chapter because each made an important and uniquely different contribution to the development of technical training. In addition, each of these figures comes from a somewhat different time during the period of the thirteenth through eighteenth centuries. This allows us to trace a rough chronology of educational developments as they affected technical training during this period.

Secular Education for Girls and Boys

In addition to the criticism Martin Luther (1483–1546) directed at the Roman Catholic Church, catalyzing the Protestant Reformation, he was also critical of the education given in monastic and ecclesiastical schools. Luther, an Augustinian monk and professor of theology at the University of Wittenburg, abhorred the rigid discipline and harsh restrictions of church education, which he described as "monkish tyranny." Consequently, he proposed that religion and the church should no longer dominate education. He felt that education should embrace both religious and secular domains and that educational reform should come through the power of the state, although existing institutional structures for delivering education developed through the centuries by the church should continue to be used.

Luther's vision of education included a remarkable notion for that period—that education be given to all people, not just the rich, and be available to girls as well as boys! His view of education was much broader than what could be provided by the schools of his time. Education should go beyond religious training to emphasize the classics, mathematics, logic, music, history, and science.

Sensory Learning

John Locke (1632–1704) possessed a broad range of intellectual interests and wrote a number of important works on many subjects. He studied philosophy at Oxford and later received a degree in medicine, which he practiced for a short time. He became a Fellow of the Royal Society of London and eventually developed a theory of education that combined practical and moral training with intellectual training. He also produced some of the most influential works on political thought ever written (Ebenstein, 1969). Yet it is his two works on the philosophy and methods of education that have had a lasting effect on the development of technical training.

In his *Essay Concerning Human Understanding,* Locke formulated his theory of knowledge, emphasizing experience and the perception of the senses as important bases of knowledge. Later known as *empiricism,* this epistemology shaped Locke's ideas on what should constitute an ideal education. Locke's *Some Thoughts on Education* was written as a series of letters to a friend who requested Locke's advice on the education of his son. This important series of writings specifically laid out the purposes of education, how problems in educating the young should be overcome, and, of significance to the development of technical training, what components of education should be provided. Locke firmly believed that education should address the development of logical thinking and preparation for practical life. Consequently, he wrote that an education should include the learning of one or more manual trades, as well as physical, moral, and intellectual training. In addition to learning the skill of drawing, Locke particularly approved of woodworking and gardening as ways in which the young could benefit from a broader, experiential education than could be gained from books alone. Although these were novel ideas at the time, Locke's generous view of the philosophy and substance of education can still be seen in the educational methods of Western nations.

Experience, the Best Teacher

The visionary ideas about education of Jean-Jacques Rousseau (1712–1778) appear to have grown out of his own life. In his earlier years, the restless, self-indulgent Rousseau moved from one work experience to another far more than was acceptable for the time. He was an engraver's apprentice, a lackey, a musician, a seminary student, a clerk, a private tutor, a music copier, and the author of a prize-winning thesis written for the Academy of Dijon on the question of "Whether the progress of the sciences and of letters has tended to corrupt or elevate morals." The later experience demonstrated his brilliant yet quite controversial ideas on the failures of contemporary social progress. His ideas on the values and moral principles that should guide the state and its obligations to the people found full expression in *The Social Contract,* Rousseau's major political treatise that was the ideological basis for the French Revolution and an important influence on our own Declaration of Independence.

Quite possibly because of the circumstances of his own life, Rousseau firmly believed that experience is the best teacher and that education must be formed around the active experience of the young. Rousseau's ideas for how education should evolve from a rigid, book-bound process to a more natural, spontaneous experience are found in his delightful and eloquent *Emile,* named for the child of Rousseau's imagination whose education and development Rousseau traces from birth to marriage. In explaining Emile's adolescent development in a section of the work entitled "The Choice of a Trade," Rousseau states:

> [S]how him the mutual dependence of men, avoid the moral aspects and direct his attention to industry and the mechanical arts that make themselves useful to each

other. As you take him from one workshop to another, never let him see any kind of work without putting his hands to it, and never let him leave till he knows perfectly the reason for all that he has observed. With that in view, set him an example by working yourself in the different occupations. To make him a master, become an apprentice. You can be sure that he will learn more by one hour of manual labor than he will retain from a whole day's verbal instructions. (Boyd, 1962, p.86)

Rousseau clearly valued handwork and the mechanical arts as a central component of the education of the young. Yet it is significant to note that as the passage cited indicates, Rousseau would have Emile learn a trade not so much for its practical use as for its value in acquiring a broader and more meaningful education. Rousseau's recognition of the value of technical training in educating youth marked the beginning of a new era in education and an important contribution to the development of technical training.

Manual Training

The contributions of Johan Heinrich Pestalozzi (1746–1827) furthered the movement from the old education of simple acquisition of knowledge to the evolving notion of education as organic development. For the spirit and energy of his work, and the importance of the educational principles he proposed, Pestalozzi has been called the "father of manual training." Pestalozzi came from a family of modest means and admitted that he was of no more than average intellectual ability. Yet his contributions not only set a new course for education and technical training in Europe but were among the strongest influences on the development of education and training in the emerging American colonies as well.

Pestalozzi concerned himself with the nature of education as a whole, and his ideas spanned the conceptual spectrum from educational theory and philosophy to institutional settings best suited to education and on to techniques for teaching skills. According to Bennett (1926), Pestalozzi's broad conception of education and training grew naturally out of a number of factors: (1) his intense desire to improve the conditions of the poor and of children in his native Switzerland; (2) his firm belief that such improvement must come through education if it was to be permanent; (3) his opinion that school should be closely connected with, and prepare one for life in, the home, rather than leading one away from it; (4) his interest in the natural, experiential education of Rousseau; (5) his successful use of manual labor, tools, and objects as means for teaching traditional school subjects; and (6) his belief that engaging children in manual labor for the primary purpose of their development might also be used to pay for their education. Through practices in the schools he established, Pestalozzi demonstrated that the subject matter of education should be part of the immediate environment of the learners and used to develop their sense perceptions and formation of judgments. Pestalozzi's methods demanded the analysis of subject matter into its component parts and the use of inductive learning methods by proceeding from simple to complex elements as the way of achieving mastery of the whole.

In his writing, Pestalozzi (1898) states, "There are two ways of instructing; either we go from words to things or from things to words. Mine is the second method." This simple yet powerful truth is at the core of Pestalozzi's work, and it has had an important effect on the development of technical training. Pestalozzi's important contributions to education and training were carried forward by other influential figures such as von Fellenberg, Herbart, and Froebel.

APPRENTICESHIP IN COLONIAL AMERICA

As the United States developed, apprenticeship training served a critical role in advancing individuals and the economy.

European Influence

The Europeans who came to settle North America were people of piety and culture who had reaped the fruits of the Renaissance and Reformation and who respected the importance of education. Apprenticeship was the dominant educational institution of the time, as it had been for centuries, so the early colonists in America brought apprenticeship with them in much the same form as it existed in the mother country of England. As Seybolt (1917) points out, however, because there were no guild or craft organizations in the colonies through which apprenticeships could be established, the scope of apprenticeships became broader and were administered by municipal authorities. Although apprenticeships eventually became displaced by a system of schooling in the wake of the industrial revolution, early Americans expanded the role of apprenticeship as the dominant method of acculturation and training of those who would build the new nation.

English laws providing for the apprenticeship of poor children were primarily enacted to insure the safety and physical welfare of the poor and only secondarily as a means of instruction. As early as 1641, colonial authorities broadened the scope of apprenticeship to emphasize its educational purpose. The colonists wanted to make apprenticeship available to all children whose education might be neglected, not just the poor. The colonists' reliance on apprenticeship was particularly important because of the strong value placed on the merits of "one's own labor." Not only did they believe that teaching young people practical skills and trades would be profitable to the community, they also held Puritan beliefs in the virtue of industry and the "sin of idleness." The Massachusetts Bay Colony consequently enacted a comprehensive apprenticeship law for all children that required training in skills needed for a "calling" and the development of the "ability to read and understand the principles of religion and the capital laws of the country" (Seybolt, 1917, p.37).

Shortly thereafter, in 1647, the beginning of what would become the American public school system first appeared. Early Americans realized that all parents and guardians were not able to teach reading and writing, despite the requirement that all children be given this elementary education. As a result, the General Court of Massachusetts ordered that every town of fifty or more homes recruit a teacher from their district and be responsible for paying the teacher's wages. Thus began the system of free public schools in the United States.

Early Leaders

Among early American leaders who influenced the development of American education, Horace Mann (1796–1859) should be singularly distinguished. Davidson (1898) writes, "[T]he first man who fully understood the needs of the nation, and undertook to meet them in large, practical ways, was Horace Mann, to whom American culture owes more than to any other person. He was exactly the influence needed by the nation in her hour of spiritual awakening" (p.246). Mann recognized the needs of the poor and uneducated in the new nation and saw the important role of education. In addition, he formulated a broad and visionary plan for a new system of education and had the persistence and energy to see it carried out. Indeed, as head of the Massachusetts Board of Education and later as a U.S. congressman, Mann worked tirelessly to establish a system of education that met the needs of the people and the nation.

Mann's belief that education should develop one's intellectual and practical skills furthered the advancement of practical and technical training in the New World. He believed that "education should be a preparation for life, domestic, economic, social, and not merely the acquisition of curious learning, elegant scholarship, or showy accomplishments. Its end should be the attainment of moral and social personality" (Davidson, 1900, p.251).

After visiting the schools of Europe in 1843, Mann issued his famous *Seventh Annual Report,* which became the basis of school reform in Massachusetts. Later, in a report to the School Committee of Boston, Mann emphasized the development of practical skills, especially drawing, in school curricula (Bennett, 1926). Indeed, as part of his contribution to the American educational system during our early history, Mann also positively influenced the integration of practical and vocational training within general education.

INDUSTRIAL ERA IN AMERICA

As America left behind its colonial beginnings and entered the eighteenth century, it slowly shifted from an agrarian to an industrial economy. Like other developing Western nations of the time, the United States underwent a traumatic yet invigorating transition in the workplace from a period of almost total reliance on manual processes to an era of continuing industrialization. Unlike in the European nations that had shaped its development, however, America's shift to an industrial economy was accompanied by a permanent decline in apprenticeship training. Apprenticeship was displaced by a number of public and private institutions for work-related training. These institutions became the basis for many of the training arrangements we use today. In this section, we examine the development of technical education and training in America as it struggled to become an industrialized nation.

Decline of Apprenticeship

Well before the onset of the industrial era in the later part of the nineteenth century, the system of apprenticeship training that had served the nation so well in earlier times was showing signs of weakness. Even before the appearance of factories, the close interaction between master and apprentice was eroding as apprenticeship became more entrepreneurial and less pedagogical. The responsibility for training apprentices was more frequently being turned over to journeymen, and rather than the one-to-one learning relationship modeled after earlier father – son apprenticeships, the number of apprentices in a single shop could be as high as ten or more. Because early apprenticeships in America were administered by local authorities and were not under the strict regulation of craft and merchant guilds as they were in England, apprenticeships were gradually losing the developmental purpose for which they had been established and were becoming more exploitative of apprentices.

Eventually, however, the decline of apprenticeship became quite pronounced as the industrial advances of the later nineteenth century created a new demand for workers trained in a different way. As early as the middle of the eighteenth century, new machinery and other inventions of the emerging industrial era began bringing about remarkable changes in how work was performed. These changes were particularly apparent in the textile industry, where processes performed manually at home were slowly moved to early "manufactories" that housed automated looms and other new inventions for textile manufacturing. Similar innovations occurred in other industries such as printing, agriculture, and furniture manufacturing.

The industrial era needed new ways to train workers. Apprenticeship was unsuited for the more automated work in the evolving factory system. In addition, it was simply unable to keep pace with the growing demand for industrial workers. The important changes in the workplace brought by the industrial revolution required corresponding changes in the preparation of workers.

Training and Corporation Schools

During the colonial era, free public schools for elementary education had been established. Secondary schools emerged after the founding of the nation's first publicly supported high school in Boston in 1821. Yet no means had been devised to provide technical and industrial education to the masses needed by the nation's expanding industries. Providing technical training in the schools along with general and academic courses was an obvious option, but this was not seriously pursued until the late nineteenth century.

Although still separate from the growing system of public education, a few private manual training schools were established throughout this period that would have lasting effects on the development of technical training. During the eighteenth century, mechanics and tradesmen formed technical societies for the purpose of mutual assistance and economic advancement modeled after the trade associations of England. A result of these associations was the establishment of "mechanics institutes," which provided formal training in mechanical arts, as well as instruction in reading, English, mathematics, and other subjects. A mechanics' institute was founded in New York City as early as 1820, and a few years later, the Franklin Institute in Philadelphia and Ohio Mechanics' Institute in Cincinnati were established. These facilities had libraries for apprentices and most offered education to the children of mechanics. Although only a small number were established, mechanics' institutes were the earliest examples in the United States of institutions that formally offered both technical and general education. They served as an important example for the later development of private manual training schools and positively influenced public perceptions of manual work and the technical training it required.

Corporation schools were the first programs of formal instruction to be sponsored by businesses held on company premises for their employees (Beatty, 1918). This precursor of today's company-based training function was first developed in the railroad industry in 1905 as a way of improving the performance and efficiency of those who worked in railroad maintenance shops. Similar training for machinists was first offered in the evening at R. Hoe and Company, a New York City manufacturer of printing presses (Bennett, 1926). Apprenticeship training in the trades that companies had previously relied on for trained workers was inadequate for current skill and production demands. Corporation schools—also called factory schools—provided technical training in the skills and trades needed in a particular industry and included instruction in mathematics, mechanical and freehand drawing, and other practical skills needed by workers. The concept of corporation schools caught on quickly as similar schools were established around the turn of the century by Westinghouse, Baldwin Locomotive, General Electric, International Harvester, Ford, Goodyear, and National Cash Register.

Public Education and Training

Although privately sponsored programs for providing training to workers had been successful, there was strong resistance to the integration of job training within the public schools. Opposition developed among conservative educators who believed that the integration of job training would lead to lower academic standards. They believed that moral training and instruction in the basic subjects would provide the best preparation for the world beyond school. Education for work had no place in the public schools.

On the other hand, criticism of the general curriculum of the public schools grew because it was seen as failing to reflect the life for which it was supposed to be preparing youth. Much of what was learned from books in the classroom had little applicability to the world beyond. Education needed more relevance. This could be provided by offering work-related training along with general education in public schools.

The struggle over what should constitute the proper education of youth, and to what degree technical education should become the responsibility of the schools, was not limited to the United States. England, France, and Russia were also dealing with changes brought on by industrialization. All three countries had achieved some progress in improving their educational systems. After studying the Russian system for providing technical training, American proponents of offering manual training in the schools came to the basic and surprising realization that principles involved in manual skills could simply be put on the same educational plane as other school subjects (Bennett, 1937).

The School of Mechanical Arts was created at the Massachusetts Institute of Technology in 1876. The Manual Training School of St. Louis was quite successful and was quickly copied in both its administration and curriculum in Chicago. Although these schools were privately funded, they demonstrated that such schools could be successfully established. Support for this training was growing, and public funding for manual training schools would soon follow.

The first high school for manual training fully supported at public expense was founded in Baltimore in 1884. In the following year, a second school supported as part of the public school system opened in Philadelphia and a third in Toledo. Although these schools were physically separate from the general high schools, the actual integration of manual training courses into general high school curricula was also beginning to occur. By 1884, manual training courses and general academic courses were offered in the same public high schools in Cleveland, Boston, Minneapolis, and other cities (Bennett, 1937).

Chautauqua Movement

A more holistic educational movement existed in the midst of the industrial era. It began in 1874 at the First Chautauqua Assembly held on Lake Chautauqua, New York. Funded by an Ohio industrialist, Lewis Miller, and led by Dr. John H. Vincent, a Methodist minister, the assembly called for broadening the education of adults under the mantra of education, recreation, and inspiration (Snyder, 1985). Permanent and traveling Chautauquas spread throughout the nation. The New York Chautauqua remains a lively intellectual community and is one of about eight operating in the United States. While adult educators rightfully look to the Chautauqua movement as important in its history, it is interesting to note the connection between this movement and the outreach mission of the land grant universities in the United States as the nation matured and moved westward. After two years in the first Chautauqua, Vincent went on to establish the Chautauqua of the Great Lakes in Lakeside, Ohio, and then to create a Chautauqua learning company that his son headed up. From 1911–1917, his son, Dr. George Vincent, became president of the University of Minnesota, a land – grant university that had overlapping values with the Chautauqua movement.

Role of Government in Training

Early support for technical training and vocational education came from state legislatures. The success and growth of early private manual training schools permanently established these technical training schools as important sources of skilled workers. In addition, demands of manufacturers, labor leaders, and the general public for more of this instruction and more skilled workers increased. Responding to these increasingly vocal and better organized con-stituencies, state legislatures funded technical training curricula within public education in schools in Massachusetts, Ohio, Pennsylvania, and in other states. Shortly after 1900, Mas-sachusetts, long a leader in promoting practical and technical training, established independent schools for industrial and technical training, funded these schools with state money equal to half of local expenditures, and allowed administration of these schools through a commission of vocational education that was established independently of the state board of education.

Similar innovations supporting the advance-ment of technical training both within and outside public education occurred thereafter in other states. State legislation promoting vocational and technical education became more common as interest spread from the industrial states of the East to the Midwest, and later to the South and far West. The greatest initiative for state legislation supporting the development of vocational and technical education came from the Morrill Act of 1862, signed into law by President Abraham Lincoln. Also called the Land – Grant Act of 1862, this legislation provided a comprehensive and far-reaching scheme of public endowment of higher education that was to bring higher education within the reach of the average citizen, not just the wealthy, for the first time. It established programs of training at the college level in agricultural education, industrial and trade education, and home economics education, and it did much to clarify the image of this type of technical training in the eyes of the public.

Another major step forward in establishing technical training as a component of public education was the enactment of the Smith – Hughes Act in 1917. It provided for a permanent, annual appropriation of $7 million for programs of industrial, agricultural, home economics, and teacher training within public education. The legislation was carefully crafted to strike balances between three sets of vested interests: (1) management and labor—with each seeking to regulate vocational training in order to control this important source of skilled labor; (2) educators who felt there should be more integration between practical and academic education and those who felt there should not be integration; and (3) among those supporting vocational education, those who felt this should occur through public institutions and those seeking to keep vocational education out of the public schools. The Smith – Hughes Act seems to have balanced these competing interests quite well, for, as Bennett (1937) states, "The law passed was probably the best compromise that could have been obtained at the time" (p.550). Since the Smith – Hughes Act, three subsequent federal laws enacted between 1929 and 1936 authorized further increases in spending on vocational education.

As America entered the twentieth century and the industrialization of its economy continued, innovations occurred in work design that fundamentally transformed the nature of work: *scientific management* and the introduction of *mass production methods.* Scientific management grew from work originated in the early eighteenth century by Charles Babbage (Davis and Taylor, 1972), and was further refined and popularized by Frederick Taylor.

Scientific management is based on two straightforward principles: break complex tasks down into simple rote tasks that can be performed with machinelike efficiency, and control the large number of workers needed for production with a hierarchical management structure (Taylor, 1912). This elegant concept of production efficiency was first implemented in manufacturing after the turn of the twentieth century, and it was soon adopted and developed into a complete system for "mass production" by Henry Ford. The mass production system required a cadre of engineers, planners, schedulers, supervisors, maintenance personnel, and quality inspectors to keep operations running smoothly and to prevent costly production delays. Direct-line workers performed simple repetitive tasks and depended on a large number of similarly specialized support staff to troubleshoot and control the production process. This approach to production permeated the industrial sectors of the economy and was responsible for our nation's dominance of the world market for manufactured goods during the middle part of the twentieth century.

TWENTIETH-CENTURY INFLUENCES IN AMERICA

Several important influences on the development of technical training emerged in the half century surrounding America's involvement in the two world wars. These include the training demands placed on our educational system by the wars themselves and the changes that resulted, the rise of the American labor movement during this period, and the impact of the technological innovations initiated during and after our war involvement. In this section we examine each of these important influences on the development of technical training.

Early 1900s

The early 1900s marked a clear shift toward the idea that other entities would need to offer work-related training. As described earlier, "corporation schools" were sponsored as early as 1905 and ensured their employees were equipped with the skills necessary to perform (Swanson and Torraco, 1995).

A parallel development emerged with the increasing importance of vocational training and schools. By the early 1900s, vocational education had become increasingly extensive. Professional associations were founded to promote the vocational education consciousness (Steinmetz, 1976). These included the National Society for the Promotion of Industrial Education in 1906 (later renamed the National Society for Vocational Education), the National Vocational Guidance Association in 1913, and the Vocational Association of the Midwest in 1914. These associations were central in furthering the interests of vocational education and, most notably, in obtaining the governmental money for vocational training—beginning with the Smith – Hughes Act of 1917.

Vocational associations grappled with a divisive issue from the beginning. Two distinct camps could be identified within many vocational associations—one composed of mostly educators, and one composed of men and women from industry. In 1913, Alvin E. Dodd, then assistant secretary of the National Society for the Promotion of Industrial Education, found that his philosophy about vocational education was more aligned with those in industry than the educators.

At a meeting in 1913, Dodd found that his desire for a different approach was shared by Channing R. Dooley, of Standard Oil, and J. Walter Dietz, of Western Electric. The National Association of Corporation Schools was formed to focus more on business issues and training needs. This organization increasingly focused on the needs of personnel, merged with the Industrial Relations Association of America in 1920, and finally became the American Management Association in 1923. We see from this evolution that present-day HRD emerged directly from this stream of increasing training consciousness born out of vocational education and its development.

World Wars

The trauma of the first and second world wars, and the rise of the American labor movement during these periods, provided ample opportunity for training and its leaders to emerge and become central in America's development.

World War I

Just four years after the founding of the National Association of Corporation Schools and at the onset of World War I, Channing Dooley was appointed director of the War Department Committee for Education and Special Training. Dooley's job was to develop materials for colleges to fill the army's needs for over one hundred trades. In 1917, Charles A. Allen was appointed head of the Emergency Fleet Corporation of United States Shipping Board, and Michael J. Kane became his assistant. When the war began, there was a desperate need to build ships quickly. The workforce needed to be expanded tenfold and trained immediately by supervisors at the shipyards. In response, Allen and Kane pioneered and ordered the now infamous four-step method of training (discussed later).

World War II

The four men mentioned previously—Dooley, Dietz, Allen, and Kane—along with Glenn Gardiner and Bill Conover, used their wartime experiences to fundamentally shape the history of training when, before and during World

War II, the War Manpower Commission established the Training within Industry (TWI) Service, naming Dooley as its leader.

Training had waned during the Depression years of the 1930s when company budgets were tightened. Industrial education primarily focused on developing skills in the unemployed to improve their personal welfare. Suddenly, World War II demanded fast mobilization of resources and exorbitant wartime production. Although the war found many people willing to work after the distress of the Depression, there was once again a significant need for training. TWI's objectives were to help contractors produce efficiently with lower costs and higher quality. Dooley (1945) wrote in a retrospective of the wartime effort that TWI "is known for the results of its programs—Job Instruction, Job Methods, Job Relations, and Program Development—which have, we believe, permanently become part of American industrial operations as accepted tools of management" (p.xi).

Indeed, TWI is known for its simple and elegant way of training incredible amounts of people. Each program had a system to support it: limited steps, key words, subpoints, documentation/work methods, and supporting training so as to obtain certification (Swanson and Torraco, 1995). TWI's four programs fostered three key contemporary elements of HRD: performance, quality, and human relations.

TWI and Performance. The philosophy under-girding the TWI Service was a clear distinction between education and training. Dooley (1945) stated, "Education is for rounding-out of the individual and the good of society; it is general, provides background, increases understanding. Training is for the good of plant production—it is a way to solve production problems through people; it is specific and helps people to acquire skill through the use of what they learned" (p.17). The programs of TWI were closely linked to organizational performance. TWI "started with performance at the organizational and process levels and ended with performance at the same levels" (Swanson and Torraco, 1995). The primary measure of success was whether a TWI program helped production, efficiency, and cost-effectiveness.

The Job Instruction Training Program (JIT) was created for first- and second-line supervisors who would train most employees. The focus of the program was to teach supervisors how to break down jobs into steps and how to instruct using a derivative of the four-step process introduced during World War I. Another program, the Job Safety Program (JST), was implemented to address the crucial need for employees to be safe in the new, unfamiliar industrial environment.

TWI and Quality. TWI also pioneered when it addressed quality issues impeding performance. Two programs are notable. First, the Job Methods Training Program (JMT) provided a specific method for teaching employees how to address production and quality problems constructively. It encouraged employees to question details of job breakdowns and to develop and apply new methods that work better.

Second, TWI partnered with General Motors in 1942 to create the Program Development Method (PDM) (Swanson and Torraco, 1995, p.33). This program introduced a four-step process designed to teach employees how to address quality problems and implement improvements. The four steps were:

- Spot a production problem.
- Develop a specific plan.
- Get the plan into action
- Check results.

This 1942 method is strikingly similar to the "plan-do-study-check-act cycle" that Edward Deming (1993) brought to the forefront in Japan during the 1950s and in America some thirty years later.

These core quality principles introduced by TWI still provide a basis from which many in HRD implement their analyses and work.

TWI and Human Relations. The TWI Service was also one of the first to address human relations issues as important aspects of production success. The Job Relations Training Program (JRT) trained supervisors to establish good relations with their employees. JRT laid important groundwork for the burgeoning of organization development in companies during the 1950s. Clearly, the TWI effort quickly went beyond training and is seen by many as the origin of contemporary HRD, as well as a springboard for the human relations perspective of the organization development component of HRD. Much of the original TWI report has recently been republished for the profession under the title *Origins of Contemporary Human Resource Development* (Swanson, 2001).

EVOLUTION OF THE ORGANIZATIONDEVELOPMENT COMPONENT OF HRD

The philosophy and methods of organization development (OD) were honed and began to affect people and work environments during the years between 1940 and 1960.

Many parallel developments occurred, including (1) a shift to the human resources school of thought, (2) the growth of laboratory training, (3) the use of survey research and feedback, (4) an increased use of action research (problem-solving) techniques, (5) an acknowledgment of sociotechnical systems and quality of work life, and (6) a new emphasis on strategic change.

Shift to the Human Resources School of Thought

From the 1940s to the early 1950s, the primary way to think about and organize work and work environments was based on the human relations model. Developed mostly in response to serious concerns about the viability of traditional and bureaucratic organizations, the human relations model attempted to move away from these classical assumptions and focused more heavily on individuals' identities, their needs, and how to facilitate stronger interpersonal communication and relationships. Leaders of the human relations school of thought included Chester Bernard, Mary Parker Follett, Frederick Roethlisberger, and Elton Mayo, who led the now infamous Hawthorne experiments that initially focused on quality of workplace lighting and its impact on worker productivity and finally concluded that productivity gains were attributed to being watched and being specially treated.

By the mid-to late 1950s, it became increasingly clear that the human relations model had not effectively impacted work environments. The human resources school of thought (Rothwell, Sullivan, and McLean, 1995) emerged to address some of its shortcomings. The human resources model was firmly rooted in humanism, "the key values of which include a firm belief in human rationality, human perfectibility through learning, and the importance of self-awareness" (Rothwell et al., 1995, p.17). Other core roots included (1) applied social science, which increasingly recognized the complexities of individuals and (2) economics, which began to recognize that individuals were as valuable as other capital such as land, machinery, and supplies.

Leaders of humanism included Carl Rogers, who pioneered client-centered consulting; Abraham Maslow, who developed the needs hierarchy; Cyril Houle and Malcolm Knowles, who focused on adult learners; and Douglas McGregor, who developed the theory of X and Y leaders. Each of these men added to new assumptions of management thought:

- Work is meaningful.

- Workers are motivated by meaningful, mutually set goals and participation.
- Workers should be increasingly self-directed and this self-control will improve efficiency and work satisfaction.
- Mangers are most effective when coaching, working to develop untapped potential, and creating an environment where potential can be fully utilized.

These assumptions continue to be the guideposts of current thinking in organization development and HRD.

Laboratory Training

Laboratory training, or the T-group, provided an early emphasis on group process and interactions. T-groups were unstructured, small-group sessions in which participants shared experiences and learned from their interactions. The first recorded T-group implementation took place under the auspices of the New Britain Workshop in 1946 under direction of leaders such as Kurt Lewin, Kenneth Benne, Leland Bradford, and Ronald Lippit. These individuals are most well known for their involvement in the founding of the National Training Laboratories (NTL) for applied behavioral science.

T-groups were first used in industry in 1953 and 1954 when Douglas McGregor and Richard Beckhard took T-groups out of the context of individual development and applied them to the context of an organization. This effort at Union Carbide focused on the team as the unit of development and, interestingly enough, aimed to address the problem of training transfer—an early indication that personnel training and OD were closely tied.

Survey Research and Feedback

Attitude surveys and data feedback have become important tools in OD. In 1947, however, they were just in their infancy as Rensis Likert pioneered the concept of survey-guided development. This process entailed measuring the attitudes of employees, providing feedback to participants, and stimulating joint planning for improvement. The first climate survey, at Detroit Edison in 1948, was used to measure management and employee attitudes. The data were fed back using a technique that Likert called an "interlocking chain of conferences"—starting at the highest level of management and flowing to successively lower levels.

Likert's work was grounded in, and resulted in, a guiding philosophy of organizational systems. Ultimately, he believed that any system could be categorized based on feedback data into one of four types: exploitative-authoritarian, benevolent-authoritative, consultative, and participative. He advocated the creation of a participative organization based on the use of influence, intrinsic rewards, and two-way communication (Rothwell et al., 1995).

Action Research (Problem-Solving) Techniques

Action research (actually a problem-solving technique rather than a research method), now acknowledged as the core method of OD, originated out of the work of social scientists John Collier, Kurt Lewin, and William Whyte in the late 1940s. Their theory asserted that problem solving must be closely linked to action if organizational members were to use it to manage change. Harwood Manufacturing Company was the site of one of the first such studies, led by Lewin and his students. Other contributors to furthering thinking behind action research included Lester Coch, John French, and Edith Hamilton. Ultimately, the cyclical nature of the action research problem-solving method is still viable—requiring data collection, analysis, planning and implementation, and evaluation.

Tavistock Sociotechnical Systems and Quality of Work Life

Also during the late 1940s to early 1950s, the Tavistock Clinic in Great Britain, known for its work in family therapy, transferred its methods to the organizational setting. Tavistock researchers conducted a work redesign experiment for coal mining teams experiencing difficulties after the introduction of new technologies. The key learning of their initial experiments was a new focus on social subsystems and people—people whose needs must be tended to during times of change.

In the 1950s, Eric Trist and his colleagues at Tavistock extended the idea of sociotechnical systems and undertook projects related to productivity and quality of work life. Their approach increasingly examined both the technical and human sides of organizations and how they interrelated (Cummings and Worley, 1993). The trend to develop interventions that more effectively integrated technology and people spread throughout Europe and to the United States during the 1960s, where the approach tended to be more eclectic, and became increasingly popular.

Strategic Change

Since 1960, much of the evolution of OD has focused on increasing the effectiveness of strategic change. Richard Beckhard's use of open-systems planning was one of the first applications of strategic change methods. He proposed that an organization's demand and response systems could be described and analyzed, the gaps reduced, and performance improved. This work represents a shift in OD away from a sole focus on the individual, and the supporting assumption that OD is completely mediated through individuals, to a more holistic and open systems view of organizations. This shift continues to this day and is evidenced in key revelations stemming from strategic change work including the importance of leadership support, multilevel involvement, and the criticality of alignment between organizational strategy, structure, culture, and systems.

Transformation of Contemporary Work Organizations

Organizations—large and small, public or private, and in a range of industry sectors—have been the primary twenty-first-century mediums through which work is accomplished. The structure of contemporary work organizations changed fundamentally in the 1980s and 1990s as a result of the globalization of the economy and information technology. Organizations are becoming flatter and less hierarchical in an effort to reduce bureaucracy, manage costs, and be more responsive to markets. Organizations or equivalent subsystems have become smaller and leaner as managers eliminate work inefficiencies and duplication of effort.

A consequence of these emerging flatter, "downsized" systems is the need for major shifts in the distribution of work tasks and roles among workers and the need for fundamental organization development. In a workplace once modeled on narrow job definitions and a wide range of functional specialists, today's workplace is often characterized by increasingly sophisticated work methods and the presence of relatively fewer workers. Narrow job definitions are giving way to broader responsibilities and a greater interdependence among workers. Jobs are being eliminated, combined, and reconfigured as organizations fundamentally rethink the ways in which work should be done. As organizational and job structures change, training for those who operate within such structures must change.

Evolving Nature of Work

The nature of contemporary work has changed. Organization development efforts underway in organizations to reduce costs, to integrate technology and work (not just in terms of labor-saving technology), and to expedite communication with customers and suppliers not only eliminate jobs throughout the organization but also increase the sophistication of work for those who remain. Today's workers increasingly need to understand work operations as a whole, rather than what used to be their specific tasks within it. Monitoring and maintaining the work system has become in today's workplace what operating a single machine had been for mass production work. Today's workers have to make sense of what is happening in the workplace based on abstract rather than physical cues. According to Zuboff (1988), this transformation of work involves the development of "intellective" rather than "action-centered" skills. Gone are the days when problem solving meant making a telephone call to management or the maintenance department.

In addition, flatter organizational structures require employees at the shop floor level to exercise more authority over a wider variety of tasks. They can no longer rely on management for planning and scheduling as these duties are integrated into production jobs themselves. Today's work requires an increasingly holistic perspective of the organizational mission, strategy, and structure along with attention to the demands of both internal and external customers. Once the mainstay of traditional forms of work, procedural thinking has become subordinate to systems thinking for all workers, not just managers.

Clearly, an important factor underlying the changing nature of contemporary work is a perceptible shortening of the half-life of knowledge. New knowledge drives the evolution of new work systems and technologies. The half-life of knowledge in technology-intensive fields such as engineering and health care is now less than four years. Conservatively, this means that the relevant expertise of an engineer completing training today will erode by fifty percent in just four years. The half-life of such knowledge is not much longer in most of the other business, professional, and technical fields upon which organizations rely for their expertise. The profound influence this constant turnover of knowledge has on the nature of work, and the way work is accomplished, is all too obvious to those who must continually update their work knowledge and skills.

Advanced technology, leaner organizational structures, and an environment of fewer resources and ever-changing demands of customers and government are powerful factors that are reshaping organizations and fundamentally changing the nature of work.

MANAGEMENT AND LEADERSHIP DEVELOPMENT IN THE UNITED STATES

Histories of HRD have largely focused on organization development and personnel training and development aimed at hourly and supervisory workers, while mostly ignoring management and leadership development (Miller, 1996; Nadler and Nadler, 1989; Knowles, 1977; Ruona and Swanson, 1998; Swanson and Torraco, 1995; Steinmetz, 1976).

A number of specialty areas of HRD have developed over the years as separate entities, spurred by unique and independent forces. Management and leadership development (MLD) is one such entity. Managers making decisions about MLD of other managers is worthy of separate consideration. Beyond MLD, other HRD arenas with unique histories are also of interest. Examples include career roles (e.g., nursing and general practice within medicine) and bodies of knowledge (e.g., computer science). Each has its own HRD history.

It is only in modern times that mainstream human resource development and MLD have converged. Consequently, there has been little systematic attempt to study the history of MLD. This section identifies the major periods or eras in MLD history.

When studying MLD, it is difficult to divorce the higher education component from the more traditional HRD components since there are important interactions between them. The whole system of MLD providers include higher education, university-based MLD, corporate-based training and development programs, association activity, private training, and others. MLD programs are designed for all levels of management, including what is often called executive development, but excludes supervisory development. Supervisory development is generally considered to be targeted toward persons supervising hourly or nonprofessional-level employees.

Management and leadership development can be thought of as any educational or developmental activity specifically designed to foster the professional growth and capability of persons in or being prepared for management and executive roles in organizations. First, it includes both formal educational activities and on-the-job type programs. As we will see, the concept of MLD has changed significantly through the years but included primarily more informal activities, though systematically planned and designed, in the early years. MLD is more than just classroom activity, and we must include all aspects of it.

Setting the Stage: American Business in the 1800s

American business prior to 1870 showed little resemblance to business after 1900 and certainly not to business today. America was primarily an agrarian society characterized by very local markets, small owner-operated companies that were largely labor- instead of capital-intensive. Highly trained personnel were not needed because business was not very complicated. America was largely rural, with only 11 percent of the population living in urban areas in 1840 (Chandler, 1959).

Early commercial schools bore little resemblance to management and leadership development, yet they were an important first step. Prior to this, business was taught through the apprenticeship method. The founders of these schools believed that commercial subjects could be taught better and more efficiently by using a systematic classroom method than the old apprenticeship method. This was a major innovation and laid the foundation for the modern business school.

By 1900, the U.S. economy had been completely transformed. More firms were involved in making goods for industrial purposes than consumer goods. Most industries were dominated by a few large firms. The nation had changed from a business to an industrial economy (Chandler, 1959).

A key outcome was that business began to need managers, at least in the modern sense of the word. As businesses grew larger, they also became bureaucratic with decisions being made in large, hierarchical structures. This great new organization—the large corporation—required careful coordination and needed people who could accomplish this. Large companies also created many specialized jobs unlike the craft-oriented small businesses. Specialists required managers to direct their activity. But there were no models or theories to guide companies in learning how to run these huge organizations. The profession of management was born and the need for MLD began.

The first formal business schools were formed in this period. The first school of business was formed in 1881 at the University of Pennsylvania with a grant from Joseph Wharton.

Other schools followed at the University of California in 1898, and New York University and the University of Wisconsin in 1900. These schools recognized two key things: formal training was needed for business, and technical training was not enough. While there was not much agreement on curricula, they did realize that a breadth of outlook was needed, more akin to other types of professional training. One can imagine much opposition in these universities since business was largely considered a trade at that time. The private commercial schools continued to prosper in this period. In 1876, there were 137 schools enrolling 25,000 students, and by 1890, they had grown to enroll almost 100,000 students (Haynes and Jackson, 1935).

The Struggle for Professionalization of Management: 1900–1928

In 1911, Frederick Taylor published *The Principles of Scientific Management* as the culmination of years of work and study into a new approach to management he began about 1900. Taylor is widely regarded as the father of American management thought and was the first to apply scientific principles to the practice of management. While many others had written about management before him, it was Taylor who first put forth a scientific theory and approach to management and the need to share it with managers and leaders in organizations.

In 1913, the National Association of Corporate Schools was formed. As the role of training broadened, the organization changed its name in 1920 to the National Association of Corporate Training. In 1922, that organization merged with the Industrial Relations Association of America (formerly the National Association of Employment Managers) to form the National Personnel Association. In 1923, this group changed its name to the American Management Association (AMA). In 1924, the AMA absorbed the National Association of Sales Managers.

The AMA continued to be a leader in the field of MLD and provided much of the early push to the field. Its principal mission was "to advance the understanding, principles, policies and practices of modern management and administration" ("50 Years of Management Education," p.5). Mary Parker Follett played a major influence in the early stages of the organization. In 1925, she voiced the need "to apply scientific methods to those problems of management which involve human relations" ("AMA Management Highlights," p.36). In 1926, the organization formed the Institute of Management "to promote scientific methods in management and to provide a forum for interchange of information" (Black, 1979, p.38).

Higher education in business also experienced tremendous growth during this period. In 1900, there were only four business schools. By 1913, there were 25 new business schools on college campuses, 37 more by 1918, and by 1925 a total of 182 business schools—thanks largely to the influx of veterans who needed training for jobs (Bossard and Dewhurst, 1931, p.252). In 1916, the American Assembly of Collegiate Schools in Business was formed; by 1930, it had forty-two member schools. Its mission was to provide accreditation for schools and to set standards for curricula.

Management theory began to take a turn away from Taylor and scientific management. In 1927, Elton Mayo became involved in a recently completed series of experiments at Western Electric's Hawthorne plant begun in 1924. Sponsored by the National Research Council of the National Academy of Science, the experiments were originally designed to determine the relationship of illumination and individual productivity. While productivity went up dramatically, it was not as a result of the lighting. It was Mayo who suggested the now famous Hawthorne effect of paying attention to workers as a likely explanation. The outcome of these experiments was a call for the development of a new set of managerial skills: human behavior and interpersonal skills. Technical skills would not be enough (Wren, 1979, p.313).

Depression Era: 1929–1939

One unfortunate result of much of the enormous growth in business during the early part of the twentieth century was the Great Depression of 1929. Even with the depressed economy, there were a few items relevant to HRD worth noting during this period. The first university-based executive or management development program was started at MIT's Sloan School in 1931 with the help and initiative of A.P. Sloan, chairman of General Motors Corporation. This program was designed for a group of selected executives with eight to ten years of experience who were released from their work for a year to attend. It was the forerunner of what would become a very important trend later.

Depression Era: 1929–1939

This was a critical era for the development of MLD. During this period business thinking changed to accept management and leadership development as a necessary part of doing business. When World War II began in 1939, corporations needed managers quickly, so they turned to MLD activities to fill that need. After the war, the successes with management training made many companies realize that management and leadership development activities should continue.

A significant new venture for university schools of business were the non-degree management and executive development programs. These programs were largely residential and required the manager or executive to leave the workplace for an extended period to return to school. In 1943, Harvard and Stanford were asked by the U.S. War Office to form the War Production Retraining Course. This was a fifteen-week course designed to retrain businessmen to manage the war production effort. By 1950, four such programs existed: MIT, Harvard, the University of Chicago, and the University of Pittsburgh.

Another postwar phenomenon was the company-based MLD program. The Industrial Conference Board reported in 1935 that only 3.1 percent of over 2,400 companies surveyed had such programs, rising to only 5.2 percent of over 3,400 companies in 1946. By 1952, the American Management Association found that 30 percent or the companies surveyed had MLD programs. While their sample was smaller and their definition a bit different, the growth trend is clear in this period and continued into the mid-1950s.

The Academy of Management began formal operations in 1941 after five years of discussions and meetings about the need for such a group (Wren, 1979, p.380). In 1942, the American Society of Training Directors was organized. This organization would become the American Society of Training and Development and was a latecomer to the MLD business. Later it adopted management and leadership development as a key part of its mission.

Management Reform Movement: 1953–1970

As MLD became a necessary part of the management profession, people in education and business began to take a close look at the quality of management education and the body of management knowledge that existed. They were not happy with what they found. Despite their growth, business schools in the 1950s remained very similar to those in the 1920s.

One of the Ford Foundation initiatives was a comprehensive study of business education that included recommendations for the future growth of management education. Started in 1955, the study was conducted by Robert A. Gordon and James E. Howell. Published in 1959, the final report is now one of the landmark works in the field of management education and development. The recommendations of this study, and the Ford Foundation's other efforts, have shaped the field of MLD ever since. The report was critical of the vocationalism and specialization prevalent in business schools of the time, in essence calling for the transformation of business schools from vocational to professional schools.

Along with the reform in business schools came a period of strong growth for all aspects of MLD. Company-based MLD programs experienced significant growth. A 1955 AMA study found that 54 percent of the 460 companies it surveyed had some systematic plan, program, or method to facilitate the development of people in or for management responsibilities *(Current Practice in the Development of Management Personnel,* p.3). A 1958 survey showed that of 492 top companies, 90.5 percent engaged in managerial development activities, with 84.8 percent of them conducting educational activity that required regular participation by management (Clark and Sloan, 1958, p.14).

Modern Management Era: 1970–2000

The early part of the modern era was really an extension of the reform movement. It was a time of consolidating gains made and continuing the progress started in the late 1950s and early 1960s. It was a time of change, although not the revolutionary change of the previous era. Business continued to change dramatically and become even more complicated. The explosion in information technologies that began in the 1960s continued into the 1970s and reshaped the way managers approached their jobs. It simplified managers' jobs by giving them new tools with which to manage, but it also complicated them because it required adapting to new technologies. The pace of technological change continues to challenge the very underpinnings of business and industry and the ability of managers to keep pace. Markets have become more complex and are now global in scope. The economic, governmental, and social environments of business have also grown more complex. The rise of the service economy and Internet commerce has reshaped much of our thinking and the workforce has grown increasingly diverse.

Beyond general expansion, this era saw the development and growth of the non-university, non-company based MLD organization. Porter and McKibbon (1988) point out that these firms fall into several categories. First are the firms whose primary business is offering MLD programs such as Wilson Learning, The Forum Corp., and the nonprofit Center for Creative Leadership. A second category includes firms whose primary business is something other than training but who provide programs as a piece of their business such as Arthur D. Little, Inc., and the major accounting-consulting firms. Nonprofit organizations offering management programs have also expanded. Notable examples include the Brookings Advanced Study Program and the Aspen Institute, a program for executives in the humanities whose growth was assisted by the interest of the Bell system in its programs. Finally, a vast array of individual consultants offer programs as well.

The concept of continuing education and learning for managers is now firmly entrenched in corporate America, although the methods, quantity, and sources vary greatly. A study of one thousand medium and large companies showed that 90 percent used some type of formal MLD program (Johnson et al., 1988, p.17). With the growth have come the critics. Two popular books that question the quality and integrity of both business schools and management consultants engaged in MLD are *Gravy Training: Inside the Shadowy World Business of Business Schools* (Crainer and Dearlove, 1999) and *The Witch Doctors: Making Sense of the Management Gurus* (Micklethwait and Wooldridge, 1996). The titles of these book challenge MLD in the twenty-first century to be theoretically sound and to demonstrate positive results.

EMERGENCE OF THE HRD RESEARCHCOMMUNITY

The HRD profession was a very large field of practice with no university academic home until the late twentieth century. Practitioners with university degrees came from many disciplines. Most were from education, business, psychology, and communication. For years universities acknowledged HRD as a career option for graduates without presenting a defined curriculum or disciplinary base.

Early University Programs

George Washington University

Leonard Nadler, who popularized the use of the term *human resource development* beginning in 1969, and his academic home base of George Washington University (GWU), deserve special status in the history of the discipline. GWU has a large and dynamic HRD graduate program in which Nadler's influence continued beyond his retirement. Specific program features of the HRD consulting role and international HRD have a long tradition at GWU.

Bowling Green State University

In the early 1970s, Bowling Green State University (BGSU) in Ohio supported separate programs in training and development and organization development. The BGSU graduate program, with a concentration in training and development, was headed by Richard A. Swanson, and the organization development graduate program was headed by Glenn Varney. Numerous innovative developments came out of BGSU for a number of years in spite of the fact that both were only master's-level programs.

Academy of Human Resource Development

The history of the Academy of Human Resource Development (AHRD) is relatively short and colorful. The academy was founded on May 7, 1993, during a passionate chartering conference. Numerous interesting events took place before and after the historic birth of AHRD. The chartering conference produced about seventy-five scholar-members in 1993. Now there are presently approximately one thousand scholar-members.

In reporting the AHRD's history, the first item to acknowledge is that HRD has been a large field of practice dominated by practical techniques and reactive thinking. HRD is very young as an academic field. Thus, the role of university-sponsored research and scholarship in the profession has been minor. During the last twenty years of the twentieth century, a cadre of HRD scholars seized opportunities to advance the status of research and scholarship in the profession. They struggled to have research lead the profession's practice. They edited special issues journals from related disciplines on the topics of HRD, training, and organization development. They joined the research committees of American Society for Training and Development (ASTD) and other practitioner societies, contributed to HRD monographs, started HRD research columns in non-research journals, and in 1990 gave birth to the first HRD research journal, the *Human Resource Development Quarterly,* under the leadership of Richard A. Swanson, founding editor.

The unwieldy Professor's Network of ASTD (most members were vendors, not professors) and the independent and elitist University Council for Research on HRD (fourteen doctoral degree-granting institutions) provided nests for the AHRD. Wayne Pace (Brigham Young University) was the driving force and founding president of AHRD. Karen E. Watkins (University of Texas) represented the Professor's Network, Richard A. Swanson (University of Minnesota) represented the University Council for Research on HRD, and both Watkins and Swanson became founding officers of the academy as they moved away from their former organizations. The altruistic goal seeking to advance the profession through research and scholarship eased the realignment of these two earlier groups into a new and independent Academy.

The vision of the Academy is to lead the HRD profession through research. The stated mission is to be the premier global organization focused on the systematic study of HRD theories, processes, and practices, the dissemination of the scholarly findings, and the application of those findings. Furthermore, the AHRD was designed to be a true community of scholars that cares deeply about advancing the scholarly underpinnings of the profession and about supporting one another in that journey.

AHRD, from its inception, was meant to be an international organization. Large involvement from a limited number of graduate faculty and students outside the United States helped (e.g., the University of Twente under the leadership of Wim J. Nijhof). AHRD also established an alliance with the *University Forum for HRD* based in the United Kingdom that helped advance the HRD international community of scholars as well as a cosponsorship of the Human Resource Development International under founding editor, Monica M. Lee. Gary N. McLean is credited with spearheading important efforts resulting in regional international AHRD chapters and annual conferences in both Asia and Europe.

The short history of the Academy is a litany of positive events and a cobweb of partnerships. Many are highlighted in the concluding "HRD History Time Line."

HRD HISTORY TIMELINE

The following timeline is a list of ideas, people, and developments of particular interest to scholars of Human Resource Development. Clearly, this timeline is neither exhaustive nor complete from a global perspective (Alagaraja and Dooley, 2003).

600-200 B.C

Confucian commitment to education as a profession
Professional classes created along with training for roles

500 B.C.–A.D. 500: INFLUENCE OF THE GREEKS AND ROMANS

Greek disdain for menial work
Socrates: The Socratic method of inquiry
Plato's *Republic:* Bringing together the domains of politics, education, and philosophy
Aristotle: The father of scientific thought
Romans: A pragmatic view

300–1300: MIDDLE AGES

Augustine: The fusion of the classics and Christianity
Monastic schools
St. Thomas Aquinas
Merchant and craft guilds
Apprenticeships

1400–1700: RENAISSANCE

Engineering and technical training in the Middle Ages
Secular education for boys and girls (Martin Luther)
Sensory learning (John Locke)
Experience, the best teacher (Jean-Jacques Rousseau)

Manual training (Johan Pestalozzi)

TRANSITION FROM THE NINETEENTH TO THE TWENTIETH CENTURIES IN AMERICA

Apprenticeship training
Industrial era
The decline of the apprenticeship in the
 United States
Technical training and corporation schools
First Chautauqua Assembly held on Lake
 Chautauqua, New York
Public education and technical training
The role of government in technical training

TWENTIETH-CENTURY AMERICA

1911	Frederick Taylor publishes The Principles of Scientific Management.
1912	Society for the Promotion of Industrial Education (later to become the American Vocational Association) is established.
1913	National Association of Corporate Schools (later to become the American Management Association) is founded.
1914–18	World War I
1914	Charles Allen develops and implements the four-step job instruction training (JIT) method as part of the war effort.
1926	American Association for Adult Education organized.

1933	Elton Mayo publishes the Hawthorne Studies.
1937	Dale Carnegie publishes How to Win Friends and Influence People.
1937	Founding of the National Association of Industrial Teacher Educators.
1941–45	World War II
1943	Abraham Maslow publishes A Theory of Human Motivation.
1944	Founding of the American Society of Training Directors (later to become the American Society for Training and Development).
1945	Channing Dooley publishes Training-within-Industry Report: 1940–1945 (this massive World War II effort is the watershed in the birthing of the contemporary human resource development profession).
1946	Kurt Lewin launches the Research Center for Group Dynamics at Massachusetts Institute of Technology.
1946	Tavistock Institute of Human Relations founded.
1947	Founding of the National Training Laboratories.
1947	Renis Likert pioneers the concept of survey-guided development.
1949	Eric Trist advances the idea of sociotechnical systems.
1954	Peter F. Drucker publishes The Practice of Management.
1956	K.E. Boulding publishes General Systems Theory: The Skeleton of a Science.
1958	B.F. Skinner builds the first teaching machine.
1958	Norm Crowder invents branching programmed instruction.
1959	Frederick Hertzberg et al. publish The Motivation to Work.
1959	Donald Kirkpatrick publishes magazine articles on the four-level evaluation model.

1961	Cyril O. Houle publishes The Inquiring Mind.
1962	Founding of the National Society for Programmed Instruction (later to become the National Society for Performance and Improvement and then the International Society for Performance Improvement).
1962	Robert Mager publishes Preparing Instructional Objectives.
1960	Douglas McGregor publishes The Human Side of the Enterprise. Training in Industry and Business magazine begins publication (later called Training).
1964	Gary S. Becker publishes Human Capital: A Theoretical and Empirical Analysis, with Special Reference to Education.
1964	The term human resource development first used by Harbison and Myers, economists focused on developing nations.
1964	Robert Craig (ed.) publishes the first edition of the Training and Development Handbook.
1965	Robert M. Gagne publishes The Conditions of Learning.
1968	Founding of the Organization Development Institute.
1969	Leonard Nadler promotes the term human resource development for the profession.
1970	Malcolm Knowles publishes The Modern Practice of Adult Education: From Pedagogy to Andragogy.
1970	Leonard and Zeace Nadler publish Developing Human Resources.
1972	Cyril O. Hoyle publishes The Design of Education.
1972	International Federation of Training and Development Organizations (IFTDO) is founded in Geneva, Switzerland.
1972	U.S. military officially adopts the instructional systems development (ISD) model.

1972	Ontario Society for Training and Development publishes Core Competencies for Training and Development.
1974	Avice M. Saint publishes Learning at Work: Human Resources and Organizational Development.
1978	Patrick Pinto and James Walker publish A Study of Professional Training and Development Roles and Competencies.
1978	Thomas Gilbert publishes Human Competence: Engineering Worthy Performance.
1983	Patricia McLagan and Richard McCullough publish Models for Excellence: The Conclusions and Recommendations of the ASTD Training and Development Competency Study.
1983	Founding of the Training and Development Research Center at the University of Minnesota (later named the Human Resource Development Research Center).
1987	Founding of the University Council for Research on Human Resource Development (later merged with the members of Professor's Network of ASTD to form the Academy of Human Resource Development in 1993).
1989	Performance Improvement Quarterly research journal begins publication. William Coscarelli is the founding editor. Sponsored by the National Society for Performance and Instruction (later called the International Society for Performance Improvement).
1990	Human Resource Development Quarterly research journal begins publication. Richard A. Swanson is the founding editor (sponsored by the American Society for Training and Development and co-sponsored since 1997 with the Academy of Human Resource Development).

1990	Peter M. Senge publishes The Fifth Discipline: The Art and Practice of the Learning Organization.
1990	Geary Rummler and Alan Brache publish Improving Performance: How to Manage the White Space on the Organizational Chart.
1992	Chris Argyris publishes On Organizational Learning.
1990	Founding of the Academy of Human Resources Development (India), an academy of practitioners and scholars with a mission of developing HRD professionals and focus on HRD professionalism.
1993	Founding of the Academy of Human Resource Development (AHRD), an international academy of HRD scholars. Wayne Pace is the founding president. Karen E. Watkins becomes president of AHRD.
1995	Founding of the University Forum for Human Resource Development (based in the U.K. and later expanded to Europe).
1996	Richard A. Swanson becomes President of AHRD.
1997	International Journal of Training and Development journal begins publication. Paul Lewis is the founding editor (published by Blackwell).
1997	Human Resource Development Research Handbook: Linking Research and Practice is sponsored by AHRD and ASTD (published by Berrett-Koehler).
1998	Elwood F. Holton III becomes President of AHRD.
1998	Human Resource Development International research journal begins publication. Monica M. Lee is the founding editor (sponsored by the AHRD and the University Forum for HRD, and published by Routledge/Taylor and Francis).

1999	Advances in Developing Human Resources scholarly topical quarterly begins publication. Richard A. Swanson is the founding editor (sponsored by the AHRD and published by Berrett-Koehler and then Sage).
1999	AHRD publishes Standards in Ethics and Integrity under the leadership of Darlene Russ-Eft.
1993.1999	Inducted into the HRD Scholar Hall of Fame:

• 1993 Channing R. Dooley (World War II Training within Industry Project)

• 1994 Malcolm S. Knowles (adult learning, andragogy)

• 1995 Lillian Gilbreth (human aspect of management)

• 1996 Kurt Lewin (change theory)

• 1997 B.F. Skinner (teaching machines)

• 1998 Donald S. Super (career development theory)

• 1999 Robert M. Gagne (conditions of learning)

TWENTY-FIRST CENTURY

2000	Gary N. McLean becomes president of AHRD.
2002	Human Resource Development Review begins publication as the theory quarterly of HRD. Elwood F. Holton III is the founding editor (sponsored by the AHRD and published by Sage).
2003	Korean Association of Human Resource Development founded.
2004	Gene Roth becomes President of AHRD.
2005	AHRD sponsors textbook titled Research in Organizations: Foundations and Methods of Inquiry (published by Berrett-Koehler).
2006	Larry Dooley becomes President of AHRD.
2000.2006	Inducted into the HRD Scholar hall of Fame

- 2000 Gary S. Becker (human capital theory)
- 2001 Leonard Nadler (foundations of HRD)
- 2002 John C. Flanagan (Critical Incident Technique)
- 2004 Richard A. Swanson (research leadership in the HRD profession)
- 2006 Gary N. McLean (international HRD research)

2007	AHRD adopts HRD Academic Program Standards for Excellence.
2008	Michael (Lane) Morris becomes President of AHRD.
2008	Paul B. Roberts produces the Human Resource Development Directory of Academic Programs in the United States-2008 (sponsored by the University of Texas at Tyler).

REFLECTION QUESTIONS

1. Identify at least three discrete times in history, report on how human beings were viewed during that time, and note the HRD implications.

2. Identify three HRD-related historical times or events of interest to you, explain why they are of interest, and what else you would like to know.

3. Why is the World War II Training within Industry (TWI) project seen as so important to HRD?

4. What unique role does the Academy of Human Resource Development play in the

140

HRD profession and what are some of its accomplishments?

5. Identify two recurring themes in the history of HRD. Name and describe them.

PART TWO

Theory and Philosophy in Human Resource Development

This section provides the critical theoretical and philosophical foundations of HRD. Both of these perspectives have generally been missing among HRD professionals and are essential for understanding and advancing the field.

CHAPTERS

4   The Role of Theory and Philosophy in Human Resource Development

5   The Theory of Human Resource Development

6   Component Theories of Human Resource Development

CHAPTER 4

The Role of Theory and Philosophy in Human Resource Development

CHAPTER OUTLINE

Introduction
- Importance of Theory
- Importance of Theory Building
- Definition of Theory.
- Theory-Development Process
Recognizing the Theory-Development Journey as Research
Requirements of a Sound Theory
Philosophy and Theory Underlying HRD
Philosophical Metaphors for HRD Theory and Practice
Contributed by Karen E. Watkins
- Organizational Problem Solver
- Organizational Change Agent/Interventionist or Helper
- Organizational Designer
- Organizational Empowerer/Meaning Maker
- Developer of Human Capital
- Summary

Conclusion
Reflection Questions

INTRODUCTION

In response to popular opinion to the contrary, Kurt Lewin, the famous early organization development innovator and scholar, presented his famous quote: "There is nothing so practical as good theory." It bears repeating. His description of practicality is in contrast to commonly held thoughts that theory is made of "half-baked ideas" disconnected from the "real world." A good theory is thorough and has been tested both intellectually and in practice. Lewin prevents us from misusing the word *theory.*

Sound theory helps direct the professional energies to models and techniques that are effective and efficient. Sound theory also confronts celebrity professionals and infomercial consultants that riddle the profession. For example, to the unsubstantiated promises of techniques for *accelerated learning,* buyers were warned to beware that it doesn't deliver on its promises (Torraco, 1992). For the unfulfilled promise and premises of Kirkpatrick's (1998) flawed four-level evaluation model, Holton (1996) warned the profession that after thirty-eight years it still does not meet any of the criteria required of sound theories or models. Science writer Michael Shermer has spent a career debunking false and flimsy ideas. He challenges practitioners and participants to step back and ask themselves if the art of the phenomenon under question is good enough, and if not, how can the science become attainable (Shermer, 2005)?

Importance of Theory

The HRD profession continues to develop its core theories and to understand that theory building is a scholarly process, not soapbox oratory. Below are a few organizing thoughts about theory. These ideas are important to highlight because some in HRD believe that it is not essential to the profession to clearly specify its underlying theory or even have one, for that matter (McLean, 1998). An interpretation of this view of theory is that the profession needs simply to have an ethical intent and to situationally draw upon as many theories as required in pursuit of its work. While practitioners need many theories in their toolkit, scholars of HRD seek an encompassing theory to define and guide the profession.

Importance of Theory Building

Theory is particularly important to a discipline that is emerging and growing (Chalofsky, 1990; Ruona, 2000; Torraco, 2005). Sound theory is not pontificating or forcefully marketing the latest fad. Rather, theory in an applied field such as HRD is required to be both scholarly and successful in practice and can be the basis of significant advances. Rhetoric that negates theory, or the promotion of the idea that theory is disconnected from practice, does not come from those who have rigorously worked to use sound theory to enhance practice.

Definition of Theory

The following two definitions from HRD scholars capture the essence of theory and the challenge facing our profession:

- *"A theory simply explains what a phenomenon is and how it works"* (Torraco, 1997, p.115). Torraco's definition poses the following questions: What is HRD, and how does it work?

- *"Theory building is the process or recurring cycle by which coherent descriptions, explanations, and representations of observed or experienced phenomena are generated, verified, and refined"* (Lynham, 2000b, p.160). Lynham's definition poses the following question: What commitments must individuals, the HRD profession, and its infrastructure make to establish and sustain theory-development research in the HRD profession?

Theory-Development Process

Theory development can be thought of as an unending journey for any discipline. Yet, it is reasonable to assume that there are points in the maturation of a field of study that cause it to press theory-development research to the forefront. We contend (1) that the demand for HRD theory is increasing, (2) that our present available understandings have taken us about as far as we can go, and (3) that what we do is too important to wallow in atheoretical explanations.

RECOGNIZING THE THEORY-DEVELOPMENTJOURNEY AS RESEARCH

When a scholar takes a serious look at the theory development research journey, it is quite intricate and rigorous. A journal theme issue titled "Theory Building in Applied Disciplines," edited by Lynham (2002), is recommended reading for all those interested in HRD theory development. In addition, there are numerous benchmark theory-prac-tice publications. "Workplace Learning: Debating the Five Critical Questions of Theory and Practice," edited by Rowden (1996), and *Systems Theory Applied to Human Resource*

Development, edited by Gradous (1989), have provided excellent contributions to the theory in HRD. Gradous's theory of HRD with arguments for and against a unifying theory for HRD. The classic monograph uses systems theory as a springboard for thinking about the perspectives in this monograph range from a call for focusing on system outputs—that is, being results driven versus activity driven (Dahl, 1989)—to the consideration of field and intervention theory, the theory of work design, critical theory, and human capital theory (Watkins, 1989). The idea of multiple theories that pay attention to people, organizational viability, and a systematic and systemic understanding of the context, emerged in this monograph. These far-ranging ideas are present in most theoretical debates about HRD.

Serious theory-development methodologies are challenging (Reynolds, 1971; Dubin, 1978; Cohen, 1991). Even comparatively simple theory-building tools and methods put forward require significant effort for the theory builder (e.g., Patterson, 1983; Storberg-Walker, 2006; Strauss and Corbin, 2007). The HRD profession needs to encourage and respect a full continuum of theory-building engagement. Examples are varied.

Seemingly elementary investigations into definitions and identification of the range of thought within HRD can be important theory-development steppingstones. Specific examples include the following:

- "Commonly Held Theories of Human Resource Development" (Weinberger, 1998). Weinberger charts the history and the evolving definition of human resource development. Up to this point, this basic information has been scattered throughout the literature.

- "Operational Definitions of Expertise and Competence" (Herling, 2000). HRD methodically analyzes the literature on knowledge, competence, and expertise—core concepts in HRD. The HRD profession lacked clear scholarly literature defining human competence and expertise until Herling's work.

- *Organization Development: An Analysis of the Definitions and Dependent Variables* (Egan, 2000). Similar to Weinberger, Egan traces the definition of organization development over time with the added identification of declared outcomes.

- On the philosophical side, an example of theory research is *An Investigation into Core Beliefs Underlying the Profession of Human Resource Development* (Ruona, 1999). This study investigates the thought and value systems the discipline of HRD. Within her extensive findings, Ruona has determined that *learning* and *performance* are the two dominant philosophical views among HRD leaders.

- "Philosophical Foundations of HRD Practice" (Ruona and Roth, 2000) exposes core values in the field, while "Theoretical Assumptions Underlying the Performance Paradigm of Human Resource Development" (Holton, 2002) pushes to articulate the underlying assumptions related to the performance and learning paradigms and their common connection to learning.

It is important to recognize that each of these studies advances understanding of the HRD phenomenon.

Examples of straightforward theory-building efforts on the part of HRD scholars include the following. Each one of these cited pieces and numerous others deserve forums with opportunity for reflection in an effort to advance the profession.

- *Systems Theory Applied to Human Resource Development* (Gradous, 1989) presents an exploration of systems theory as being foundational to HRD.
- "A Theory of Knowledge Management" (Torraco, 2000) helps us think theoretically about the supportive systems required of the phenomenon of knowledge management.

- "Human Resource Development and its Underlying Theory" (Swanson, 2001) discusses the underlying theory of HRD when performance improvement is viewed as the desired outcome.
- "A Theory of Scenario Planning" (Chermack, 2002) emphasizes the dynamic impact scenario planning can have on an organization preparedness for uncertain futures.
- "The Evolution of Social Capital Theory" (Storberg, 2002) emphasizes the importance of social capital theory to HRD and its impact on organizational effectiveness.
- "Responsible Leadership for Performance: A Theoretical Model and Hypotheses" (Lynham and Chermack, 2006) looks at leadership in the context of purpose rather than the limited lens of leaders' traits and behaviors.

REQUIREMENTS OF A SOUND THEORY

Critics of HRD have chided the large number of HRD practitioners and commercial HRD products as being atheoretical (Swanson, 1998; Holton, 1996). *Atheoretical* means there is no thorough scholarly or scientific basis for the ideas and products being promoted. Organizations seeking quick or magical solutions are vulnerable to the exaggerated promises of suppliers. Patterson (1983) has provided the following criteria for assessing the theory that undergirds sound practice: (1) importance, (2) preciseness and clarity, (3) parsimony and simplicity, (4) comprehensiveness, (5) operationality, (6) empirical validity or verifiability, (7) fruitfulness,

Reflective practitioners and scholars want to know about the completeness and integrity of ideas they adopt. Certainly there are always new ideas, and those ideas generally deserve to be tried and tested. An ethical problem arises when unjustified claims are made in an attempt to market these ideas before they are fully developed and assessed.

PHILOSOPHY AND THEORY UNDERLYING HRD

There is tension in the academic world about the distinction between disciplines and fields of study. Some of the tension is rooted in history and tradition, some with singularity of focus in some fields, and some has to do with knowledge apart from practice. The debates around academic "turf" contain a number of issues. First, HRD is an old and established realm of practice and yet a relatively young academic field of study. While HRD continues to mature, the stage of maturation varies within nations and between nations.

Most academic fields of study are *applied* (e.g., medicine, engineering, education, business, and communication) and draw upon multiple theories in articulating their disciplinary base. HRD is not alone. It is common for applied disciplines to create specializations that over time come to outgrow their hosts and break away as independent disciplines. For example, university departments of adult education and vocational education have historically supported HRD in the United States. In the late 1990s, many of these HRD programs became larger than their adult education and vocational education academic university hosts and carried with them particular emphases. A simple example would be a higher interest in self-directed learning in programs from those nurtured in an adult education department, performance-based learning from those nurtured in a vocational education department, and human capital development from those nurtured in a human resource department.

Another point of confusion is that most disciplines are rooted in a set of theories, and some of those theories are shared by other disciplines. A major question is, "What core theories help define the HRD discipline?" If psychological theory were determined to be one

154

of them, note that HRD programs are hosted in colleges of the arts, engineering, business, and education—all draw upon some aspect of psychological theory. What slice of psychological theory, and for what purpose, are the questions that help select the specific psychological theories that help frame the discipline? In that HRD has specific purposes, those purposes are instrumental in guiding the profession to general theories and specific theories as being core. Thoughtfully identifying core component theories of HRD and their fusion is essential for advancing HRD's academic status (Swanson, 2007).

Choosing core contributing theories is not a casual exercise. Take two theories often considered as foundational to HRD: systems and anthropological theories. Systems theory is not as value laden as anthropology. Anthropologists are generally committed to not disturbing or changing the culture they study. In contrast, systems theory is almost always thinking about understanding the system and the potential of improving it. Thus, it can be paradoxical to have HRD people espouse anthropological views while intending to change the culture. This is a simple illustration of the missing logic that can occur when theory development is bypassed. Given the nature and purpose of HRD, easy arguments can be made that systems theory is core to HRD and that anthropology is secondary. Anthropology can provide important situational methods and tools to be called upon as needed while never being core to the theory and practice of HRD. Recently, social capital theory has been seriously entertained by HRD scholars (Akdere, 2008; Storberg, 2002; Tuttle, 2002). By itself, social capital theory is particularly useful for the organization development side of HRD. Yet, it could be argued that social capital theory, like HRD, is a fusion of economic, psychological, and systems theories for its own purposes.

A second example of missing logic within HRD is seen when HRD professionals claim a whole systems view (of the world, the organization, and the people in it) without having the rigorous systems theory and tools to match those claims. Putting people into a guided group process and relying only on those interaction skills is inadequate for whole systems understanding. Such a limited view would reduce the skill of the HRD professional to group interaction facilitation.

Theory has an enormous challenge and opportunity in the growing HRD profession. The concurrent questions are questions of philosophy: What is there? (ontology); How do you know? (epistemology), and Why should I? (ethics). The following essay by Dr. Karen

Watkins, a noted HRD scholar, provides alternative philosophical metaphors for thinking about HRD theory and practice.

PHILOSOPHICAL METAPHORS FORHRD THEORY AND PRACTICE

Contributed by Karen E. Watkins

Theories from different disciplines attempt to explain the universe, using the tools and perspectives of that discipline. An interdisciplinary applied field like HRD can thus be expected to make use of many different theories. For example, general systems theory is a robust and useful diagnostic theory, which befits a particular philosphic metaphor.

Just as different disciplines and different system levels may call for different theories, so may alternative *philosophies* for the role of human resource development call for different theories. Five such philosphic metaphors will be considered and are depicted in Figure 4.1: The human resource developer as organizational problem solver, organizational change agent/interventionist or helper, organizational designer, organizational empowerer/meaning maker, and developer of human capital.

Organizational Problem Solver

For many years, the dominant image of the trainer has been one of a person who designs instructional programs to respond to organizationally defined problems. Training has been largely behavior oriented, in keeping with the emphasis on skills training. Systems theory is a useful tool for designing programs to respond to clearly defined problems. It enables people to attend to the whole and to classify and define the parts of a system. Depending on how broadly they define the system, they can think about the problem in increasingly broad terms. From the level of the individual to the "whole wide world environment," systems are made up of the same parts—context, inputs, processes, outputs, and feedback loops. These parts not only help clarify the elements of a system, but they have definable characteristics that can be tinkered with to produce alternative outputs. By increasing the number of inputs, by improving the processes that produce the outputs, or by drawing resources more effectively from the environment, or context, we can alter the cost and effectiveness of our outputs. Because systems theory has been so useful for helping trainers think about the nature of the problems they are trying to solve, the theory has been widely favored. But there are problems with relying on it.

158

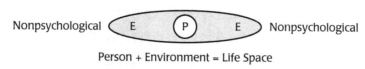

Person + Environment = Life Space

Figure 4.1 The Psychological Life Span

Systems theory is a useful diagnostic theory, but it does not help us decide which parts are working and which are not. It is not normative, so there is no hint about what might be a more ideal solution to the present situation. Moreover, systems theory focuses more on problem solving than on problem finding, yet the complex, turbulent environments in which organizations find themselves today demand much greater emphasis on the problem-identification phase of the problem-solving process.

Systems theory has grown out of the recognition that to solve the problems of the world, we need models that are more holistic than analytic, as were those in favor previously. Greenman (1978) suggested that efficient system models help people and organizations maintain purposeful, goal-directed behavior. He pointed out that there are inherent dilemmas in the use of systems models, such as the dilemma of oversimplifying complex environments or the dilemma of idealism versus realism. To accompany the classic systems model, Greenman developed a decision-making cycle that moves through three phases: *policy making, preplanning evaluation,* and *action implementation,* which therefore incorporates problem solving. Senge (1987) has noted that decision making is where most problems occur. Decision making is the product of a mental model, and if a manager's mental model is inadequate, he or she will make poor decisions.

Senge hypothesizes that managerial learning processes will be more effective if they are the result of a systemic and dynamic perspective or worldview. He concludes that the task of HRD professions is to map, challenge, and improve existing mental models. The systems approach, when conceptualized broadly, may be a useful model for addressing short-term perspectives, truncated problem-solving processes, or limited worldviews.

Because systems theory does not include even an implicit normative model, it is often coupled with other theories of organizational change or effectiveness to enable decision makers to move from diagnosing problems in a system to prescribing action. Systems thinking is often at a fairly macro or abstract level and some other model or theory is needed to identify operational constructs that can be enacted in organizations. The following metaphors are often used in concert with systems theory.

Organizational Change Agent/Interventionist or Helper

Many would argue that the most compelling metaphor for HRD is that of organizational change agent or helper (see Mink and Watkins, 1983). In this conception, human resource developers help people and organizations change. To do this, they need a theory of how human beings and groups are led to act as they do and what interventions might influence them to act differently. To start at the beginning, we must start with Kurt Lewin, the father of organizational change agentry.

Lewin's field theory is a comprehensive depiction of human behavior. First there was Freud, who gave us a theory to help us understand the importance of individual history, and then there was Lewin, who helped us understand the group, especially as a means of understanding people (Argyris, 1952). These two remain two of the most influential thinkers in psychology. Lewin developed field theory out of the field concept in physics—the study of electromagnetic fields—which eventually led to Einstein's theory of relativity. The first psychologists to use field theory were the gestalt psychologists, who believed that the way an object is perceived is determined by the context in which it is embedded and that the relationship between the parts of that perceptual field is more important than the characteristics of those separate parts (Hall and Lindzey, 1970). Lewin, who was associated with these early Gestalt psychologists while at the University of Berlin, developed field theory as a way to represent psychological reality. He had three major premises:

- Behavior is a function of the field that exists at the time the behavior occurs. This has often been expressed as the equation $B=f$ (P, E), or behavior (B) is a function (f) of the interaction between a person (P) and his or her psychological environment (E).
- Analysis begins with the situation as a whole (the Gestalt) from which we may differentiate parts.
- The concrete person in a concrete situation can be represented mathematically (Hall and Lindzey, 1970).

To amplify the first premise, Lewin termed the environment, as the person perceives and organizes it, the psychological field, or the *life space.* Lewin suggested that the life space was made up of the person and his or her environment. He believed these parts were dynamically interrelated and held in equilibrium, with changes in any part affecting the whole just as in an electromagnetic field. Field theorists believe that a field not only surrounds the individual, but it also combines or overlaps with that of others to make up the *social field* (Argyris, 1952). Thus, by studying the organization in the individual, we can know the organization. A related idea in field theory is that past events only influence behavior in the present in terms of present conditions. For example, growing up with an alcoholic does not affect one's present behavior, but the mental "tapes" and embedded shame-based behavior one carries over from the past may.

Lewin sought to understand the psychological field with enough rigor that it could be represented mathematically. He even developed a new mathematic to help him represent psychological reality. Using topology, he could mathematically depict the connectedness of regions in the life space. Such concepts as Karl Weick's (1976) loose and tight coupling and the idea of having no permeable boundaries for the self illustrate ways we have conceptualized the degree of connectedness between regions. Although that degree of connectedness is more psychological than spatial, it is nevertheless clear and observable and hence may be represented mathematically. Organizational researchers, for example, sometimes measure the degree of loose or tight coupling in decision making by the number of decisions that organizational members say must go to the top of the organization.

Lewin developed "hodology," or a mathematic of path, to express psychological distance and direction. Lewin's concern was for powerful, scientific discourse, and the language of mathematics was considered the most powerful. He chose the mathematics of spatial relationships to explain the person in his or her life space. He depicted the person as a circle within a larger circle, much like the boy in a bubble. Thus, people have boundaries that differentiate them from each other and from their environment. Yet they are included in a larger area or context, which also defines who they are. Bordering the entire life space is a *foreign hull,* which Lewin described as made up of all the data to which a person is not now attending but which is nevertheless part of his or her environment (Hall and Lindzey, 1970).

By varying the thickness of the circle around *P,* we can indicate a person's accessibility or inaccessibility. Lewin divided the life space into regions based on relevant psychological facts at any given moment. Those that are relevant to the person are *needs;* those that are relevant to the environment are *valences.* Needs are a system in a state of tension, or psychological energy, directed toward the boundaries of the system (Argyris, 1952). Needs are directed toward *goals*—regions in the life space that are attractive to the person or, in other words, have a positive valence. Here the analogy seems clear. Lewin said there may be *barriers* in the life space that create resistance to goal attainment, and these barriers may be social, physical, or psychological. The clarity with which a person perceives the field in terms of structure, the amount of differentiation, and the relationships between regions is the *cognitive structure.* The regions of the personality are organized in definite relationships to each other; this arrangement is called the *psychological structure.*

Force in the psychological field is the tendency toward movement in people or groups. *It is the cause of change.* It is a vector with direction and magnitude or size. Every force in one direction has its opposite, so the direction of movement will depend on the strength of a given force. A force field is a constellation of forces. Human resource developers commonly use force-field analysis to analyze conflict situations, to problem solve, or to identify change strategies. It consists of analyzing the forces promoting and inhibiting change and determining the strength of each of those forces, followed by developing strategies to reduce the strength of the restraining forces and testing those strategies in action.

Lewin's theory can also be viewed in terms of adult development. Adults, he said, have more regions in their personality and are thus more differentiated than children. The boundaries between regions of the adult are less permeable, making adults more rigid but also less affected in one region by frustrations in another. In contrast, the child who wants an apple and can't have it will find that his frustration spreads to his play, his ability to concentrate, and so on. Long periods of frustration may produce de-differentiation in adults. For example, when workers are underutilized, their behavior deteriorates in all areas of their lives.

The *social field* is made up of the group life space and may contain many subgroups or regions. The group has its own unique properties, both structural (the degrees of differentiation, stratification, and unity, as well as the type of organization or social hierarchy) and dynamic (group goals, ideal goals, style of living, and psychological and social climate) (Argyris, 1952).

Most people are part of many groups. Often these groups create *overlapping situations* for people. Chris Argyris (1952) used the example of a foreman who is both part of the worker groups and part of the management group. The degree of *consonance,* or similarity in values, norms, and goals between the groups will increase or decrease the amount of overlap, the valence or desirability of that overlap, and the nature of the barriers between the groups (Argyris, 1952). A clearer understanding of the nature of groups, intergroup conflicts, and the psychological reality internalized by individuals as members of groups grew out of Lewin's work.

Finally, people vary in terms of the relative accessibility of various regions in their life spaces. This concept is defined as their *space of free movement.* A person may view a region negatively or may have a barrier imposed around a region. In either case, movement toward personal goals will be impeded. For example, adults who have difficulty playing have limited their space of free movement. Also, in the case of a foreman in a newly unionized company, the union will circumscribe the foreman's ability to hire, fire, and work directly with the workers. Psychologically, the foreman's space of free movement also will be circumscribed.

Perhaps the most significant aspect of field theory is that it does not purport to be or to explain objective reality, but rather to explain a person's psychological reality, which is not what *is* but what that person perceives reality to be. But Lewin did not develop his theory only to explain human behavior at an abstract level. Like most human resource developers, he was interested in observing these abstract concepts at work at the practical level. He believed that one had to have a theory that was broad enough to encompass the multifaceted nature of human action, and that the way to test that theory was through a process called *action research.*

Action research can be thought of as a series of successive approximations. Interventions are developed while looking at the whole (at the individual level, at the life space, at the organizational level, and at the social field). Interventions are made and their effects studied. They are followed by new interventions, which are developed upon reflection of the previous effects on the whole. Lewin depicted the process of movement from a present state to a desired state through action and reflection as a process of unfreezing, changing, and refreezing.

Lewin's concepts will not lead to simple prescriptions or step-by-step instructions for human resource developers wondering what to do on Monday, but they do bring into sharper focus the architectural structure of human and organizational relationships in a way that permits a rich analysis of organizational life.

The work of Chris Argyris, who was one of Lewin's last students, furthers our understanding of how to use field theory in organizational change efforts. He defined intervention as entering "into an ongoing system of relationship, to come between or among persons, groups, or objects for the purpose of helping them" (1970, p.15). In field-theory terms, to intervene is to interrupt the forces in the life space in such a way as to disrupt the quasi-stationary equilibrium.

Argyris emphasized that the system exists independently of the intervenor and that despite the interdependencies that develop between the client system and the intervenor, the intervenor should focus on how to maintain or increase the autonomy of the client system, how to differentiate even more clearly the boundaries between the client system and the intervenor, and how to conceptualize and define the client system's health, independent of the intervenor. *The client must be the system as a whole regardless of where one initially begins to work,* he said. Interventions, must, over time, provide all members with opportunities to enhance their competence and effectiveness (Argyris, 1970). Perhaps because of the ethical implications of tinkering with a person's or an organization's life space, the intervenor's primary tasks are to seek valid information, to provide for free and informed choice, and to encourage the client's internal commitment to the choices made in the interventions.

As HRD practitioners, our theories of practice usually contain intervention theories—theories of action aimed at increasing our effectiveness (Argyris and Schon, 1982). Because these theories are largely tacit, we need to reflect critically on what we actually do in order to examine and test our assumptions about what causes us to be effective. Argyris developed a normative theory of intervention. Having observed repeated patterns in people's theories of practice, he identified the pattern most commonly found in people's actual practice as a control orientation. In contrast to this pattern is a learning-oriented intervention theory that encapsulates Argyris's prescription for effective intervention.

Viewed from the perspective of field theory, Argyris can be seen to have defined the intervenor-client relationship in a way that will minimize the potential conflict in an overlapping situation (or field) in order to decrease the conflict that might be produced by attempts to control others and in order to permit learning to occur. His primary tasks for intervenors are designed to minimize the production of perceptual barriers in the form of defensiveness, negative attributions about the intervenor's motives, and other self-protective responses that could limit the intervenor's space of free movement and subsequent learning. By emphasizing the need for shared meaning between client and intervenor about goals and the personal causal responsibility of the client for actions and choices, Argyris hoped to increase the consonance between the two overlapping situations.

Action science (Argyris, Putnam, and Smith, 1985) has been defined as "an inquiry into how human beings design and implement action in relation to one another." It has three key features:

- empirically disconfirmable propositions that are organized into a theory;
- knowledge that human beings can implement in an action context;
- alternatives to the status quo that both illuminate what exists and inform fundamental change, in light of values freely chosen by social actors (p.4).

These three propositions have traveled far from Lewin's three key tenets. Like Lewin, Argyris believed that human action is the result of subjective human perception that occurs within a behavioral world or a life space. Both agreed that this knowledge of the perceptual world could inform and reform action. Lewin believed that for adults, education was most often reeducation, a process of unfreezing that begins with a disconfirmation of one's present beliefs or perception of reality, which leads to anxiety or guilt and finally to a search for psychological safety. The critical theory that people change as a result of an internal critique in which they perceive that their own action is in conflict with their own values has refined Argyris's concept of reeducation.

Argyris described re-education as a process of disconfirmation based on internal critique, which leads to a sense of personal causal responsibility (as in, "I produced this mismatch—this action that conflicts with my values"), which can then lead to psychological success or congruence between one's internal critique and the external feedback one receives. Argyris noted that people and organizations develop elaborate defensive routines to deny that these mismatches occur and to save face. Only by interrupting those defensive routines will people and organizations experience psychological success.

In both Lewin's and Argyris's work, the emphasis is on a way of understanding people, especially in their social context. They offer not a technical prescription of action for change agents, but rather a rich conceptual framework for action in any change situation.

Organizational Designer

A third metaphor for HRD is that of organizational designer. Organizational design is the process of first diagnosing and then selecting the structure and formal system of communication, authority, and responsibility to achieve organizational goals. Organizational designers attend to environmental flux, strategic choices, and the uncertainty or certainty of task or technology (Hellriegel, Slocum, and Woodman, 1986). People who work from this conception see a clear connection between the structure of work and work organizations and the development of the organization's human resources. A foundational theory for students of organization design is Herb Simon's administrative decision-making theory.

Simon (1965) theorized that individuals have a bounded rationality that leads to satisfaction in decision making. Given the quantity of information we deal with, we need to find boundaries within which to make rational decisions. We may use heuristics or rules of thumb, which, experience suggests, usually lead to acceptable solutions; but heuristics may limit the search for solutions, especially in large, complex problem spaces (note the Lewinian image). In contrast, algorithms are more rigorous, systematic procedures. One goal of management science is to discover more algorithms by which managers may make more consistently effective decisions.

To meet this goal, we need to have a concept of the elements that make up decision-making activity. The typical response of managers to stimuli is a program, the basic element of Simon's theory. A program has basic parts:

- stimuli—the information that evokes a program
- inputs—both facts and values
- content—a series of execution steps
- outputs

There are programmed and unprogrammed activities: A programmed activity is prompted by a single clear stimulus. An unprogrammed activity is evoked when there is no tried-and-true method for handling the stimulus, either because it is a new situation, its nature is elusive and complex, or because it is so important that it deserves a customized response. Unprogrammed activity has three stages of individual activity, each stage of which is so rich that the stage itself has theories. The stages are:

- intelligence activity—searching the environment for conditions calling for a decision
- design activity—inventing, developing, and analyzing a course of action
- choice activity—selecting a course of action from those available

For intelligence activity, theorists have explored the differences in problem framing between novices and experts. Schon (1983) found that experts frame problems through a kind of artistry that defies routinization, whereas novices follow more of a technical, by-the-numbers process. Jaques (1985) suggested that individuals vary in cognitive complexity, or work capacity. Work capacity is the longest time period one can plan a project or work without the need of feedback. This variable, Jaques said, is a given in individuals, like their height, and it varies enormously. Most people have a work capacity between three months and one year. A few scientists, politicians, and leaders have work capacities that exceed their lifetimes; they are designing new worlds. People with limited work capacities cannot fall back far enough to view a problem with a wide-angle lens, nor can they conceive of long-term solutions or parallel implications. Thus, they are limited in the scope of work that they can design.

Design activity has also been studied extensively. We see design as having both a conceptual and an aesthetic quality, whether we conceive of it

- in the dictionary sense, as in conceiving an idea or a form, planning and shaping a structure, using tools and materials creatively, and making something useful;

- in the broader context used by Simon, as in converting actual to preferred situations;
- or in accordance with C. West Churchman's (1971) notion that design is occurring whenever we consciously attempt to change ourselves and our environment to improve the quality of our lives (p.vii).

Churchman (1971) stated that design is "thinking behavior which conceptually selects among a set of alternatives in order to figure out which alternative leads to the desired goals or set of goals" (p.5). Schon (1983, 1987) understands design to be a process of problem framing or problem setting, in which the artistry of expert practitioners is a "reflective conversation with a situation," which may lead to a reframing of the situation and thence to an architectural plan or a therapeutic intervention. Pfeiffer and Jones (1973) described the design process in training as dependent on four considerations:

- the parameters of the situation (time, place, resources, staff, etc.)
- the skill needed to design
- the components to be designed
- outcome criteria, which are defined in terms of client needs.

Those considerations will be influenced greatly by the conceptual skill (thinking behavior) and the design expertise (artistry) of the designer. Design is artistic, because in these nonroutine, unprogrammed activities, we must create a new artifact, plan, or training program.

Most of what human resource developers do is unprogrammed activity. Organizational design has emerged as a distinct field within the study of organizations. Galbraith (1974) noted that "the ability of the organization to successfully utilize coordination by goal setting, hierarchy, and rules depends on the combination of the frequency of exceptions and the capacity of the hierarchy to handle them" (p.29).

Organizational design was thus the creation of responses to uncertainty, which he said could be done either by

- reducing the need for information processing through creating slack resources or self-contained tasks, or by
- increasing the organization's capacity to process information through investment in vertical information systems or through the creation of lateral relationships.

Lorsch (1971) focused on the design dimensions of differentiation and integration. In each of these theoretical models, organizational design is triggered through a process of assessing the gap between where the organization is now and where it needs to be, based on a normative model of organizational effectiveness.

Design theory has emerged from the literature of art, architecture, computer science, decision making, and education. Houle, in *The Design of Education* (1972), found that design is a two-part process consisting of first examining the situation in which the learning activity occurs and then applying a framework to that situation. The framework can be systems theory, field theory, or some other theory; although designers who operate only out of a credo or belief system, such as Malcolm Knowles's andragogy, will find that their frameworks are not broad enough to guide a program design process. Thus, the systems approach is a useful theoretical tool to guide the design stage, but other theories may be more useful for Simon's other two stages of unprogrammed activity.

Organizations increase productivity by increasing the level of routinization. Thus, a major task for human resource developers is to help managers design routine responses for nonroutine, unprogrammed activities. There are many ways to do this, from designing a learning program for training machine operators to use a new machine, to designing strategic systems for monitoring unstable or unpredictable processes. General systems theory is an analytical process model, not a content model. In order to develop models for diagnosis and prescriptions for action, organizational design theorists add to systems theory other normative content theories, such as a theory of an open, healthy person or a theory of organizational effectiveness.

Organizational Empowerer/Meaning Maker

Theorists who embrace this metaphor seek to transform people and organizations in order to foster long-term health and effectiveness. They view the organization and its people as repressed and disenfranchised. As adherents of the philosophy that meanings are in people, they would agree with Smirich (1983) that "organizations are socially constructed systems of shared meaning" (p.221). In modern terms, they follow the prescripts of critical theory. Critical theories are aimed at producing enlightenment in those who hold them and are inherently emancipatory in that they help people free themselves from self-imposed coercion.

Critical theorists contrast their type of knowledge, which is "reflective," with that of normal science, which is "objectifying." They argue that because knowledge is never objective, the search for objectivity in normal science tends to objectify people and natural phenomena. Critical theory emancipates by offering a critique of "what is" from the perspective of "what might be." It seeks to stimulate self-reflection so that people may freely choose to transform their world. Geuss (1981) has defined

emancipation as a movement, or transformation, from an initial state to a final state. The
initial state is one of false consciousness, error,
and unfree existence, in which
- this false consciousness is interconnected
  with the oppression
- the false consciousness is self-designed, and
  the oppression is self-imposed
- the power in the above lies in the fact that
  people do not realize their oppression is self-
  imposed.

The final stage is one in which people are
free of false consciousness (enlightened) and
free of self-imposed constraints (emancipated).

People move from one state to another by
engaging in a process of self-reflection, or critical reflectivity, in which they
- dissolve the illusion of objectivity
- become aware of their own origin and
- bring to consciousness the unconscious determinants of their action (Geuss, 1981).

As a result of this reflection, a perspective
transformation will occur (Mezirow, 1981), and
the person will generate new knowledge, which
may be generalized into a critical theory. This
reflective thinking has also been referred to as
an internal critique of a person's epistemic beliefs (second-order beliefs about which beliefs
are acceptable), in which the person's values

are seen to contradict his or her ideal of a good life.

The critical theory so generated will consist of three parts:

- a demonstration that change is possible
- a depiction of the practical necessity of the change, as the present situation has produced frustration and suffering and is only thus because people hold a particular world-view that, upon critical reflection, is no longer acceptable
- an assertion that the movement or transformation can only come about if people accept the critical theory as their "self-consciousness" (Geuss, 1981, p.76).

The best-known critical theories are psychoanalysis for individuals and Marxism for social systems. Action science comes closest to operationalizing the idea of a critical theory for organizations.

The strategies used to transform perspectives in action science include determining the potential unintended or unjust consequences of action strategies, ensuring that participants feel personal causal responsibility for their actions, and offering an alternative for action in the form of learning-oriented behavior rather than coercive or control-oriented behavior.

Developer of Human Capital

The fifth and final metaphor of the human resource developer is that of the developer of human capital. A derivative of economics, human capital theory refers to "the productive capabilities of human beings that are acquired at some cost and that command a price in the labor market because they are useful in producing goods and services" (Parnes, 1986, p.1). Flamholtz (1985) emphasized that it is the "expected realizable value" of a person, given opportunities for training, expected turnover, age to retirement, promotability, and so on, that has ultimate value in a human resource accounting system. Value is typically perceived as the relationship between costs and benefits (or the return on investment). Gordon (in LaBelle, 1988) outlines the economic assumptions that underlie human capital theory: "Product and labor markets are competitive, firms attempt to maximize profits, workers seek to maximize earnings, and the labor force has both knowledge and mobility to take advantage of the best opportunities available" (p.206).

Salaries are seen in supply-and-demand terms. A worker's skills and abilities are a form of capital because they influence the worker's productivity for the organization as well as the worker's opportunities for higher wages, greater economic security, and increased employment prospects. Education, or training, is seen in the human capital model as a major tool to influence workers' acquisition of the needed knowledge and skills.

Dierkes and Coppock (1975) suggest that human needs are met in organizations as the result of a chain of interventions that have allowed a problem to bubble up from a state of recognition by subgroups in society, to legislation, to organizational enforcement of new human resource standards. An example is the human need for equal pay for equal work. A more proactive approach—one that attends to the organization's long-term human resource needs—is human resource accounting.

To illustrate how difficult it is to justify training without the concept of human resource accounting, Dierkes and Coppock compared how we now account for management's spending $100,000 on a new piece of equipment and how we account for spending the same amount on employee training or on efforts to improve the quality of the work environment. When purchasing equipment, the manager anticipates amortizing the costs over the expected life of the equipment and being able to document benefits by listing the equipment as an asset over a number of years. When purchasing human resource development, the manager anticipates incurring costs for the current year, with no amoritization over the useful life of the skills gained.

Human resource accounting systems have been developed to attempt to overcome this short-range distortion in measuring organizational economic effectiveness. Initially, the focus was on developing accounting procedures to determine investments in human capabilities. Human resource information systems attempted to inventory human resources, determine outlay and replacement costs, and determine the economic value of the human resources employed in the organization. Succession plans and lists of high-potential employees are recent outgrowths of organizational attempts to develop inventories of their human resource assets. These approaches led to a definition of the economic value of human resources as "the present discounted value of their [individuals'] future contributions less the costs of acquiring, maintaining, and utilizing these resources in the organization (Pyle, in Dierkes and Coppock, 1975, p.313).

The first extension of the application of human resource accounting systems was to health and safety measures, because, if people are assets, anything that diminishes those assets will diminish the organization's expected realizable value. The costs of investments in employee health, rehabilitation, safety measures, and safety training can be compared with the costs of days lost because of accidents and illnesses. It is a short step from there to examining the economic impact of the psychological work environment. The research and literature on job satisfaction, matching jobs and people, climate, leadership, motivation, etc., illustrate the high degree of interest in this approach. However, research linking these tertiary effects to productivity typically involves assumptions of correlation when, for example, a change in both climate and productivity occurs without careful concomitant control of any intervening social, historical, demographic, or political variables. Such research is difficult to conduct. Rensis Likert and David Bowers (1973) made perhaps the most comprehensive attempt to capture such relationships. In analyzing the result of a large number of studies, they found a .67 correlation between organizational climate and subordinates' satisfaction and a .42 correlation between subordinates' satisfaction and total productive efficiency. Given the large number of studies they used, these are fairly strong relationships, which suggest that climate influences satisfaction and leads to at least modest gains in productivity.

Human capital theory provides a strong, bottom-line-oriented justification for HRD. It breaks down the barriers that now exist between organizational development approaches that attempt to influence climate and quality of work life, employee assistance, and other employee health and safety areas, and the more conventional training and development arena of HRD. Each area makes its contribution to the organization's long-term effectiveness. The human capital, or human resource accounting approach, is perhaps most valuable for this long-term emphasis.

Changing demographics and higher labor participation by women and minorities along with recent technological changes are creating an enormous need for long-range thinking. "It becomes increasingly clear that economic security in the post-industrial economy depends less on expertise and more on *flexpertise*—the ability to continually adapt individual knowledge and skill.... Virtually the entire adult population needs retraining and new learning to be economically productive.... The emergence of a knowledge-based economy requires a new synthesis of the functions of training, education, and other forms of communication and learning under the single umbrella of the learning enterprise" (Perelman, 1984, pp.xvi–xvii).

Carevale (1984) has offered a similar analysis of the role of training and development in developing human capital. According to Carevale, workplace learning and formal education account for more growth in economic output than employee health, capital, the composition of the workforce, population size, or resource adaptation. Workplace learning, he said, accounts for 85 percent of the variance in lifetime earnings. The relationship between learning and training and economic returns for both people and organizations enjoys a distinguished, currently prominent place among the theoretical underpinnings for HRD.

Critics of human capital theory point to the limits of capitalism and to economic explanations of what people gain from investments in learning. In the first instance, they discuss the role of training as a means of social control, using as examples

- training as a means of despoiling, or "cooling out" the aspirations of many people so they will accept low-level jobs, and
- organizational training programs to socialize newcomers into conforming to the organization's norms and values.

Moreover, the inherent class structure and objectification of workers in bureaucratic organizations may produce lower productivity despite training efforts (La-Belle, 1988).

People gain considerably more from training than simply an enhanced economic value. Intrinsic satisfaction, enhanced life skills, the increased capacity to function effectively as parents, as citizens, are alternative benefits derived from training. In fact, people often regard training as a fringe benefit—a view human resource developers deplore, as it often leaves training budgets seeming as expendable as other fringe benefits. Yet this perspective may also correctly capture a more holistic, value-added approach to understanding the benefits of training.

Summary

The underlying root philosophies and theories of HRD are rich and varied. Increasing understanding among practitioners of their potential to enrich and improve practice often requires translations, such as Peter Senge's translation of systems theory to management practice and Argyris's translation of field theory to HRD practice. When human resource developers come to embrace many different theoretical foundations, practice will be enlarged and will rise to the level demanded by the present complex, nonroutine, ambiguous business environment. Not one, but many metaphors can be used to guide our understanding of the field of our practice.

CONCLUSION

Theory, research, development, and practice together compose a vital cycle that allows ideas to be progressively refined as they evolve from concepts to practices and from practices to concepts (Swanson, 2007). The Theory-Research-Development-Practice Cycle (Figure 4.2) illustrates the systematic application of inquiry methods working to advance the knowledge used by both HRD researchers and practitioners.

There are those that caution us in constructing the relationships among theory, research, development, and practice. In offering the notion of a scientific *paradigm,* Kuhn (1970) compelled philosophers and researchers to rethink the assumptions underlying the scientific method and paved the way for alternative, postpositivistic approaches to research in the behavioral sciences. Ethnography and naturalistic inquiry allow theory to emerge from data derived from practice and experience; theory does not necessarily precede research as theory can be generated *through* it. The model of theory, research, development, and practice for HRD embraces these cautions (see Figure 4.2).

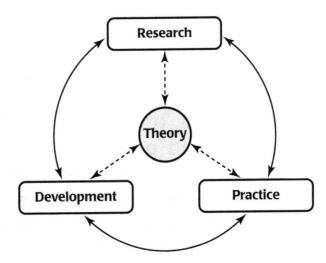

Figure 4.2 Theory-Research-Development-Practice Cycle Source: Swanson, 2005, p.8.

The cyclical model brings HRD theory, research, development, and practice together in the same forum. The union of these domains is itself an important purpose of the model. Two other purposes also exist. First, each of the four domains makes a necessary contribution to HRD. There is no presumption about the importance to the profession of contributions from research, practice, punctuated development efforts, and theory itself. The model demonstrates the need for all domains to inform each other in order to enrich the profession as a whole. Second, exchange among the domains is multidirectional. Any of the domains can serve as an appropriate starting point for proceeding through the cycle. Improvements in the profession can occur whether one begins with theory, research, development, or practice. Thus, each of the cycle's domains both *informs* and *is informed by* each of the other domains.

In summary, HRD philosophy and theory results in powerful and practical *explanations, principles,* and *models* for professionals to carry out their work in organizations. The problem facing almost every organization, and those who work in them, is in meeting the constant demand for high performance. In that organizations are human-made entities, they require human expertise to perform, grow, and adapt. These demands include everything from assuring sustainable financial growth of the organization to satisfying the next customer standing in the front row. Without a holistic mental model of human resource development within an organizational system and improvement context working through people, the practitioner is left with the task of dissecting and interpreting each and every HRD situation in isolation. Or worse yet, they simply charge ahead in a trial-and-error mode.

REFLECTION QUESTIONS

1. Why would someone argue that good theory is practical?
2. What is theory? Give a definition and an explanation.

3. Of the HRD theory references cited on pages 77–90, which one interests you the most? Why?

4. Which of the five philosophical metaphors for HRD theory presented by Dr. Karen Watkins makes the most sense to you? Explain why?

5. Which of the five philosophical metaphors for HRD theory makes the most sense to a high-tech business organization? Explain why.

CHAPTER 5

Theory of Human Resource Development

CHAPTER OUTLINE

Introduction
Perspectives on Theory and Practice
Theory Framework for Applied Disciplines
- Boundary of the Theory
- Contributing Theories
- Core Theory
- Useful Theory
- Novel Theory
- Irrelevant Theory
  Theory of Human Resource Development
- Assumptions, Context, Definition, and Models of HRD
- Theoretical and Disciplinary Foundations of HRD
- Economic Theory Component of HRD
- Psychological Theory Component of HRD
- Systems Theory Component of HRD
- Ethics in HRD
- Summary
  Conclusion
  Reflection Questions

INTRODUCTION

Models of HRD have been developed and disseminated through books, seminars, and consulting projects. Many models are based on extensive practical experience with development and improvement (Brache, 2002; Nadler, Gerstein, and Shaw, 1992; Rummler and Brache, 1995; Schwartz, 1996; Weisbord, 1987). Other models have been embraced as ways to solve problems then casually called "multidisciplinary" to demand that the user apply multidimensional thinking.

Armed with a flowchart and a description of its components, HRD professionals often find that while their personal models may be powerful enough to create change, those models and their explanations are almost always too superficial to *explain* the complex dynamics of HRD and its connection to results. In short, a model derived from logic is no substitute for sound theory. Such models can guide improvement efforts through hypothesized relationships without having those relationships ever tested. You can have a model and no theory and you can have a theory with no model. Yet, most theories are accompanied by a model. A model by itself is not theory.

PERSPECTIVES ON THEORY AND PRACTICE

Perspectives on the link between theory and practice are wide-ranging. In the lay world, theory is a very loose construct, even to the point of ridicule in noting that something is "just a theory"—an untested speculative idea or antithesis of reality. In the academic world, theories require extensive development and verification before earning the label "theory." In an applied discipline, verification must take place in both the laboratory and in practice.

Bacharach's (1989) definition of theory states that "A theory is a statement of relations among concepts within a set of boundary assumptions and constraints" (p.496). Many definitions of theory use the words phenomenon or phenomena. For example, Torraco (1997) says, "A theory explains what a phenomenon is and how it works" (p.115). Gioia and Pitre (1990) described theory as "a coherent description, explanation, and presentation of observed or experienced phenomena" (p.587). Lynham (2000) described theory development as "the purposeful process or recurring cycle by which coherent description, explanations, and representations of observed or experienced phenomena are generated, verified, and refined" (p.161).

Unfortunately, the popular use of the words *phenomenon* and *phenomena* often suggest a narrow realm of concern, event, or occurrence. It is important to note that a phenomenon can be long lasting, large, and broad—such as democracy, global warming, and civil engineering. As an example, human resource development scholars can pay attention to training transfer theory while others focus on the theory of the broader realm of workplace learning, or even broader to the human resource development discipline itself.

Within any discipline or field of study, rival views regarding its purposes and practices exist at almost every level. The rival perspectives can be very broad, such as the focus and the nature of the discipline itself, or narrow, such as the explanation of a simple elemental aspect of the discipline. In applied disciplines, where matters of both theory and practice are of great concern, the range of perspectives expands even further in an effort to satisfy the demands of both scholars and practitioners.

Having rival theories in a discipline is not disturbing. Not having well-developed theory is disturbing, however. This holds true when framing an entire discipline or when considering even the smallest phenomena within a discipline. The assumption is that theoretical challenges from within can only help to advance the theory. For applied disciplines rooted in professional practice (such as human resource development or management), a problem emerges that is less likely to exist in more staid disciplines that are disconnected from practical matters (such as history, religion, or philosophy). The theory development challenge in applied disciplines is exacerbated by the dynamic that comes from practice and the relative youthfulness of most applied disciplines.

Beyond a few traditional academic disciplines, the majority of disciplines in contemporary institutions of higher learning are applied, dynamic, and relatively young—such as management, information technology, interior design, or dental hygiene. Applied disciplines almost always have both a strong theory component and a strong practice component. The focus of this chapter is on HRD, an applied discipline, and the quest to bring disciplinary coherence to both the theory and practice of the field

Most applied disciplines are attempting to make significant advancements in articulating the theoretical foundation of their fields of study. Management (Weick, 1979), human resource development (Swanson, 2001) and information science (Benbasat,

1999) are just a few. Most theory discussions and theory research are not held together in a manner that allows interpretation and integration. For example, theory development related to the essence of HRD can be held up against a theory effort focused on an extremely narrow sub-phenomenon within HRD, such as emotional intelligence theory, with no clear means of connecting the two. Without a theory framework, there is a sense of randomness and incoherence to theory discussions and developments.

THEORY FRAMEWORK FORAPPLIED DISCIPLINES

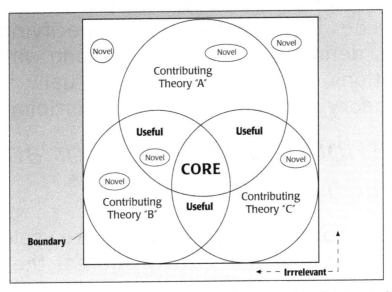

Figure 5.1 Theory Framework for Applied Disciplines: Boundaries, Contributing, Core, Useful, Novel, and

Irrelevant Components Source: Swanson, 2007, p.328.

The Theory Framework for Applied Disciplines (Swanson, 2007) helps scholars and practitioners think about, develop, and critique the status of the theory in their disciplines through a holistic perspective. It is made up of six components that are displayed in a graphic presentation (Figure 5.1).

Each of the six theory components for applied disciplines is described below. These descriptions establish the purpose and features of each theory framework component.

Boundary of the Theory of an Applied Discipline

The boundary of the theory of an applied discipline is established by specifying its name, definition, and purpose along with assumptions or beliefs that conceptually frame the theory and practice of that discipline.

Contributing Theories for an Applied Discipline

The contributing theories are selected theories that fundamentally address the definition, purpose, and assumptions under-girding an applied discipline.

Core Theory for an Applied Discipline

The core theory of an applied discipline is the intersection and integration of the contributing theories that operationalize the definition, purpose, and assumptions of an applied discipline.

Useful Theory for an Applied Discipline

The theory of a phenomenon that is outside the *core theory* of an applied discipline and within the intersection of two *contributing theories* has utility in explaining an important realm of practice within the discipline.

Novel Theory for an Applied Discipline

The theory of a narrow phenomenon that is related to an aspect of the applied discipline under consideration could logically provide an unusual explanation of how the phenomenon works.

Irrelevant Theory for an Applied Discipline

Any theory that falls outside the theory boundary, contributing theories, core theory, and useful theory of the applied discipline under consideration with no compelling evidence as to its *usefulness* or logic supporting its potential for a *novel* contribution.

The remainder of this chapter articulates a theory of HRD and the following chapter expands on the three primary contributing theories to HRD. These four updated writings are rooted in papers presented at an Academy of Human Resource Development theory symposium by Holton, Ruona, Swanson, and Torraco. The first section, "Theory of Human Resource Development," was written by Richard A. Swanson. The purpose of this section is to frame the discipline of HRD by identifying definitions and explanatory models along with the theory boundaries, contributing theories, (psychological theory, economic theory, and systems theory), core theory, and propositions arising from the theory. Each of three contributing core theories to HRD are discussed in depth in the following chapter.

THEORY OF HUMAN RESOURCE DEVELOPMENT

Contributed by Richard A. Swanson

The purpose of this section is to propose one theory of HRD that is supported by both research and practice.

Assumptions, Context, Definition, and Models of HRD

The bias of HRD has been the belief that organization, work process, group, and individual performance are mediated through human expertise and effort. In contrast to this belief, the performance scorecards available to organizational decision makers generally ignore the human element. The most evident example is the short-term financial view of company performance as judged by daily stock market data.

The journey of understanding performance improvement for those having the "human resource perspective" has not been easy. The range of performance perspectives in organizations forces the HRD profession to face the realities of how others strategically view HRD and how HRD views itself (Torraco and Swanson, 1995; Swanson, 1995a,

1995b). It appears as though HRD has taken a detour during the past fifty years. The clear vision and practice during World War II was lost in the 1950s and began returning in the 1980s.

The massive Training within Industry (TWI) project, that culminated with the ending of World War II, is seen as the origin of contemporary HRD (Dooley, 1945; Ruona and Swanson, 1998; Swanson and Torraco, 1994; Swanson, 2001). The performance language was simpler then—"Is it a production problem?" they would ask. If yes, they would use performance improvement tools that were masquerading under the name of "training." Besides operating under a training title that they quickly outgrew, the TWI project delivered on organization, process, and individual performance outputs using simple and powerful tools they called *job instruction, job relations,* and *job methods.*

In the 1950s, a psychology-only perspective took over the training and development professions. As far back as 1950, Peter Drucker warned that while this thinking freed managers from viciously bad ideas about working with people, it never provided substantive alternatives (1964, p.278). He went on to chide the profession for an inadequate focus on the work and for inadequate awareness of the economic dimensions of work (pp.278–279).

The reality is that most decision makers in organizations pursue performance and improvement, with or without professional HRD interventions. This simple fact confronts the HRD profession with the need to think about performance with and without the human resource perspective. The willingness to *temporarily* let go of the human bias in favor of performance improvement at all levels is the key to elevating HRD to its fullest potential. Without this fundamental mental shift, HRD will awkwardly keep trying to claim system performance (organizational system) through subsystem thinking (individuals). The best HRD theory and practice has invariably validated the contribution of human expertise and the unleashing of it as integral to performance at multiple levels.

The basic decision to begin with the host system of HRD (usually the organization) as the primary avenue to performance alters the models, thinking, and tools of HRD effort. Without this shift beyond the individual, the human resource development lens remains clouded, the HRD model is fragmented, and the underlying theory remains unclear.

Performance as the Key Outcome Variable of HRD

To *perform* is "to fulfill an obligation or requirement; accomplish something as promised or expected" *(American Heritage College Dictionary,* 1993, p.1015). Performance is not system design, capability, motivation, competence, or expertise. These, or other similar performance taxonomies, can best be thought of as *performance variables* (or *performance drivers),* but not performance. Performance may be aligned within missions, goals, and strategies—but not always. *Performance is the valued productive output of a system in the form of goods or services.* The actual fulfillment of the goods and/or services requirement is thought of in terms of *units of performance.* Once these goods and/or services units of performance are identified, they are typically measured in terms of production quantity, time, and quality features (Swanson and Holton, 1999; Swanson, 2001).

Chasing after individual or organizational change without first specifying a valid unit of performance is foolhardy and a waste of time. Change can take place while "real" performance decreases. One example is to pursue employee satisfaction with the assumption that production will increase. Numerous studies have demonstrated that employee satisfaction can increase while actual production decreases or remains the same. The reengineering fad is another example of the pursuit of change with the majority of instances ending up in losses in performance instead of gains (Micklethwait and Wooldridge, 1996). There are those in the profession speaking directly to the topic of performance in an attempt to clarify the relationships among performance *drivers* (Holton, 1998) and/or performance *variables* (Swanson, 2007).

Systems theory informs us that (1) there are systems and subsystems, and (2) all systems are open systems. It is humbling to realize that there are tiers of subsystems and larger host systems and that systems are open entities constantly changing. These realizations help prevent professionals from thinking and acting simply and mechanically. HRD practitioners and scholars should not lose sight of the constantly evolving state of overall systems.

The larger frame in which HRD operates includes organizational systems and the milieu in which they function. Organizations are the host systems for most HRD activity. Some of these systems are profit-making organizations that produce goods and/or services for consumers. Some are nonprofit or government organizations that produce goods and/or services for consumers. Some are publicly owned, some are shareholder owned and publicly traded, and some are owned by individuals or a group of individuals. All these organizations function in an ever present political, cultural, and economic milieu. Each has its own mission/strategy, structure, technology, and human resource mix. And, each has core processes related to producing the goods and services it produces.

Definition and Model of Human Resource Development

The expectation is that HRD efforts will logically culminate with important performance improvements for its host organization. Thus, the operational definition of HRD is as follows:

> Human resource development (HRD) is a process of developing and unleashing expertise for the purpose of improving performance.

The realms of performance improvement include organizational systems, processes, groups, and individuals. The two primary components of HRD include (1) organization development (OD), the unleashing of expertise for the purpose of improving performance, and (2) training and development (T&D), systematically developing expertise for the purpose of improving performance. These definitions and their connection to application areas and contexts are portrayed in Figure 5.2.

Additionally, HRD itself can be viewed and pursued as an improvement process functioning within the host organization. This is graphically portrayed in Figure 5.2. This model of HRD illustrates HRD as a five-phase process working in concert with other core organizational processes, all functioning in the organizational system context and the larger environmental context. The boundaries of HRD relate to the system hosting HRD. In most instances, this is an organization such as a business, industry, government, or nonprofit agency. In some instances, the host organization for HRD could be a geopolitical region or a nation.

Figure 5.2 Human Resource Development: Definitions, Components, Applications, and Contexts Source: Swanson, 2008.

While performance will likely always demand multiple interpretations, performance and, more importantly, performance improvement, are not simply abstract notions about desirable ways to reach a better state. In every organization, the concrete determinants of performance are reflected in people, their ideas, and the material resources through which their ideas reach the marketplace. Performance cannot be described or improved without specifying its determinants, accounting for the sophisticated processes through which performance is expressed (e.g., human behavior, work process innovation, stock market performance), and making some judgment about whether performance has, in fact, improved. Performance improvement can only be manifested through outputs, and change in outputs can only be assessed through some form of measurement. Thus, performance is a concept that can be systematically operationalized in any organization when we set out to demonstrate whether or not it has improved.

Theoretical and Disciplinary Foundations of HRD

HRD as a discipline is broader than any single theory. Reflecting the reality that most successful strategies for system and subsystem improvement require multifaceted interventions, HRD draws from multiple theories and integrates them in a unique manner for the purposes of HRD. This section develops a core theoretical foundation for HRD that draws upon contributions from several respected theoretical domains. For the purpose of a deeper under-standing, refer to the Model of Human Resource Development within the Organization and Environment (Figure 5.3).

While "a theory simply explains what a phenomenon is and how it works" (Torraco, 1997, p.115), "a discipline is a body of knowledge with its own organizing concepts, codified knowledge,epistemologicalapproach,undergirding theories, particular methodologies, and technical jargon" (Passmore, 1997, p.201). The belief that HRD is a discipline that draws upon many theories is widely held. This overly generous idea has served as fool's gold to the profession. In the attempt to be inclusive of so many theories—staking its claim so broadly—HRD has come up with no theory using this approach. However, many believe that efforts in developing core HRD theory are essential to the maturation of the profession.

Having well-defined core HRD theories in no way limits the utility of hundreds of available theories that could *inform* HRD research or the development of specific practitioner tools and methods.

Contributing and Useful Theory Components of HRD

Presently there is no universal view or agreement on the theory or multiple theories that support HRD as a discipline. Furthermore, there are no HRD theory alternatives being visibly proposed in the literature and being debated by the profession. On one hand, some have called for systems theory to serve as a unifying theory for HRD to access all useful theories as required (Gradous, 1989; Jacobs, 1989; McLagan, 1989); on the other hand, many have proposed sets of principles in the forms of comparative lists of added value, products, processes, and expertise (e.g., Gilley and Maycunich, 2000).

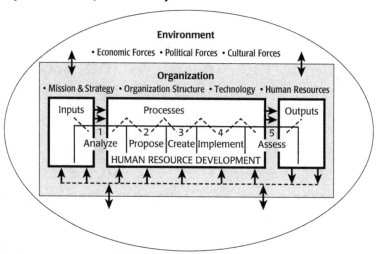

Figure 5.3 Model of Human Resource Development within the Organization and Environment Source: Swanson, 2001, p.305.

The alternative to having a sound theoretical and disciplinary base for the HRD profession is the present state of rudderless random activity aggressively sponsored by atheoretical professional associations and greedy consultants (Micklethwait and Wooldridge, 1996; Swanson,

1997). This present state celebrates short-term results without having deep understanding of the ability to replicate the results or the utility of those results. For this reason, a discrete and logical set of theories as the foundation of HRD is proposed as a means of understanding the Model of Human Resource Development within the Organization and Environment. The discipline, definition, and the model of HRD are believed to be supported and explained through the three contributing core theory domains of psychological theory, economic theory, and systems theory (Passmore, 1997; Swanson, 1995a, 1995b). Economic theory is recognized as a primary driver and survival metric of organizations; systems theory recognizes purpose, pieces, and relationships that can maximize or strangle systems and subsystems; and psychological theory acknowledges human beings as brokers of productivity and renewal along with the cultural and behavioral nuances. Each of these three theories is unique, complementary, and robust. Together they make up the foundational contributing theory underlying the discipline of HRD.

The theories have been visually presented as a three-legged stool, with the three legs providing great stability for HRD as a discipline and field of practice required to function in the midst of uneven and changing conditions (see

Figure 5.4). The seat represents their fusion into the unique core theory of HRD. In recent years, particularly with the demands of the global economy and an unbridled free-market condition, the stool has been positioned on an ethical rug—a filter, if you will—between its three contributing theories and the context in which HRD functions. Thus, the three contributing theories are poised to shape the core of the HRD discipline, and ethics plays an important moderating role (Hatcher, 2002). Furthermore, the ethical concerns are believed to be best expressed through recognition and adherence to the following basic beliefs:

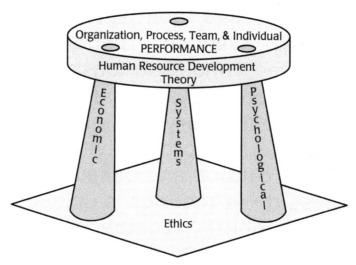

Figure 5.4 The Theoretical Foundations of Human Resource Development Source: Swanson, 2001, p.306.

1.   Organizational systems are human-made entities that rely on human expertise in order to establish and achieve their goals.

2. Human expertise is developed and maximized through HRD processes for the mutual long-and/or short-term benefits of the sponsoring organization and the individuals involved.

3. HRD professionals are advocates of individual, group, work process, and organizational system integrity.

The *whole* or core theory of HRD is proposed to be the fusion of psychological, economic, and systems theories while being filtered by a filter of ethical beliefs. This integrative state is central to securing HRD as a discipline, not in just knowing the elements. The journey to this disciplinary fusion results in the organizing concepts, codified knowledge, underpinning theories, particular methodologies, and the unique technical jargon of HRD. The *core* of an integrated HRD theory will be larger than the sum of the parts and unique to HRD. On their own, psychological theory, economic theory, or systems theory are inadequate for understanding HRD and for producing reliable results. Thus, the overarching proposition for HRD is as follows:

The theory integration proposition: HRD must integrate its contributing and useful psychological, economic, and systems theories into a core HRD theory and model for practice.

214

For example, business process reengineering, according to Hammer and Champy (1994), focused on cost reductions through low-level system analysis. Had they considered the larger frame system and sustainable economic performance and not ignored the psychological domain, the intervention and its total effects would have been very different. The premise is that the three theories constitute the contributing useful and core theory for the discipline of HRD. As such, they must be understood not only individually but, more important, in their wholeness and integration. The implications of economic, systems, and psychological theories in guiding the overarching approach to HRD practice follows.

Economic Theory Component of HRD

Any minimization of economic theory in HRD is untenable. The widely used book on organization development, *Organization Development and Change* (Cummings and Worley, 1993), does not have the words *economic, financial,* or *cost-benefit analysis* in its index. The organization development literature addresses the psychological theory leg of the theory stool and a portion of the systems theory leg, but it regularly ignores the economic leg. As a result, what is called organization development is reduced to individual development or team development in hopes of achieving improvement in organizational performance. While there is still much to be learned, a substantial amount of information about the economics of short-term interventions (Swanson, 2001) and broader-based investments is available (Becker, Huselid, and Ulrich, 2001; Fitz-enz, 2000; Lyau and Pucel, 1995).

How could responsible HRD not include direct analysis, action, and measurement of economic outcomes? Over time, organizations must generate more income than they spend in order to exist. Unless expenditures on HRD contribute to the viability and profitability of an organization, those expenditures will almost certainly be reduced or eliminated. Three specific economic theory perspectives are believed to be most appropriate and useful to the discipline of HRD: (1) scarce resource theory, (2) sustainable resource theory, and (3) human capital theory.

Scarce Resource Theory

Scarce resource theory informs us that there are limitations to everything. The limitations in money, raw materials, time, and so on, require us to make choices as to how capital will be utilized in order to gain the greatest return. Decision makers choose among options based on their forecasted return on investment. This is a simple and powerful notion that forces decision makers to separate the most valuable and worthy initiatives from the many things that they would like to do if there were no resource limitations (Swanson and Gradous, 1986).

Sustainable Resource Theory

Sustainable resource theory is much like scarce resource theory except for one major point: The concern for the long-term versus short-term agenda. Thurow (1993) informs us that, "in the future, sustainable advantage will depend on new process technologies and less on new product technology. New industries of the future depend ... on brain power. Man-made competitive advantages replace the comparative advantage of Mother Nature (natural-resources endowment) or history (capital endowments)" (p.16). Economist David Warsh (2006) punctuates these points throughout his recent book titled *Knowledge and the Wealth of Nations: A story of Economic Discovery.*

Human Capital Theory

Becker's (1993) classic book, *Human Capital: A Theoretical and Empirical Analysis with Special Reference to Education* (1993), illustrates this domain. Becker implores the reader, "I am going to talk about a different kind of capital. Schooling, a computer training course, expenditures on medical care, and lectures on the virtues of punctuality and honesty are capital too, in the true sense that they improve health, raise earnings, or add to a person's appreciation of literature over a lifetime. Consequently, it is fully in keeping with the capital concept as traditionally defined to say that expenditures on education, training, and medical care, etc., are investments in capital" (pp.15–16). These are not simply costs but investments with valuable returns that can be calculated.

The Economic Theory Propositions for HRD

The economic principles for HRD revolve around managing scarce resources and the production of wealth. Most people who talk about performance can mentally convert units of performance into monetary units. HRD itself has costs and benefits that need to be understood and are not always favorable. As they are better understood in terms of theory and practice, the HRD discipline and profession will mature. The economic propositions for HRD appear elementary, yet must be addressed through sound economic theory and practice:

> *Scarce resource theory:* HRD must justify its own use of scarce resources. *Sustainable resource theory:* HRD must add value to creating sustainable long-term economic performance.

Human capital theory: HRD must add short-term and long-term value from investments in the development of knowledge and expertise in individuals and groups of individuals.

In conclusion, economist Alfred Marshall (1949) argues that the most valuable of all capital is that invested in human beings. Since HRD takes place in organizations that are economic entities, HRD must call upon economic theory in shaping its core theory (Wang and Dobbs, 2009). In addition, most management theories and methods should be properly viewed as useful extensions of economic theory (see Drucker, 1964).

Psychological Theory Component of HRD

The psychological theory which HRD can draw on is immense. It includes theories of learning, human motivation, information processing, group dynamics, and psychology-based theories of how we make decisions and behave in organizations. Yet it has been poorly interpreted by the profession. Most practitioners grab onto a small and relatively irrelevant slice of psychological theory and act upon it in exaggerated ways. Examples include the fascination with whole-brain theory, personality types, and emotional intelligence. Passmore (1997) informs us, "Psychology is the science of behavior and mental processes of humans and other animals.

Beyond that, we have something that resembles a teenager's closet" (p.210).

While psychological theory may have something for everybody, HRD has yet to capitalize fully on its psychology leverage to improve performance. Interestingly, the widely used book on training, *Training in Organizations: Needs Assessment, Development and Evaluation* (Goldstein, 1993), is almost exclusively focused on the behaviorist school of psychology and does not deal in any meaningful way with Gestalt psychology or cognitive (purposive-behaviorism) psychology. At best, the HRD literature addresses the psychological theory leg of the theory stool in an unpredictable manner. Add to this the fact that HRD interventions are rarely systematically connected to the economic agenda via a systematic analysis of the organization and its goals (Brache, 2002; Swanson, 2007), it is no wonder that HRD interventions based only on psychological theory are often dismissed as irrelevant by organization leaders.

Fascination appears be the watchword of the psychological leg, as questions from psychology are typically narrow and/or disconnected from the core purpose of the organization, the work process, and often even the individual. For example, the continued intrigue of such topics as transfer of training from the psychology perspective mostly focuses on the individual and individual perceptions. The response to this limited perspective in HRD is best expanded through the addition of systems and economic theory, not by psychological theory alone (Holton, 1996c).

How could responsible HRD not integrate and use the vast body of knowledge from psychological theory? With such vast and divergent psychological theory available, it is more appropriate to focus on core understandings related to behavior and learning rather than fringe psychology theories and techniques. Three specific psychological theory perspectives are proposed here to be most appropriate to the discipline of HRD: (1) Gestalt psychology, (2) behavioral psychology, and (3) cognitive (purposive-behaviorism) psychology.

Gestalt Psychology

Gestalt is the German term for configuration or organization. Gestalt psychologists inform us that we do not see isolated stimuli but instead see stimuli gathered together in meaningful configurations. We see people, chairs, cars, trees, and flowers—not lines and patches of color. Gestaltists believe that people add something to experience that is not contained in the sensory data, and that we experience the world in meaningful wholes (Hergenhahn and Olson, 1993). Thus, learning involves moving from one whole to another. Words associated with gestalt psychology include introspection, meaning, closure, insight, life space, field theory, humanism, phenomenology, and relational theory. The holistic view of individuals and their own need for holistic understanding is in sharp contrast to a mechanistic and elemental view of human beings.

Behavioral Psychology

Behavioral psychology is concerned with what can be seen, and therefore behavior is what is studied. Behavioral psychologists inform us that individuals respond the only way they can given their capacity, experience, and present forces working on them. No more introspection, no more talk of instinctive behavior, and no more attempts to study the vague notions of human conscious or unconscious mind. Words associated with behaviorism include *readiness, law effect, exercise, recency, frequency, stimulus, response, reinforcement, punishment, programmed learning,* and *drives.*

Cognitive Psychology

Tolman's (1932) term of *purposive-behaviorism* has been selected as the exemplar of this third important perspective from psychology. Purposive-behaviorism attempts to explain goal-directed behavior and the idea that human beings organize their lives around purposes. Purposive-behaviorism (and other cognitive psychologies) attempts to integrate theory from Gestalt and behavioral psychology.

"For Purposive Behaviorism, behavior, as we have seen, is purposeful, cognitive, and molar, i.e., 'Gestalted.' Purposive Behaviorism is molar, not a molecular" (Tolman, 1932, p.419). Words associated with cognitive psychology, including purposive-behaviorism, include *drive discriminations, field-cognition modes, cognitive map, learning by analogy, learned helplessness, structuring, information processing, short-and long-term memory,* and *artificial intelligence.*

The Psychological Theory Propositions for HRD

The psychology principles for practice revolve around the mental processes of humans and the determinants of human behavior. Among scholars and practitioners of psychology, the schisms and gimmicks reported under the psychology banner abound with little integration. As the three useful psychology theories here are interpreted in terms of the theory and practice relevant to HRD, the discipline and profession will mature. While the psychological propositions appear to be elementary, they are regularly ignored in practice:

> *Gestalt psychology theory:* HRD must clarify the goals of individual contributors, work process owners, and/or organization leaders.

Behavioral psychology theory: HRD must develop the knowledge and expertise of individual contributors, work process owners, and organization leaders.

Cognitive psychology (purposive behaviorism) theory: HRD must harmonize the goals and behaviors among individual contributors, work groups, work process owners, and organization leaders.

In conclusion, since HRD takes place in organizations that are psychologically framed by those who invented them, operate in them, and renew them, HRD must call on psychology as a contributor for its useful and core theory (see Argyris, 1993; Bereiter and Scardamalia, 1993; Dubin, 1976). In addition, learning theories such as constructivism and situated cognition should be properly viewed as useful derivatives of psychological theory. Performance cannot be improved if people choose not to perform, put forth little effort, or do not persist in their efforts (Bereiter and Scardamalia, 1993). Moreover, systematically designed learning experiences and workplace systems provide a durable foundation for performance improvement. Thus, specific theories of learning, human motivation, information processing, and other psychologically based phenomenon complement core theoretical foundation for the discipline of HRD and have high utility for specialized (novel) challenges.

Systems Theory Component of HRD

Systems theory, a small body of knowledge compared to economics and psychology, contains a harvest of low-hanging fruit for HRD. From a systems theory perspective, a wide range of systemic disconnects is adversely affecting performance. They include (1) not being able to clearly specify the required outcomes of the host organization and (2) not having a systematically defined HRD process (see Brache, 2002; Rummler and Brache, 1995; Swanson, 2007).

Systems theory is a relatively young discipline made up of "a collection of general concepts, principles, tools, problems and methods associated with systems of any kind" (Passmore, 1997, pp.206–207). Gradous's (1989) classic mono graph set the stage for serious consideration of systems theory by the HRD profession. Jacobs's (1989) chapter, "Systems Theory Applied to Human Resource Development," called for the profession to adopt an individual contributor view of systems theory as the unifying theory. Seeing this as limited, McLagan (1989) proposed the larger organization and societal views in her chapter titled "Systems Model 2000: Matching Systems Theory to Future HRD Issues." Her challenge was for HRD to think about, and work within, a more expansive and tiered world of systems.

Three specific systems theory perspectives are proposed here to be appropriate to HRD: (1) general systems theory, (2) chaos theory, and (3) futures theory.

General Systems Theory

At the core, general systems theory (GST) forces us to talk intelligently about inputs, processes, outputs, and feedback. Furthermore, GST informs us of the reality of open systems (vs. closed systems), that systems engineering focuses on the less dynamic aspects of the organization, and of the limitations of a single personality theory in predicting human behavior (Bertalanffy, 1962).

Boulding's (1956a) classic article on general systems theory describes the paradox of a theory so general as to mean nothing and the seeming inability of a single theory from a single field of study to ever reach a satisfactory level of theory generality. He goes on to talk about the power of a "spectrum of theories"—a "system of systems" that would perform the function of a "gestalt" in theory building. "General Systems Theory may at times be an embarrassment in pointing out how far we still have to go" (Boulding, 1956a, p.10).

Chaos Theory

"Where chaos begins, classical science stops.... chaos is a science of process rather than a state, of becoming rather than of being" (Gleick, 1987, pp.3–5). Chaos theory confronts Newtonian logic head-on by offering a revised motto away from determinism to something much softer: "Given an approximate knowledge of a system's initial conditions and an understanding of natural law, one can calculate the approximate behavior of the system" (Gleick, 1987, p.15). Chaos theory purposefully acknowledges and studies phenomena that are unsystematic and do not appear to follow the rules.

Futures Theory

Futures theory is "not necessarily interested in predicting the future, it is about the liberation of people's insights" (Schwartz, 1996, p.9). Thus, futures theory, in the context of planning for the future in uncertain conditions, in no way resembles the reductionist view of most strategic planning efforts that end up with a single strategy. The language and tools of *alternative futures* and *scenario building* are intended to create a true picture of the facts, the potential flux in those facts, and the decision-making agility required of the future. Futures theory is critical for sustainable performance in that it prepares one to recognize and cope with an evolving future state (Chermack, 2005).

Systems Theory Propositions for HRD

The systems theory principles for practice are organic. The system elements, their arrangements, the interdependencies—the complex nature of the phenomenon under study—must be faced. The systems theory principles for practice require serious thinking, sound theory-building research, and the utilization of new tools for sound practice. A full pursuit of the following simple propositions in HRD would re-shape the HRD purpose and the tools utilized in practice:

General systems theory: HRD must understand how it and other subsystems connect and disconnect from the host organizational system.

Chaos theory: HRD must help its host organizational system retain its purpose and effectiveness given the chaos it faces.

Futures theory: HRD must help its host organizational system shape alternative futures.

In conclusion, since HRD takes place in organizations that are themselves systems and subsystems functioning within an environmental system that is ever-changing, systems theory is both useful and at its core (see Buckley, 1968; Gradous, 1989). Furthermore, engineering-technology theories and methods should be viewed as useful extensions of systems theory, even though they have a longer scholarly history (see FitzGerald and FitzGerald, 1973; Davenport, 1993).

Ethics in HRD

As noted earlier, the rug of ethics is viewed as the supporting theory for HRD, but not a core theory. It serves as the filter among the three core theories of economics, psychology, and systems within the performance improvement context.

From the ethical beliefs perspective, some argue about the exploitive nature of organizations and would criticize HRD as an unthinking arm of management (Korten, 2001), challenging the profession to act as the agent of democracy and equity (Dirkx, 1996). Others argue that exploitation is a much more expansive concept (e.g., employees can exploit their employers) and that it must be dealt with as such (Swanson, Horton, and Kelly, 1986). The ethical issue is not with performance. It is the distribution of the gains realized from performance. Such distribution among contributors and stakeholders is the bogeyman behind most of the emotional performance discussions in HRD. It should be dealt with directly and apart from the pursuit of performance (Hatcher, 2002).

Summary

The purpose of this theory of HRD discussion was to frame the discipline and theory of human resource development by identifying its definition, model, component theories, and the propositions of the theory.

Research in the realm of theory requires that theories be developed through rigorous theory-building research methods (Dubin, 1969; Hearn, 1953; Torraco, 1997; Lynham, 2000b) and that the journey be continuous. If theory just happened as a result of practice, the development of an HRD theory bucket would be overflowing. Instead, the massive field of HRD practice is still experiencing a "theory application deficit disorder" (Swanson, 1997). Fulfilling HRD's performance improvement mission by advancing the HRD discipline around sound theory, proven in practice, is fundamental to the maturation of the profession. The following chapter provides extended and alternative views of the contributions of psychological, economic, and systems theories to HRD.

CONCLUSION

This has been an attempt to investigate the contribution of systems theory to HRD. It is hoped that it offers a unique synthesis of the literature in describing its scope and meaning as well as a framework to organize its multiple contributions to HRD theory and practice.

The twenty-first century is seeing a burst of HRD theory-building research. It is being spurred on by the maturing of the academic side of the HRD profession and the high expectations organizations have for the HRD contribution. The *Human Resource Development Review* and the Academy of Management Review have provided a boost to HRD theory research and theory visibility.

REFLECTION QUESTIONS

1. Explain how models and theories differ and discuss if it is possible to have one without the other.
2. What general idea about theory from this chapter did you find most interesting and why?
3. What is the argument for multiple contributing theories being used and fused for creating a unique theory of HRD?
4. From the section on the discipline of HRD, what do you see as the connection between the definition of HRD (Figure 5.2) and the model of HRD (Figure 5.3)?
5. What do you think the main contribution of psychological theory is to HRD? Why?

6. What do you think the main contribution of economic theory is to HRD? Why?
7. What do you think the main contribution of systems theory is to HRD? Why?

CHAPTER 6

Component Theories of Human Resource Development

CHAPTER OUTLINE

Introduction
Psychology and the Discipline of HRD
Contributed by Elwood F. Holton III
- Psychology and HRD
- Emerging Foundational Theories of Psychology
- Limits of Psychology
- Summary
Economics, Human Capital Theory, and HRD
Contributed by Richard J. Torraco
- What is Economics?
- What is Human Capital Theory?
- Human Capital Theory and Human Resource Development
- Summary
Systems Theory as a Foundation for HRD
Contributed by Wendy E.A. Ruona
- What Is Systems Theory?
- Why Systems Theory?

- The Support Provided to HRD by Systems Theory
- Summary
  Conclusion
  Reflection Questions

INTRODUCTION

The preceding chapter presented a theory of Human Resource Development (HRD) and advocated three primary theory components and a purposeful fusion of them. The fusion of the three theory components was done in context of the definition and purpose of HRD and is now presented as the core theory of the HRD discipline. The following three sections in this chapter provide extended views of the contributions of psychological, economic, and systems component theories to HRD.

Elwood F. Holton's section, titled "Psychology and the Discipline of Human Resource Development," addresses psychological theory. He notes that psychology has long provided a core theoretical base for HRD. Contemporary HRD extends beyond psychology to embrace multiple theoretical bases. This section examines psychology's theoretical contributions to the discipline of HRD. It argues that psychological theories are both powerful and yet limited as a foundation for HRD. Specific psychological theories and their conceptual relationships with economics and systems theory are discussed.

The second section, "Economics, Human Capital Theory, and Human Resource Development," was written by Richard J. Torraco.

He argues that the development of a theory base to support the rapidly growing field of HRD is the most important issue facing HRD scholars today. The pressures on HRD to meet the needs of a diverse workforce in a rapidly changing work environment demand the inclusion of economics as a foundational theory of HRD. He further argues for human capital theory as the primary economic theory relevant to HRD.

The final section, "Systems Theory as a Foundation for Human Resource Development," by Wendy E. A Ruona, investigates the contribution of systems theory to HRD. The treatise offers a framework to organize themes emerging from the literature on how systems theory supports HRD. Finally, some current challenges and how systems theory relates to the disciplines of economics and psychology are discussed.

PSYCHOLOGY AND THE DISCIPLINE OF

HUMANRESOURCE DEVELOPMENT

Contributed by Elwood F. Holton III

Psychology has been identified as one of the core theories of human resource development (Passmore, 1997; Swanson, 1994). There can be little question that the discipline of psychology has made, and continues to make, major contributions to the discipline of HRD. Indeed, references from industrial psychology, educational psychology, cognitive psychology, and developmental psychology are common in our research. It is psychology that keeps HRD's focus on the individual.

However, there are those who practice HRD as if it were little more than applied psychology. This approach results in overemphasis on the individual to the exclusion of other vital components of our discipline. The thesis of this section is that there can also be little question that psychology is inadequate *by itself* to define the discipline of HRD. The purpose of this section is to systematically identify some key issues surrounding psychology's contribution to defining the discipline of HRD.

Psychology and HRD

Understanding Psychology as a Discipline

To understand psychology as a field, one must first differentiate between what are alternately called foundational or framework theories (Wellman and Gellman, 1992) and systems of psychology (Lundin, 1991) versus specific theories. "Framework theories outline the ontology and the basic causal devices for their specific theories, thereby defining a coherent form of reasoning about a particular set of phenomena" (Wellman and Gellman, 1992, p.342). A *system* has been defined as "a framework or scaffolding which permits the scientist to arrange his data in an orderly meaningful way" (Lundin, 1991, p.2). In psychology, these systems are also known as *movements* or *schools.*

Systems or framework theories, then, inspire specific theories that propose specific formal propositions. For example, behaviorism is a framework theory or system because it defines a particular set of assumptions about human behavior. Within that system are a variety of theorists (e.g., Watson, Skinner) who vary in their specific propositions about behaviorism but nonetheless agree as to the underlying epistemology. Our interest here is not in specific theories but rather the underlying framework theories or systems from psychology that are in turn foundational theories for the discipline of HRD. Continuing the previous example, we will not discuss which theory of behaviorism is appropriate but rather whether behaviorism is a foundational theory for HRD.

No universal agreement prevails among psychology scholars as to which theories are specific versus foundational theories, and some theorists are "bridge" theorists in that they attempt to integrate multiple systems. Furthermore, many noted psychologists can be classified in multiple categories (e.g., Is Bandura a behaviorist or a cognitivist?). Thus, it is difficult to find one "best" classification. For this discussion, Lundin's (1991) and Brennan's (1994) classifications of twentieth-century psychology systems have been integrated to generate the following list of candidates to be included as foundational theories for HRD: functionalism, behaviorism, Gestalt (classic and field theory), psychoanalysis, "third force" (humanistic and existential), cognitive, and emerging systems (social psychology and developmental psychology).

Interestingly, some psychologists have called for the creation of a "metadiscipline" of theoretical psychology to recapture the theoretical roots of psychology (Slife and Williams, 1997). They use some of the same language that scholars in HRD do to bemoan movement away from theory "toward models, techniques, and microtheories in the more modern sense" (Slife and Williams, 1997, p.118). Due in large part to the emergence of applied or functional psychology in the early 1900s (Watson and Evans, 1991), psychology has moved away from the creation of broad theories such as behaviorism and cognitivism, to the scientific testing of theories and models.

Psychological Theories for HRD
   Within psychology, Swanson (1998a) proposes three foundational psychological theories: Gestalt, behavioral, and cognitive psychology. Figure 6.1 summarizes these three foundational theories and selected contributions to the discipline of HRD.

Relationship to Other Core Theories of HRD
   Swanson (1998a) also proposes that the other two foundation theories of HRD are economics and systems theory. Yet unresolved is the relationship between psychology and the other two core domains. While there may be many microlevel linkages, at the macrolevel possible relationships are as follows:
- *Behaviorism* provides the link between psychology of the individual and economic theory. One of behaviorism's strengths is its emphasis on external reinforcers of human behavior. Human behavior within organizations is deeply affected by organizational

performance goals as represented by individual performance criteria and associated rewards. This performance system is largely economic, as described by Torraco (1998). Behaviorism provides the theoretical linkage between the external performance system and individual behavior.

- *Gestalt* psychology is primarily concerned with the integration of the parts of the self into the whole person. Conceptually, this is the same contribution that systems theory makes to understanding organizations—the focus on the whole and the interaction of the parts, rather than reducing it to just its parts. In addition to helping the HRD profession focus on the whole person, the emphasis on holism also logically leads to a holistic view of the person embedded in the organizational system.

Figure 6.1 Foundational Psychological Theories and their Contribution to HRD

Foundation Theory	Representative Theorists	Contributions to HRD
Gestalt	Wertheimer, Kofka, Kohler, Lewin	• Focus on the whole person
		• Holistic view of organizations and individuals
Behaviorism	Watson, Pavlov, Thorndike	• How external environments affect human behavior

Foundation Theory	Representative Theorists	Contributions to HRD
Cognitive	Piaget, Bruner, Tolman	• Reward and motivation systems • Goal setting • How humans process information • Foundation for instructional design • How humans make meaning of their experiences

- *Cognitivism* is primarily focused on the self. Cognitive psychology explains how individuals make meaning of what they experience. It emphasizes that individuals are not simply influenced by external factors but make decisions about those influences and their meaning. In the constellation of psychological theories relevant to HRD, it is cognitive psychology that exclusively focuses on the internal processes of individuals. It helps explain how people learn and how they make sense of the organizational system.

Emerging Foundational Theories of Psychology

There is little question that, of the well-established foundation theories in psychology, these three are the appropriate ones. Others, such as functionalism and psychoanalytic theory, simply don't fit. That said, two other emerging psychological theories point out possible weaknesses in this scheme and offer possible theoretical solutions.

Individual Growth Perspective

None of these three theories fully recognizes the potential that humans have to expand and develop capabilities well beyond those immediately apparent. Gestalt psychology comes closest but still is focused primarily on how people perceive, think, and learn in the here and now (Hunt, 1993). It still leaves unexplained the human processes that underlie the motivation to grow and develop. It is this potential for growth and expansion of human capabilities that undergirds human capital theory in economics.

Humanistic psychology is still a somewhat loosely formed movement that views humans as self-actualizing, self-directing beings. It is one of the roots for much of adult learning theory (Knowles, Holton, and Swanson, 2005). Two of its most recognizable names are Carl Rogers and Abraham Maslow. While still not as theoretically "tight" as behaviorism or cognitivism, it nonetheless makes contributions in explaining individuals' motivation and potential. A core presumption of some HRD models is that employees have intrinsic motivation to grow.

While some growth can be explained from the behavioristic notion that people grow to seek organizational rewards, a strictly behaviorist view of this phenomenon is much too limited. The three psychological theories proposed earlier (Gestalt, behaviorism, and cognitive) may fall short in supporting HRD's position that humans are capable of reaching far higher potential, justifying long-term investment to build expertise.

Social System of Organizations

A second area of concern is whether these three psychological theories, along with systems theory and economic theory, provide adequate theory to account for individuals within the social system of organizations. Organization development specialists are particularly focused on elements of the social system such as organizational culture, power and politics, group dynamics, intergroup communication, and how these social systems change (Cummings and Worley, 1997). The question is whether the core theories proposed provide an adequate foundation to understand the individual within the organizational social system.

It is these very concerns that have led to the emergence of social psychology that studies interactions between people and groups. It, too, is seen by some as an eclectic discipline lacking any unifying theory (Hunt, 1993), while others are more generous in describing it as still emerging in its theoretical base (Brennan, 1994). In some respects, social psychology is much like HRD, building on other theories while creating a new theory of its own. Wiggins, Wiggins, and Vander Zanden (1994) define *social psychology* as "the study of behavior, thoughts, and feelings of an individual or interacting individuals and their relationships with larger social units" (p.17). According to them, social psychology consists of four theoretical streams, the first two from psychology and the second two from sociology:

1. *Behavioral perspective*—Social learning and social exchange theory
2. *Cognitive perspective*—Field theory, attribution theory, and social learning of attitudes
3. *Structural perspective*—Role theory, expectation states theory, and postmodernism,
4. *Interactionist perspective*—Symbolic interaction theory, identity theory, and ethnomethodology

Frankly, I offer it more as a "placeholder" than with certainty that it is a foundational theory. What social psychology emphasizes, and which seems lacking in this HRD discipline model, is some theory base that defines the social system of an organization. There are deep roots in some aspects of HRD that have relationships with social psychology. For example, social psychologist Lewin's force field theory is a core model for organizational change and development. Social psychology also focuses on humans in groups, which is clearly a major issue in HRD. If social psychology is not the correct foundational theory, then we must identify a component that provides a base for HRD's work in the social systems of organizations.

In summary, Kuhn (1970) cautions us that the emergence of new theory is rarely an orderly or quick process. While both humanistic and social psychology lack the conceptual clarity of cognitivism, behaviorism, and Gestalt psychology, they emerged to fill the need to explain human phenomena that the others did not adequately explain. The question for HRD to debate is whether these same holes are important considerations for HRD theory. If so, then these two emerging areas of psychology—or some other theory—should be carefully considered.

Limits of Psychology
Issue 1: Domains of Performance

Two predominant performance frameworks are the Rummler and Brache (1995) model and Swanson's (1994) expanded framework. Because Swanson's framework uses five performance variables, it is a more powerful lens for this analysis. He suggests that there are three levels of performance and five performance variables. By definition, psychology's primary focus is on the individual. Psychologists do consider organizational context, but as environmental influences on the individual, not as a core area of focus.

Historically, HRD was also defined at the individual level (Ruona and Swanson, 1997). It is increasingly considering multiple levels (individual, group, work process, and organizational) as core areas of focus. The implications of this for HRD as a discipline are significant. If the discipline of HRD is a multilevel discipline, then we can draw heavily upon psychology as a foundation discipline but must also realize it is inadequate by itself.

The psychological lens, while powerful, leads to incorrect or inadequate conceptions of HRD when used alone. For example, Barrie and Pace (1997) state:

> The question of whether the field of human resource development is in the business of improving *performance* or of enhancing learning in organizations has not been sufficiently explored. Succinctly put, advocates argue that the field should focus on creating *behavioral* changes or on fostering a cognitive perspective in organization members. (p.335, emphasis added)

The authors equate the performance perspective with the behavioral perspective in psychology, which is incorrect. Performance theory is concerned with the outputs and outcomes of humans in organizations, and the extent to which cognitive strategies improve them. From an applied psychology definition of HRD, theirs is the logical conclusion. From a broader theoretical base, their argument is incorrect.

Issue 2: Building Capacity for Performance

Holton (1999) presents an expanded framework for conceptualizing performance domains in HRD that offers another lens within which to consider psychology's contribution to HRD. One important addition is the integration of Kaplan and Norton (1996) to two categories of performance measures: outcomes and drivers. Unfortunately, they do not offer concise definitions of either. For our purposes, *outcomes* are measures of effectiveness or efficiency relative to core outputs of the system, subsystem, process, or individual. The most typical are financial indicators (profit, return on investment [ROI], etc.) and productivity measures (units of goods or services produced) and are often generic across companies. According to Kaplan and Norton, these measures tend to be lag indicators in that they reflect what has occurred or has been accomplished in relation to core outcomes.

Drivers measure elements of performance that are expected to sustain or increase system, subsystem, process, or individual ability and capacity to be more effective or efficient in the future. Thus, they are leading indicators of future outcomes and tend to be unique for particular business units. Together with outcome measures, they describe the hypothesized cause-and-effect relationships in the organization's strategy (Kaplan and Norton, 1996). Thus, drivers should predict future outcomes. For example, for a particular company, ROI might be the appropriate outcome measure that might be driven by customer loyalty and on-time delivery, which in turn might be driven by employee learning so that internal processes are optimized. Conceptually, performance drivers could be added as a third axis to Swanson's performance levels and performance variables. This lens further defines the limits of psychology's contribution to HRD:

- At the individual level, psychology pays only limited attention to building future capacity for individual performance.
- At other levels, performance drivers are not an area of focus for psychology.

Some areas of psychology are preoccupied with current performance and outcomes, while HRD has a more balanced view of building capacity for future performance in addition to present performance (see Figure 6.2).

Summary

As part of a series of papers on the core theories of HRD, this treatise was primarily designed to initiate an ongoing dialogue to continue defining the discipline of HRD. HRD has, and always will have, psychology as one of its core theories. It is psychology that reminds us that our discipline is one concerned with humans in organizations. It is important that we recognize its contributions, as well as its limitations as a lens through which to view HRD.

ECONOMICS, HUMAN CAPITAL THEORY, AND HUMAN RESOURCE DEVELOPMENT

Contributed by Richard J. Torraco

Economics offers a distinctive perspective for analyzing social conditions and making choices about how scarce resources can be distributed among competing needs. This section addresses economics, human capital theory, and the economic realities faced by the organizations in which human resource development professionals carry out their work. The application of human capital theory to human resource development reveals the importance of economic considerations to the human resource development practice and demonstrates the central role of economics in the theoretical foundation of human resource development.

Figure 6.2 Performance Domains and Metrics

Domains of Performance	Typical Metrics for Measuring Performance Domains	
	PERFORMANCE OUTCOMES	PERFORMANCE DRIVERS
Mission	Economic returns	Societal benefits
	External metrics	Innovation
	Market share	Knowledge capital
	Profitability	Management/leadership
	Mortality rate	Strategy
	Poverty level	Social responsibility
Process	Customers	Customer (needs satisfaction)
	Quality	Quality
	Cost	Innovation
	Time	
	Product features	
	Market share (in product category)	
Critical performance subsystem (team, department, etc.)	Team effectiveness	Team/group climate
	Structural subunits performance	Management/leadership
	Productivity (resource efficiency)	Ethical performance
	Internal metrics	
	Work outputs	
Individual	Productivity	Knowledge, expertise
	Work output	Learning
		Renewal and growth
		Human relations
		Ethical performance
		Turnover
		Absenteeism

What is Economics?

Economics addresses the allocation of scarce resources among a variety of human wants and needs. Economics represents human wants and the scarcity of resources as essential and perennial elements in the study of any human activity. Like other social sciences, economics deals with human behavior that cannot be controlled as can, for example, the physical mechanisms of automated equipment used by an engineer. Economics uses society as its laboratory and cannot engage in the kind of experimentation favored by the physicist or chemist. As with the social sciences in general, economics is not an exact science and its predictions about economic developments are subject to error. Nonetheless, according to Lewis (1977), economics is the social science "with the most sophisticated body of theory—that is, the one with the greatest predictability accuracy of all the social sciences" (p.43). For comprehensive treatments of economics, see Samuelson (1980), Milgrom and John (1992), and Shughart, Chappell and Cottle (1994).

What is Human Capital Theory?

Human capital theory is considered the branch of economics most applicable to human resource development. Human capital theory offers an increasingly influential perspective to social and economic policy. While Theodore Schultz's (1961) address to the American Economic Association was the first presentation of research on the return-on-investment in human capital, Gary S. Becker is generally credited with developing human capital theory. Classical economic theory considers labor as a commodity that can be bought and sold. Because of the negative connotations associated with the exploitation of labor by capital, it is understandable that human capital theory is still suspect in some circles. However, unlike the meaning traditionally associated with the term "labor," human capital refers to the knowledge and expertise one accumulates through education and training. Emphasizing the social and economic importance of human capital theory, Becker (1993) quotes the economist Alfred Marshall's dictum that, "the most valuable of all capital is that invested in human beings" (p.27).

Becker distinguished *specific* human capital from *general* human capital. General human capital development increases the skills and productivity of people by the same amount in the organizations providing the training as it would if they went to work for another organization. However, organization specific training increases the productivity of people working in that organization and not in other organizations if people decided to leave. Becker refers to training that increases productivity more in the organizations providing it as specific training. Examples of specific human capital include training in firm-specific purchasing procedures, management information systems, and most types of on-the-job training since they address skills that are specific to a particular organization. General human capital is knowledge gained through education and training in areas of value to a variety of organizations. Examples include leadership, problem solving, and communication skills. Both specific training and general training are means of human capital development. Both are important to those acquiring the knowledge and skill and to the organizations and communities where trainees use these skills. However, the incentives for an organization to invest in training are different for these two types of training. Because general training develops expertise that can increase productivity by the same amount in the organization providing the training as in other organizations, competitors could benefit by hiring trained employees away from the organizations providing the general training. For this reason organizations may be less likely to offer general training. This distinction notwithstanding, Becker (1993) states that "education and training are the most important investments in human capital" (p.17).

The rates of return on education analyzed by Becker are impressive and contributed substantially to advancing human capital theory into the forefront of social and economic policy. The findings of Becker's empirical analysis of the rates of return on education conclude that the average rate of return on a college education to white males is between 11 and 13 percent, with higher rates on a high school

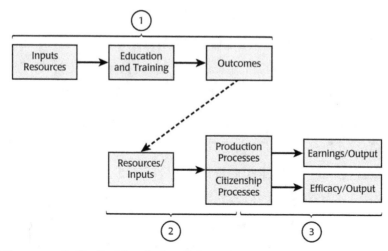

Figure 6.3 A Model of Human Capital Theory

education, and even higher rates on an elementary school education.

Investing in the education and training of those who are more educated to begin with is justified by the concept of rates of return. Within the present knowledge economy that demands more human capital, there are increasingly strong market-based incentives to produce expertise more efficiently. The need to produce more human capital cheaper, faster, and better inevitably leads to an investment bias that favors the most highly skilled and educated. An additional dollar invested in a more highly skilled person brings higher economic returns than an additional dollar invested in a less skilled youth or adult. As a result, economic incentives alone are unlikely to lead to greater investments in the least skilled workers (Carnevale and Fry, 2001).

A Model of Human Capital Theory (see Figure 6.3) presents the key relationships in human capital theory and the assumptions underlying these relationships. Key relationships and assumptions of human capital theory are represented in Figure 6.3 by the numbered brackets 1, 2, and 3. Based on systems theory, the relationships in Figure 6.3 are process models, each composed of *inputs, processes,* and *outputs.*

- *Relationship 1* represents the concept of *production functions* as applied to education and training. This relationship shows the potential of education as a means to foster learning and human capital development. Relationship 1 is a process model showing that inputs/resources to education and training (e.g., investments in schools, instructors, learning materials, and so on) should produce learning outcomes. Presumably as people participate in education and training, they are involved in learning and acquire knowledge and skill. The key assumption underlying this relationship is that investments in education and training, in fact, do result in increased learning. Relationship 1 includes the human capital variables assessed using cost-effectiveness analysis.

- *Relationship 2* represents the human capital relationship between learning and increased productivity. This relationship shows the potential contribution of education and learning to increased productivity. The process model in relationship 2 shows that increased learning should produce increased productivity. Presumably as people acquire more knowledge and skill, they apply this expertise in their work and thereby enhance productivity. The key assumption underlying this relationship is that increased learning, in fact, does result in increased productivity.

- *Relationship 3* represents the human capital relationships between increased productivity and increased wages and business earnings, and between increased citizenship processes and increased social efficacy. Presumably as productivity increases, business revenues are generated that result in higher wages for employees and higher earnings for businesses. Similarly, as citizenship processes affected by education are enhanced (e.g., community involvement, voting, socially responsible action), social efficacy would be expected to increase (e.g., social equity and opportunity, enhancements to the environment). The key assumption underlying this relationship is that increased productivity, in fact, does result in increased wages for individuals and earnings for businesses. An equally important assumption of human capital theory represented by Relationship

3 is that increased citizenship processes affected by education, in fact, do enhance social efficacy.

- The entire human capital continuum represented in Figure 6.3 (i.e., all the bracketed relationships as a single continuum) are assessed using return-on-investment analysis or cost-benefit analysis.

Human Capital Theory and Human Resource Development

The theory and practice of human resource development is grounded in economics and human capital theory. In this section, concepts of human capital theory are briefly reviewed and applied to human resource development, revealing the importance of economics and human capital theory to human resource development.

Macroeconomic Theory

Macroeconomic theory addresses the aggregate performance of an entire economy or economic system (e.g., the European economy or world economy).

Macroeconomics is concerned with fiscal and monetary policy and the interaction of major determinants of economic developments such as wages, prices, employment levels, interest rates, capital investments, the distribution of income, and other factors. Macroeconomics is contrasted with microeconomics, which focuses on the individual consumer, family or firm and the determinants of each of these factors (i.e., wages, interest rates) in particular.

Human capital theory has both macroeconomic and microeconomic implications for human resource development. Human resource development on a regional or national level is what economists might call "human capital deepening" on a macroeconomic scale. The increased value of human capital derived from human resource development is likely to influence productivity, wages, prices, and other factors at an aggregate level of the economy. Conversely, the decisions made by human resource development professionals in organizations are microeconomic in scope—that is, they influence the economic performance of a particular community, organization, group, or its members.

Supply and Demand

The supply of, and demand for, education and training affects the competitive position of organizations such that human resource development's role becomes central to the organization's long-term viability. Classical economics posits that, on average, scarce resources are more valuable than plentiful resources. Grounded in economic theory, Wright, McMahan and McWilliams's (1994) resource-based view of the firm is based on the concept of supply and demand. They suggest that human resources, and skilled workers in particular, substantially increase the competitive position of the firm because they enhance the value of the firm's human resources in ways that are (a) rare, (b) inimitable, (c) valuable, and (d) non-substitutable. It is difficult to stay competitive with organizations whose greatest assets are embedded in people—their human capital (Barney, 1991).

Elasticity of Demand

This concept is an elaboration of the concept of supply and demand. Elasticity of demand indicates the degree of responsiveness of the quantity of a product or service demanded by consumers to changes in the market price of the product or service. Elastic demand exists when a price reduction leads to a substantial increase in demand for the product or service (and an increase in total revenue despite the price cut). Inelastic demand exists when a price reduction leads to a decrease in total revenue despite the price cut. Elastic demand is said to exist for some leisure and recreation-related goods (e.g., airfares, vacation cruises, and hotel and resort rates). Inelastic demand is said to exist for gasoline prices, railroad service, and certain necessities (e.g., foods, medicine) for which acceptable substitutes are unavailable.

The elasticity of demand for human resource development can be viewed in a number of contexts. For example, how elastic is the demand for education/training when its cost increases relative to the cost of alternative activities in the workplace (e.g., attend training versus remain on the job)? Will attendance or support for human resource development increase, despite its increased cost, if the intervention is perceived as crucial to organizational growth or survival (e.g., an organization development or performance improvement intervention)? To what degree does the availability of substitutes for training (e.g., outsourcing, hiring versus training skilled personnel) influence the elasticity of demand for training?

Opportunity Costs

Opportunity costs are the value of opportunities foregone due to participation in a given project or activity. By electing a particular course of action among alternatives, one necessarily foregoes the opportunities offered by the alternatives. Human capital theory involves opportunity costs at several levels of human resource development practice. At the organizational level, opportunity costs in human resource development occur with programs that have been established to prepare groups of employees for particular positions or career opportunities. By adopting these programs in an environment of scarce resources, the organization necessarily foregoes the opportunities to provide programs for other positions or employee populations.

At the individual level, participation in employer-sponsored training, especially during normal working hours, incurs the opportunity costs associated with lost productivity on the job. This opportunity cost has traditionally been a major source of management reluctance to support certain types of training. Similar opportunity costs are incurred at the department level when work activities are foregone to participate in training. At the organization level, the value of opportunity costs is necessarily higher, as is the value of human capital, because it is applied across the organization. Opportunity costs are the flip side (and sometimes the unnoticed side) of the benefits of education and human resource development.

Agency Theory

Agency theory derives from a branch of organization theory concerned with reconciling the behavior of self-interested individuals with conflicting goals within a larger organizational context where collaboration among individuals is sought. Levinthal's (1988) agency theory proposes that principals (i.e., owners) monitor the performance of agents (i.e., employees) and use incentives such that employees work to achieve the principals' goals in spite of employees' self-interests. Given discretion in the direction and degree of investments in human capital, agency theory suggests that principals are far more likely to promote firm-specific human capital over general-purpose human capital, which increases the ease with which employees can move to other firms.

Production Functions

Production functions are the technical or physical relationships between the inputs and outputs in a value-added process. With respect to educational investments in human capital, we wish to know the precise inputs (i.e., resources) that enter the production process (i.e., education), the precise relationship between factors within the production process, and the outputs (i.e., benefits, outcomes) which result from the educational production process (Lewis, 1977). The production function for education is represented as relationship 1 in Figure 6.3. Educational economists are not disinterested in the learning process and the best ways for people to acquire skills. On the contrary, studies of the way people learn and the way people use their skills in the workplace should reflect economic considerations and human capital theory. Production functions in human resource development are represented by choices such as internal training (i.e., provided by the employer) versus external training (i.e., provided by a training vendor), classroom versus on-line training, the direct involvement of supervisors or subject matter experts in developing programs, and other means of "producing" education and training.

Screening Theory of Education

The screening theory of education suggests that, as opposed to affecting the productivity increases espoused by human capital theory, education serves a screening function in which individuals are ranked by ability, achievement levels, and grading. Any productivity gains apparent from education are, therefore, a function of the traits of those being educated, not a product of the education process. That is, increased productivity derives from the abilities of individuals, not from the education. Education serves to screen out those who do not have the ability; individuals with ability complete their educations, others do not. Some evidence exists in support of the screening theory of education (Stiglitz, 1975). The implications of this theory extend to human resource development in that training might be seen as a screening activity and thus perceived as not improving productivity. Education also may be viewed as a screening process for promotion, transfer or other personnel action.

Summary

Human capital development is critical not only to organizations, but to all areas of work-force and human resource development. The economic realities facing human resource development professionals strongly influence human resource development research and practice. These realities are:

- The measurements used most frequently in organizations, of any kind, are financial measures.
- Efficiency is a universal value, not limited to economics. Efficiency is simply a ratio of the optimal level of accomplishments relative to the effort and resources required to achieve them.
- Human resource development professionals are reluctant to express their work in financial terms, even though their organizations are economically driven.

Principles of economics and human capital theory are part of the fabric of the organizations in which human resource development professionals carry out their work. Ideology aside, the reality in our culture is that economic choices are among the most important decisions made in the workplace. These considerations support economics and human capital theory having a central place in the theoretical foundation of human resource development.

SYSTEMS THEORY AS A FOUNDATION FORHUMAN RESOURCE DEVELOPMENT

Contributed by Wendy E.A. Ruona

It is widely acknowledged that HRD is a discipline rooted in multiple theories. While it is true that HRD utilizes many theories, all of these theories are not foundational or core to HRD. A foundation is the basis on which a thing stands and comprises those elements that are essential to its survival. For a profession such as HRD, a foundation must be theoretically sound and its professionals must be well-versed in what comprises that core. Indeed, Warfield (1995) regards the specification of foundations as central to the progress of a discipline when he stated that, "Science is a body of knowledge consisting of three variously integrated components: foundations, theory, and methodology. Foundations inform theory and the theory informs the methodology" (p.81).

Systems theory has been proposed here as one of three theories that are integrated to constitute HRD theory. While many are committed to systems theory implicitly, if not explicitly, its incorporation into HRD's foundational base has yet to fully take hold. The goal of this section is to investigate the contribution of systems theory to HRD.

What is Systems Theory?

Systems theory is fundamentally a theory concerned with systems and their interdependent relationships. Beyond this elementary description, there is not one correct way to define it. The father of general systems theory was von Bertalanffy, who in 1968 first forwarded his revolutionary ideas on complex systems. General systems theory, as forwarded by von Bertalanffy, actually birthed a new organized body of science and a new scientific paradigm. Systems theory today includes *many* specific theories. All of them share a fundamental interest in understanding *systems*—with a particular emphasis on the *interdependencies* and *dynamics* of the parts, how they are organized, and how they work together to produce results.

Scope

Describing this burgeoning field of science is difficult. Multiple fields are direct descendants of systems theory and operate as part of the larger conceptual system of systems inquiry. Although all these related fields are distinctive, they align in their concern with the system. Four of these fields, in particular, dominate the discussion in systems theory.

General Systems Theory. As described above, General Systems Theory is known for focusing multiple disciplines on wholes, parts, the organization and connectedness of the various parts, and, especially, the relationships of systems to their environment. Von Bertalanffy (1968) challenged traditional conceptions of organization by forwarding the notion of open systems; and, in so doing, laid the foundation for the other major fields of study described below.

Cybernetics. Cybernetics is the science of information, communication, feedback, and control both *within* a system as well as *between* a system and its environment. Its focus is more on *how* systems function—how they react to and process information. The result of much of its core work has been in defining heterogeneous interacting components such as mutuality, complementarily, evolvability, constructively, and reflexivity (Joslyn, 1992). It is cybernetics which is the foundation for the emphasis on feedback loops that is commonly associated with modern-day systems thinking.

Chaos. Chaos theory is the "qualitative study of unstable aperiodic behavior in deterministic non-linear dynamic systems" (Kellert, 1993, p.2). A parallel and highly related field of study growing predominantly out of physics, this theory revolutionized science through its discovery that complex and unpredictable results were actually not random but, rather, could be expected in systems that are sensitive to their initial conditions. Behavior that had been assumed to be random in systems of every type was actually found to be bounded and operating within recognizable patterns. Now it is widely recognized that forces in a system endlessly rearrange themselves in different, yet similar patterns. The resulting hidden pattern is coined chaos, fractal, or strange. Chaos theory seeks to understand this ordered randomness and enables scientists to discover and study chaotic behavior.

Complex Adaptive Systems. This field inquires into a special kind of system and strives for an even more holistic view. These systems are *complex* because they are diverse and nonlinear and they are *adaptive* in that they have the capacity to change and learn from experience. Founded by the Santa Fe Institute, the field of complex adaptive systems (CAS) proposes that systems function in a unique area of complexity and conduct self-organizing and learning processes which include structural change through self-renewal (replication, copy and reproduction), nonlinear flows of information and resources, and "far-from-equilibrium conditions that create a dynamic stability where paradox abounds" (Dooley, 1996, p.20). The field of CAS, then, is vitally important to our understanding of how systems emerge, change, and learn from experience in a way that makes the future of a system unpredictable and, ultimately, determined by a dynamic network of agents acting and reacting in parallel (Holland, 1995).

Why Systems Theory?

Even after this brief review of systems theory, the question must be raised as to whether HRD has any choice but to fully embrace systems theory. If HRD agrees that it serves organizations and the people in them, it *must* adopt the science of systems as a core foundation. Organizations *are* systems. A system is defined here as a collection of elements where the performance of the whole is affected by every one of the parts and the way that any part affects the whole depends on what at least one other part is doing. Although there remains some critique of using the "organization as organism" metaphor (Morgan, 1996), organizations can be viewed as living systems of discernible wholes that have lives of their own which they manifest through their processes, structures, and subsystems (Jaros and Dostal, 1995; Wheatley, 1999). One of the largest differences between organizations and other living systems is that they are multi-minded, a fact which HRD has long accepted, and that newer systems theories such as those coming out of complex adaptive systems embraces.

Systems theory provides a common conception of organizations—an organizer or conceptual frame through which HRD can ensure a holistic understanding of its subject. It also provides analysis methodologies capable of including multiple variables. For these important two reasons, systems theory/inquiry is viewed as the only meaningful way to comprehend an organization.

The Support Provided to HRD by Systems Theory

It is not possible to provide a comprehensive review here of the multiple ways in which systems theory contributes valuable knowledge to HRD. However, some general themes can be drawn from the literature and grouped into conceptual categories. A cross-section of the systems leg of the three-legged stool proposed by Swanson (1998) visually depicts these three categories—three ways that systems theory supports HRD (Figure 6.4). Systems inquiry provides (a) information: knowledge or data about systems, (b) capabilities: the potential to act, and (c) direction: guidance for a field's activities and development.

Information Provided by Systems Theory

A primary goal of systems theory is to uncover information about systems. During the last forty to fifty years a large amount of knowledge has been compiled that can help HRD professionals understand the basic structure and essences of systems' parts and wholes. Four distinct areas of information have emerged from the literature review conducted by this author. A description of each area as well as a cursory discussion of the implications resulting from that knowledge is provided below.

Structure of Systems. Systems theory has sought to understand the basic structure of systems—the way that their parts are arranged, the interrelation of parts to other parts and of wholes to the environment, and the purposes of the system design. Although some systems scientists propose that the structure of a system is hardly separable from its functioning or behavior, others study structure specifically and agree that there are specific elements that provide necessary infrastructure (such as boundaries, feedback structures, and mechanisms that serve specific purposes). Prigogine and Stengers (1984), for example, discovered that systems in disequilibrium produce new structures spontaneously from the disorder. Field theory, commonly discussed

272

as related to organizational development, emerged in the 1970s as an explanation of the empty space in systems that affect the structure. Finally, the issue of levels in complex systems has begun to attract scholarly attention.

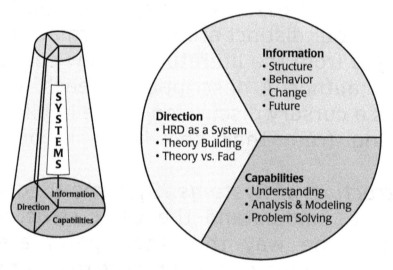

Figure 6.4 A Cross-section of the Systems Leg: Contributions of Systems Theory

Behavior of Systems. The behavior of a system must be understood before it can be influenced. Systems theorists conduct considerable research into the processes and behaviors of a system. While it is not possible here to offer a comprehensive inventory of the plethora of information in this area, a brief account demonstrates how extensive it is and how much information is available for HRD to tap to better understand how systems behave.

Katz and Kahn (1966) identified nine common characteristics of open systems that help to inform HRD of the basic character of systems. To date, seventeen laws of complexity have been discovered and can be classified in a matrix particularly relevant to behavior outcomes (Warfield, 1995). McLagan (1989) discusses processes unique to self-creating systems. Dooley (1996) offers theoretical propositions of complex adaptive systems. The entire field of cybernetics exists for the primary goal of understanding information processing and how nonlinear feedback guides systems behavior. Finally, chaos and emerging fields of complexity inform us that apparent random behavior of a system actually reveals an underlying pattern and order and that complex systems are deterministic (that is, they have something that is determining their behavior).

Change Processes. Systems theory acknowledges that change is part of the very fabric of systems. A systems sub-field, *population ecology,* focuses almost entirely on the potential evolution of the system and posits that actual equilibrium in a system is equal to death; underscoring how systems must evolve, grow, and change to survive. It has taught us to view change as the activation of a system's inherent potential for transformation. The field of *ontogeny* supports this evolutionary perspective in developing ways to study the history of structural change in a unity without loss of organization in that unity (Dooley, 1995).

Systems theory is also increasingly probing for a deeper understanding of the nature and processes of change in systems. Findings in systems theory inform us that systems sensitive to initial conditions are fairly unpredictable in that minor changes can cause huge fluctuations through amplification or, conversely, that some changes in systems can have no apparent effect at all. We also know from the theory that (a) systems behavior gets worse before it grows better, (b) systems tend toward equilibrium (thus, to expect resistance to incremental change), and (c) changes in the essential nature of a system take place when a control parameter passes a critical threshold or bifurcation point (Dooley, 1996). From the field of chaos and complexity, we are beginning to understand that a system is creative not when all of its components pull in same direction, but when they generate tension by pulling in contradictory directions (Stacey, 1992). Systems theory renders the complex dynamics of change more comprehensible through the uncovering of general principles about the nature of change.

The Future in Systems. There have been many distinguished systems scientists who have also been very active in the study of the future. Systems theory contributed a rather revolutionary element to futures theory in that it surfaced the reality that the future is *emergent*—it is created by, and emerges from, self-organization and the interaction of its members (Banathy, 1997; Hammond, 2005; Stacey, 1992).

What does this mean? This means that emergent systems are adaptable, evolvable, boundless, and resilient and are *not* optimal, controllable, or predictable. The literature emerging out of chaos, in particular, informs us that the future is unpredictable due to a system's sensitivity to initial conditions as well as specific characteristics being discovered about emergent systems. Attempting to perform traditional strategic planning given this information has extreme limitations. In a systems approach, rather, the focus of inquiry is on the general character of a system's long-term behavior. There is ongoing pressure to develop improved ways of understanding the qualitative patterns that emerge, how to increase the ability of a system to cope with its emerging future, and how to use evolution as a tool. The emphasis in modern organizations on core competencies, strategic thinking, and scenario planning reflects the application of these principles.

Capabilities Offered by Systems Theory

Systems theory offers a specific contribution that, beyond simply the information described above, affects how things are seen or done. It is in this way that systems theory provides HRD with *capabilities*—the potential to act.

Understanding of Wholes and Complexity. Some might find it strange that this theme has been categorized as a capability. However, it is placed here to sufficiently recognize the perspective contributed by the ontology and epistemology discussed earlier in this paper. Information provided by systems theory is simply raw data without professionals using it to act in ways that are unique in what can often be a mechanistic, reductionist environment. If we accept and utilize systems as a foundational theory, it enables us to set critical standards for our profession that demand a deep analysis of the whole to seek understanding. The conceptual importance of the whole cannot be minimized in HRD, and it has great implications. While there are many frameworks emerging from organization theory that seek to model the parts of an organization, systems theories remind us that we must use these only as a starting point. Systems theories acknowledges that systems have a life of their own separate from their parts, focuses on the interactions *between* the parts rather than the variables themselves, concedes that cause and effect are distant in time and space, and reminds us that the properties of the parts and the whole system are constantly interacting, emerging, and evolving. Systems theories should help to remind the HRD practitioner that the nature of a system is a continuing perception and deception—a continual reviewing of the world.

Systems theory also offers a unique capability rooted in its perspective on the complexity that organizations face. This includes understanding the environment and its impact on systems as well as the complexities within systems. These types of understandings better position systems professionals to deal with the unpredictability inherent in systems and, in fact, to recognize the need for nonlinear feedback and structural instability as a source of innovation and growth. Furthermore, current literature reveals that chaos methods are being discussed as tools to simplify decisions made in conditions of complexity. Guastello (1995) asserts that the tool kit of nonlinear dynamical systems theory consists of: attractor and repellor forces, stabilities and instabilities, bifurcation and self-organization, fractal geometry, the distinction between evolutionary and revolutionary change, and catastrophes and discontinuous change. All of this redirects the potential of HRD to act and forces the development of new capabilities.

Methodologies for Analysis and Modeling. Systems theory offers much in the way of describing, analyzing, and creating models of systems. These methods facilitate the analysis and modeling of complex interpersonal, inter-group, and human/nature interactions without reducing the subject matter to the level of individual agents. The key is to utilize methods that allow the abstraction of certain details of structure and component, while concentrating on the *dynamics* that define the characteristic functions, properties, and relationships—this simplification is coined "reduction to dynamics" (Laszlo and Laszlo, 1997). There are multiple analysis and modeling approaches grounded in the systems approach to be reviewed in the literature. Generally they entail identification of multiple elements around and in a system and a refocusing on the whole, integrating what was learned in an understanding of the overall phenomena.

Problem-Solving Approaches. Systems theory offers two things in terms of approaching problem solving in applied sciences such as HRD. First, systems theorists actually start from the problem, not some preconceived notion of a model or a solution. Once the manifestation of the problem has been identified and described, they proceed inward to the subsystems and outward to the environment (Laszlo and Laszlo, 1997). Second, systems theory is the antithesis of the "one-tool-fits all" mentality. Rather, the theory accepts complexity, freeing problem solvers from causality and linearity and fostering the identification of patterns and tools that apply to different entities. Furthermore, systems theory encourages drawing on multiple disciplines without being unduly restricted from points of view within those disciplines (McLagan, 1989).

Direction Provided by Systems Theory

Finally, it is suggested that systems theory can serve as a guiding force that offers direction for a discipline's activities and future. Interpretations grounded in systems theory can help to build the case for the structure and behavior of HRD.

HRD as a System. There continues to be much discussion about the purpose, function, and definition of HRD. Further work on how HRD will conceive of itself is imperative to ensure a robust future for the field. While there have been multiple proposals to conceive of HRD as a system, there continues to be no firm agreement or discussion of the implications of such a conception. Systems theory provides guidance for identifying the field's contexts and boundaries, actual versus desired goals, inputs, processes, and outputs, modes of operation, constraints, various systems states, and roles.

Theory Building in HRD. Systems theory can enhance the development of theory in HRD in a few ways. First, it serves as a unifier with other disciplines and sciences in the spirit of its founder. Von Bertalanffy (1968) called for the unity of science through an interdisciplinary theory that sought to integrate findings into "an isomorphy of laws in different fields" (p.48). This isomorphy needs to be built at two levels. On a microlevel, it can assist in the organization of HRD's "various practical experiences into some formal, theoretical structure that will be useful in advancing our practice and that in turn will provide a basis for further theory building" (Jacobs, 1989, p.27). On a macrolevel, systems theory provides a foundation on which to acknowledge how interdisciplinary it really is and contribute to the isomorphy integrating those disciplines.

Secondly, systems theory provides relief from mechanistic approaches and a rationale for rejecting principles based on the closed-system mentality (Kast and Rosenzwig, 1972). The theory requires a new heuristic other than reducing things to their components—that is, focusing on wholes, dynamics, and general theory constructs.

Finally, systems theory provides great insight into the process of theory-building. It offers guidance about the limits of theoretical generalization. Although a motivation undergirding the theory is the unity of science and discovery of general systems principles and laws, it should be noted that systems scientists take great pains to avoid the trap of creating theory that explains 'everything' but actually explains nothing. The goal of systems theory is to build theory that explains a lot and has tentacles linking it to other general theories whose purposes it is to describe a particular class of phenomena (Guastello, 1995).

Theory versus "Fad." Systems theory provides knowledge of the nature and behavior of systems. In this knowledge is once again found a capability—the capability to fight against the propagation of fads. Most of these types of solutions are only partial, focusing on parts that gurus can easily see or market, rather than the holistic view that is needed. They typically lack an overall understanding of complexity and how a system copes with the implications. Systems theory is not a panacea or an easy "six-step" kind of thing. It is hard. However, it provides a foundation that facilitates a thorough understanding of complex situations and systems. This is the strongest way to increase the likelihood of appropriate action. Professionals embracing systems theory as a foundation of HRD are best positioned to influence other practitioners to change their perception of the development and the unleashing of expertise in systems. This is the very nature of scientific revolution (Kuhn, 1970).

Summary

Even in the limited space of these pages, it would be incomplete not to acknowledge that systems theory poses challenges to the field. Some of these are noted in Figure 6.5 in terms of how they impact theory and practice. These issues provide ample challenges to HRD professionals; however, most of them can be overcome through research, development, and increased dialogue between theoreticians and practitioners.

Attending to these challenges will certainly make the field of HRD more capable of being a strategic partner and more able to effectively work to achieve the aims to which we espouse. Systems theories offer much wisdom for HRD professionals and should certainly be requisite for foundational knowledge and effective practice. Hammond (2005), sums it up well in saying that, "Systems thinking nurtures a way of thinking that engenders a different kind of practice and cultivates an ethic of integration and collaboration that has the potential to transform the nature of social organization ... the challenge is to integrate what we have learned, to communicate these insights to a larger audience, and to nurture institutional practices that honor the ethical principles inherent in the systems view" (p.20).

Figure 6.5 Challenges Posed by Systems Theory as a Foundation for HRD

Theoretical Challenges	Practical Challenges
• Provides more information about dynamics between the parts than it does about the parts themselves	• Theories are complex
• Biological model may ignore social psychological nature of social systems (Katz and Kahn, 1966)	• Responsibilities of systems practitioners have yet to be clearly articulated and developed
• Can be misinterpreted as not offering a definite body of knowledge since there is not one mainstream approach	• Necessitates interventions that may lie outside of the mandate of the "client" (Dash, 1995)
• Lacking in reliable methods of "total" conception of the whole	• Can be viewed as constraint to practitioners because time-consuming and costly
• Requires subjectivity, which is still a "stretch" for strict positivists	• Coercive structures in organizations have to be confronted as they undermine the pluralist spirit of systems approach (Dash, 1995)
• Normative implications of systems theory not clarified (Dash, 1995)	• Raises the risk of becoming obsessed with system and forgetting individual (Bierema, 1997)

Theoretical Challenges	Practical Challenges
• Requires more empirical data on systems applications and concepts relative to theoretical formulations	• Places great demands on the field in terms of theory building
• Risk of losing scientific depth in favor of breadth	• Requires knowledge and skills that are not readily available in academia†

CONCLUSION

Three component theories have been proposed as constituting the theoretical foundation of HRD. Explicit in this proposal is that the *integration* of these three theories is what will equip HRD to contend with the challenges it is called upon to address. In this sense, the whole of the theory of HRD stemming from these foundations will be larger than the sum of the parts and must be unique to HRD (Ruona and Swanson, 1998). The component theories complement one another in explaining the phenomenon of HRD.

REFLECTION QUESTIONS

1. What aspect of psychological theory interests you the most? Why?
2. What aspect of economic theory interests you the most? Why?

3. What aspect of systems theory interests you the most? Why?
4. How do you see the three component theories working together for HRD?

PART THREE

Perspectives of Human Resource Development

This section explains the performance and learning paradigms of HRD and associated models within each. It clarifies the learning – performance perspectives and their logical connection.

CHAPTERS

7 Paradigms of Human Resource Development
8 Perspectives on Performance in Human Resource Development
9 Perspectives on Learning in Human Resource Development

CHAPTER 7

Paradigms of Human Resource Development

CHAPTER OUTLINE

Introduction
Overview of the HRD Paradigms
Debates about Learning and Performance
Philosophical Views of Learning and Performance

- Three Views of Performance
- Three Views of Learning
- Comparing Philosophical Foundations
  Learning Paradigm of HRD
- Definition of the Learning Paradigm
- Core Theoretical Assumptions of the Learning
  Paradigm Performance Paradigm of HRD
- Definition of the Performance Paradigm
- Core Theoretical Assumptions of the Performance
  Paradigm
- Myths about the Performance Paradigm
  Fusing the Two Paradigms
  Conclusion
  Reflection Questions

INTRODUCTION

Like most professional disciplines, Human Resource Development (HRD) includes multiple paradigms for practice and research. A paradigm is defined as a "coherent tradition of scientific research" (Kuhn, 1996, p.10). Thus, multiple paradigms represent fundamentally different views of HRD, including its goals and aims, values, and guidelines for practice. It is important to understand each paradigm, as they often lead to different approaches to solving HRD problems and to different research questions and methodologies. It is also important that each person develops a personal belief system about which paradigm or blend of paradigms will guide his or her practice. This chapter reviews the major paradigms, discusses the learning versus performance debate, examines core philosophical and theoretical assumptions of each paradigm, and examines their merger.

OVERVIEW OF THE HRD PARADIGMS

For our purposes, we divide HRD into two paradigms, the learning paradigm and the performance paradigm (Figure 7.1) These two paradigms are the most clearly defined and dominate most HRD thinking and practice. A third paradigm, the meaning of work and work-life integration is an emerging perspective (Morris and Madsen, 2007). It seems to have arisen out of a backlash against the workplace as a result of downsizings, layoffs, and other corporate actions that have left workers unemployed or otherwise feeling disenfranchised. One important HRD role from this perspective is helping people create a sense of meaning in their work and balance in their lives.

The first paradigm, the learning paradigm, has been the predominant paradigm in HRD practice in the United States. As shown in Figure 7.1, this perspective has three different streams. The first, *individual learning* (column 1a), focuses primarily on individual learning as an outcome and the individual learner as the target of interventions. Two characteristic approaches within this stream are adult learning (Knowles et al., 2005; Yang, 2003) and instructional design (Allen, 2006; Gagne, 1965; Gagne, Briggs, and Wagner, 1992; Gagne and Medsker, 1996).

Most HRD practice has now advanced to *performance-based learning* (column 1b) or *whole systems learning* (column 1c). The key change when moving from individual learning to these two streams is that the outcome focus changes to performance, though it is still

Figure 7.1 Comparison of the Learning and Performance Paradigms

	1 *Learning Paradigm*			*2* *Performance Paradigm*	
	(A) **INDIVIDUAL LEARNING**	**(B)** **PERFORMANCE-BASED LEARNING**	**(C)** **WHOLE SYSTEMS LEARNING**	**(A)** **INDIVIDUAL PERFORMANCE IMPROVEMENT**	**(B)** **WHOLE SYSTEMS PERFORMANCE IMPROVEMENT**
Outcome focus	Enhancing individual learning	Enhancing individual performance through learning	Enhancing multiple levels of performance through learning	Enhancing individual performance	Enhancing multiple levels of performance
Intervention focus	▪ Individual learning	▪ Individual learning ▪ Organization systems to support individual learning	▪ Individual, team, and organizational learning ▪ Organizational systems to support multiple levels of learning	▪ Nonlearning individual performance system interventions ▪ Learning if appropriate	▪ Nonlearning multiple-level performance system interventions ▪ Multiple-level learning if appropriate
Representative research streams	▪ Adult learning ▪ Instructional design	▪ Performance-based instruction ▪ Transfer of learning	▪ Learning organization	▪ Human performance technology	▪ Performance improvement

individual performance improvement as a result of learning. The primary intervention continues to be learning, but interventions are also focused on building organizational systems to maximize the likelihood that learning will improve broader performance. *Performance-based learning* (column 1b) is focused on individual performance resulting from learning. Performance-based instruction (Brethower and Smalley, 1998) and systematic training (Allen, 2006) are two examples of this paradigm. *Whole systems learning* (column 1c) focuses on enhancing team and organizational performance through learning in addition to individual performance. It does so by building systems that enhance learning at the individual, team, and organizational levels. Most representative of this perspective is learning organization theory (Dibella and Nevis, 1998; Marquardt, 1995, 2002; Watkins and Marsick, 1993).

The second paradigm, the *performance paradigm,* is quite familiar to those who have embraced performance improvement or human performance technology (HPT) (Brethower, 1995). From these perspectives, the outcome focus is on total performance, but the intervention focus is on nonlearning as well as learning interventions. It is the incorporation of nonlearning components of performance and associated interventions that distinguishes this group from the learning systems perspective.

Within the performance systems perspective are also two streams. The *individual performance improvement* approach (column 2a) focuses mostly on individual level performance systems. Human performance technology (Gilbert, 1978; Stolovich and Keeps, 1992) represents this approach. *Whole systems performance improvement* is the broadest perspective, encompassing learning and nonlearning interventions occurring at multiple levels in the organization. What is generically called *performance improvement* (Holton, 1999; Rummler and Brache, 1995) or *performance consulting* (Robinson and Robinson, 1995) is representative of this approach.

DEBATES ABOUT LEARNING AND PERFORMANCE

Since 1995, an intense debate in the U.S. research literature has revolved around the learning versus performance paradigms of HRD (Watkins and Marsick, 1995; Swanson, 1995a, 1995b). This has occurred in spite of the fact that HRD practice in the U.S. has been found to be increasingly focused on performance outcomes and developing systems to support high performance (Bassi and Van Buren, 1999).

In this debate, the performance paradigm of HRD has come under increasing criticism, some of which reflects misconceptions about the basic tenets of performance-based HRD. For example, Barrie and Pace (1998) argue for a more educational approach to HRD manifested through an organizational learning approach. They are also particularly critical of the performance paradigm with respect to the individual:

Improvements in performance are usually achieved through behavioral control and conditioning. Indeed, performance may be changed or improved through methods that allow for very little if any willingness and voluntariness on the part of the performers. In fact, behavioral performance may be enhanced decidedly by processes that allow for minimal or no rational improvement on the part of performers in the change process. Their willingness of consciousness as rational agents is neither encouraged nor required. Such persons function in a change process purely as "means" and not "ends." (Holding, 1981, p.50)

Their criticisms became even harsher: "It is the performance perspective that denies a person's fundamental and inherent agency and self-determination, not the learning perspective. All of the negative effects of training come from a performance perspective" (Barrie and Pace, 1999, p.295).

Bierema (1997) calls for a return to a focus on individual development and appears to equate the performance perspective to the mechanistic model of work. She says, "The machine mentality in the workplace, coupled with obsessive focus on performance, has created a crisis in individual development" (p.23). She goes on to say that "valuing development only if it contributes to productivity is a viewpoint that has perpetuated the mechanistic model of the past three hundred years" (p.24). Peterson and Provo (1999) also equate the performance paradigm with behaviorism.

Dirkx (1997) offers a somewhat similar view when he says that "HRD continues to be influenced by an ideology of scientific management and reflects a view of education where the power and control over what is learned, how, and why is located in the leadership, corporate structure, and HRD staff" (p.42). He goes on to say that the traditional view in which learning is intended to contribute to bottom-line performance leads "practitioners to focus on designing and implementing programs that transmit to passive workers the knowledge and skills needed to improve the company's overall performance and, ultimately, society's economic competitiveness. In this market-driven view of education, learning itself is defined in particular ways, largely by the perceived needs of the sponsoring corporation and the work individuals are required to perform" (p.43).

What is striking about these comments and others offered by critics of the performance paradigm of HRD is that they all contain rather gross errors and misunderstandings. In reality, there is less of a gap between the performance and learning paradigms than is represented by learning paradigm advocates. Simply put, when properly and clearly framed, the performance paradigm is not what the learning paradigm advocates present it to be. While there can be no denying that some tension will always exist between the learning systems and work systems in an organization (Van der Krogt, 1998), there is actually more common ground than has been portrayed by critics of performance.

Our purpose in this chapter is *not* to argue for a unifying definition or perspective of HRD. Rather, we present a framework for understanding paradigms of HRD to highlight both the common ground and the differences between the perspectives. As Kuchinke (1998) has articulated, it is probably not possible or even desirable to resolve paradigmatic debates, but the sharp dualism that has characterized this debate is also not appropriate or necessary. Others would argue to at least search for common ground.

PHILOSOPHICAL VIEWS OF LEARNINGAND PERFORMANCE

Underlying this debate is tension about whether performance is inherently "bad" and learning "good." From a philosophical perspective, this is a discussion about the ontology of learning and performance because it focuses on making the fundamental assumptions about the nature of these phenomena explicit and clearly articulated (Gioia and Pitre, 1990; Ruona, 1999, 2000). In this section, we define the multiple perspectives of performance and learning that can be identified within the learning versus performance debate and argue that neither performance or learning can be considered inherently "good" or "bad," and that human resource development can embrace both as humanistic (Holton, 2000).

Three Views of Performance

Performance has largely been a practice-based phenomenon with little philosophical consideration. Three basic views pervade the thinking about the performance paradigm: Performance as (1) a natural outcome of human activity, (2) necessary for economic activity, and (3) an instrument of oppression.

Performance as a Natural Outcome of Human Activity

In this view, performance is accepted as a natural part of human existence. Human beings are seen as engaging in wide varieties of purposeful activities with performance as a natural and valued outcome. Furthermore, the accomplishment of certain outcomes in these purposeful activities is regarded as a basic human need. In other words, few people are content not to perform.

Many of these activities occur in work settings where we traditionally think of performance; however, they may also take place in leisure settings. For example, a person may play softball for leisure but be quite interested in winning games. Or, a person might be heavily involved with church activities such as membership drives or outreach programs and exert great effort to make them successful. In both of these examples, performance is a desired aspect of their freely chosen behavior.

In this view, for HRD to embrace performance is also to embrace enhancing human existence. It is this perspective that many, although not all, performance-based HRD professionals advocate. This view of performance-based HRD views advancing performance and enhancing human potential as perfectly complementary (Holton, 2000).

Performance as Necessary for Economic Activity

This perspective is a more utilitarian view that considers performance to be an instrumental activity that enhances individuals and society because it supports economic gains. More value-neutral than the first perspective, this view sees performance as neither inherently good nor bad but rather as a means to other ends. It is largely a work-based view of performance. Performance is seen as necessary for individuals to earn livelihoods, be productive members of society, and build a good society. In this recursive process, performance at the individual level leads to enhanced work and careers, and performance at the organizational level leads to stronger economic entities capable of providing good jobs to individuals.

Some models and concepts of performance improvement can be associated with this perspective as they attempt to enhance the utility of learning by linking learning to individual and organizational performance outcomes. While this objective is worthy by itself, it is criticized for lacking the intrinsic "goodness" of the first ontological perspective. As the performance paradigm has matured, it has broadened to embrace the first perspective.

Performance as an Instrument of Organizational Oppression

From this perspective, performance is seen as a means of control and dehumanization. Through focusing on performance, organizations are seen as coercing and demanding behaviors from individuals in return for compensation. Performance is viewed as threatening to humans and potentially abusive. As such, it is largely a necessary evil that denies human potential.

It is this perspective that seems to be represented in critics of performance-based HRD. For example, Barrie and Pace (1998) say that "it is the performance perspective that denies a person's fundamental and inherent agency and self-determination" (p.295). Others (Bierema, 1997; Peterson and Provo, 1999) refer to the mechanistic or machine model of work when referring to the performance perspective.

The underlying presumption of this perspective is that performance is antithetical to human potential. It seems to be most closely aligned with critical theorists who wish HRD to challenge organizational power structures that seek to control performance outcomes.

Three Views of Learning

Much philosophical work has focused on learning and adult education since ancient times (Gutek, 1998; Elias and Merriam, 1995; Lindeman,1926; Bryson 1936; Hewitt and Mather, 1937). For purposes of this discussion, we group the views of learning into three analogous ontological views of learning as (1) a humanistic endeavor, (2) value-neutral transfer of information, and (3) a tool for societal oppression.

Learning as a Humanistic Endeavor

The primary purpose of learning in this perspective is to enhance human potential. Most closely aligned with humanistic psychology and existentialist philosophy, humans are seen as growing, developing beings. Learning is viewed as a key element in helping individuals become more self-actualized and inherently good for the person. Most HRD scholars view learning from this perspective. They believe deeply in the power of learning to enhance human potential. It is important to note that most within performance-based HRD also see learning in this way.

Learning as a Value-Neutral Transmission of Information

Learning in this view has instrumental value in that it transfers information that individuals need and desire. Closely aligned with Dewey's (1938) pragmatic philosophy, learning is seen as a means to solve problems of everyday living. Instructional designers and many organizational trainers approach learning from this perspective as their primary task is to transfer information effectively. A large part of training practice in the United States is grounded in this perspective that sees learning as largely value-neutral and instrumental.

Learning as a Tool for Societal Oppression

Largely overlooked by most HRD scholars in the United States is the fact that learning can also be a tool for oppression, particularly outside organizational settings. For example, communist use of learning to control people, cults use learning to brainwash people, religion has used learning to restrict worldviews of people, and education has used learning to restrict or misrepresent Native American, African American, and female history. Freire (1970) and Mezirow (1991) are examples of scholars who have warned about the potentially oppressive nature of learning. Thus, learning can also be a tool for oppression and control.

Comparing Philosophical Foundations

The first conclusion is that neither learning nor performance are inherently good or bad. Both can be instruments of oppression or means to elevate human potential. We maintain that human resource development can elevate human potential and enhance the human experience by focusing on *both* performance and learning.

It is disturbing that debates in the literature have reflected diverse ontological assumptions about performance without explicitly owning and acknowledging them. Specifically, critics of "the" performance-based HRD have categorized all emerging views of performance into the third perspective, an instrument of organizational oppression. As a result, learning has been incorrectly portrayed as inherently "good" and performance as inherently "bad." It is equally possible for performance to be "good" and learning to be "bad" in a given situation. Any notion that either performance or learning has these inherent qualities should be abandoned in future exchanges.

Performance-based HRD should adopt the perspective that *both* learning and performance are inherently good for the individual because both are natural parts of human existence. It is hard to imagine a life without learning or without performance. The challenge for the human resource development profession is to ensure that neither one becomes a tool for oppression but rather elevates human potential.

LEARNING PARADIGM OF HRD

The learning paradigm is familiar territory to most HRD professionals. In this section the learning paradigm is defined and its core assumptions presented.

Definition of the Learning Paradigm

Watkins (1995) offers a useful definition of the learning paradigm of HRD: "HRD is the field of study and practice responsible for the fostering of a long-term work-related learning capacity at the individual, group, and organizational level of organizations" (p.2). Furthermore, she says that HRD "works to enhance individuals' capacity to learn, to help groups overcome barriers to learning, and to help organizations create a culture which promotes conscious learning" (p.2).

Core Theoretical Assumptions of the Learning Paradigm

The core assumptions of the learning paradigm have not been clearly articulated by any one individual. Ruona (1998, 2000) provides particularly good insights in her study of the core beliefs of HRD scholarly leaders. Others have offered strong arguments in favor of what we are calling the learning paradigm (Barrie and Pace,1998; Watkins and Marsick, 1995; Bierema, 1997; Dirkx, 1997). Drawing on these and other sources, the following ten core assumptions from the learning paradigm have emerged.

Learning Paradigm Assumption 1: Individual education, growth, learning and development are inherently good for the individual. At the heart of the learning paradigm is the notion that learning, development, and growth are inherently good for each individual. This assumption is drawn from humanistic psychology that stresses self-actualization of the individual. This assumption is also central to all of human resource development practice and is unchallenged by any paradigm of HRD.

Learning Paradigm Assumption 2: People should be valued for their intrinsic worth as people, not just as resources to achieve an outcome. Learning advocates object to characterizing people as "resources" to be utilized to achieve a goal, particularly in an organization. For HRD to value people only with regard to their contribution to performance outcomes is offensive because it invalidates them as human beings. Furthermore, it leads to workplaces that devalue people and can quickly become abusive to employees. From this perspective, HRD should value people for their inherent worth and not seek to use them to accomplish a goal. Thus, learning and development should be a means to enhance people and their humanness, not merely to accomplish performance goals.

Learning Paradigm Assumption 3: The primary purpose of HRD is development of the individual. From this paradigm, the needs of the individual should be more important than the needs of the organization, or equally important at a minimum. Those learning advocates who are concerned about power structures in society would argue that the learning and development needs of the individual should take precedence over the needs of the organization (Bierema, 2000; Dirkx, 1997). Others might take a more moderate view that the needs of the individual need to be balanced against the needs of the organization. Regardless, the primary goal of HRD from this perspective is to help individuals develop to their fullest potential.

Learning Paradigm Assumption 4: The primary outcome of HRD is learning and development. In this paradigm, learning is considered to be the primary outcome of human resource development. While performance is acknowledged, the core outcome variable is learning. As stated in the overview, there are variations within this paradigm such that some focus mostly on individual learning while others take a whole systems approach (individual, team, and organizational). Regardless, the end result is some form of learning and development.

Learning Paradigm Assumption 5: Organizations are best advanced by having fully developed individuals. Performance outcomes that benefit the individual and the organization are presumed to occur if the individual is developed to full potential. That is, the specific performance behaviors desired by the organization are best achieved by focusing on the individual's development. Performance, then, flows naturally from development instead of having performance drive development. As Bierema (1996) states, "A holistic approach to the development of individuals in the context of a learning organizationproduceswell-informed,knowledge-able, critical-thinking adults who have a sense of fulfillment and inherently make decisions that cause an organization to prosper" (p.22). Indeed, learning and development are presumed to be able to nourish the individual to higher levels of performance than can be achieved by a focus on well-defined performance outcomes.

Learning Paradigm Assumption 6: Individuals should control their own learning process. This assumption is deeply rooted in the democratic as well as humanistic principles of adult learning. Individuals are presumed to have the inherent capacity and motivation to direct their own learning in a way that is most beneficial to them. Because of this, HRD is presumed not to need to specify performance outcomes because learners are able to determine their own course to high performance and will actively seek to do so. Deeply rooted in the inherent belief of the goodness of people and the concept of self-organizing systems, this assumption frees HRD from focusing on performance outcomes by striving to create nourishing learning situations.

Learning Paradigm Assumption 7: Development of the individual should be holistic. For people in organizations to achieve their fullest potential, they must be developed holistically, not just with specific skills or competencies for specific tasks (Barrie and Pace, 1998; Yang,

2003). HRD, from this paradigm, should focus on all aspects of individual development.

Holistic development integrates personal and professional life in career planning, development, and assessment. Holistic development is not necessarily linked to the present or future job tasks, but the overall growth of the individual with the recognition that this growth will have an effect on the organizational system. (Bierema, 1996, p.25)

Learning Paradigm Assumption 8: The organization must provide people a means to achieve their fullest human potential through meaningful work. This assumption extends assumption 3 to say that organizations have a duty and responsibility to help individuals develop to their full potential. Furthermore, one of the primary vehicles for this is human resource development.

Learning Paradigm Assumption 9: An emphasis on performance or organizational benefits creates a mechanistic view of people that prevents them from reaching their full potential. This assumption is particularly important because it creates the largest gap with the performance paradigm. Learning advocates tend to think that emphasizing performance outcomes in HRD, and targeting HRD interventions to improve performance, results in an overly mechanistic approach to HRD and organizational life. As a result, people in organizations are limited and many fail to reach their full potential. Such an approach fails to tap into the capabilities people have to accomplish great things, leaving them more alienated from the organization and ultimately hurting the organization.

PERFORMANCE PARADIGM OF HRD

The performance paradigm of HRD has seen renewed interest in the 1990s. As shown in chapter 3, it actually has very deep roots in training practices throughout history. It has come to the forefront of HRD debates because changes in the global economy have put renewed pressure on HRD for accountability.

Definition of the Performance Paradigm

Holton (1999) points out that the performance paradigm of HRD has not been formally defined in the literature, although there are definitions of HRD that are performance based (Weinberger, 1998). Holton offers several useful definitions. *Performance* is defined as:

accomplishing units of mission-related outcomes or outputs.

A *performance system* was defined as

any system organized to accomplish a mission or purpose.

It is important to note that the term *performance system* was used instead of *organization.* Performance systems are simply purposeful systems that have a specified mission. All organizations are performance systems, but some performance systems are not an organization. For example, a community could become a performance system if it adopts a mission.

Then, the performance paradigm of HRD was defined as follows:

The performance paradigm of HRD holds that the purpose of HRD is to advance the mission of the performance system that sponsors the HRD efforts by improving the capabilities of individuals working in the system and improving the systems in which they perform their work.

Core Theoretical Assumptions of the Performance Paradigm

In this section, eleven core assumptions are presented (Holton, 2002). It is important to remember that the performance paradigm has evolved over the last decade with only limited work to explicitly define it (Swanson, 1999; Holton, 1999). Thus, these core assumptions represent a snapshot of the performance paradigm at this point. Clearly literature from ten years ago might appear to represent different perspectives because the performance paradigm was just emerging. Indeed, in their zeal to get performance added to the HRD framework, early performance advocates focused mostly on performance variables and may have unintentionally appeared to exclude learning and human potential.

Performance Paradigm Assumption 1: Performance systems must perform to survive and prosper, and individuals who work within them must perform if they wish to advance their careers and maintain employment or membership. The performance paradigm views performance as a fact of life in performance systems (e.g., organizations) that is not optional. For example, if organizations do not perform, they decline and eventually disappear. Performance is not defined only as profit, but rather by whatever means the organization uses to define its core outcomes (e.g., citizen services for a government organization). Every performance system has core outcomes and constituents or customers who expect them to be achieved. Even nonprofit and government organizations face restructuring or extinction if they do not achieve their core outcomes.

By extension, then, if individual employees do not perform in a manner that supports the system's long-term interests, they are unlikely to be seen as productive members of the system. Thus, in an organization persons may not advance and may ultimately lose their jobs. This is not to suggest that employees must blindly follow the organization's mandates. In the short term they are expected to challenge the organization when necessary, but over the long term every employee must make contributions to core outcomes. Thus, the greatest service HRD can provide to the individual and to the performance system is to help improve performance by enhancing individual expertise and building effective performance systems.

Performance Paradigm Assumption 2: The ultimate purpose of HRD is to improve performance of the system in which it is embedded and which provides the resources to support it. The purpose of HRD is to improve performance of the system in which it is embedded (or within which it is working in the case of consultants) and that provides the resources to support it (Swanson and Arnold, 1997). All interventions and activities undertaken by HRD must ultimately enhance that system's mission-related performance by improving performance at the mission, social sub-system, process and individual levels (Holton, 1999). Aside from general ethical responsibilities (Dean, 1993), HRD's primary accountability is to the system within which it resides.

The system's mission and the goals derived from it specify the expected outcomes of that system. Every purposefully organized system operates with a mission, either explicitly or implicitly, and the role of the mission is to reflect the system's relationship with its *external* environment. If the system has a purpose, then it also has desired outputs, so performance theory is applicable. Performance occurs in everything from churches (e.g., number of members, money raised, individuals helped), to government (e.g., health care in a community, driver's licenses issued, crime rates), to nonprofits (e.g., research funded, members), and, of course, to profit-making organizations. Under this broad definition, performance is not seen as inherently harmful or nonhumanistic but rather as an important fact of life in systems organized for purposeful activity.

The particular system's definition of its performance relationship with the external environment is fully captured by the mission and goals of the organization. In that sense, this model differs from that of Kaufman and his associates (see Kaufman, Watkins, Triner, and Smith, 1998; Kaufman, 1997) who have argued that societal benefits should be included as a level of performance. This difference should not be interpreted to mean that societal benefits are unimportant. Rather, the relationship between the performance system and society is most appropriately captured by the mission of that system.

Performance Paradigm Assumption 3: The primary outcome of HRD is not just learning but also performance. The argument over learning versus performance has positioned the two as equal and competing outcomes. In reality, this is an inappropriate theoretical argument. Performance and learning really represent two different levels of outcomes that are complementary, not competing. Multilevel theory building has become increasingly popular as a means to integrate competing perspectives (Klein, Tosi, and Cannella, 1999). In management, this divide has been characterized as the "micro" domain where the focus is on the individual and the "macro" domain where the focus is on the organization. Multilevel theory integrates the two by acknowledging the influence of the organization on the individual, and vice versa:

> Multilevel theories illuminate the context surrounding individual-level processes,

clarifying precisely when and where such processes are likely to occur within organization. Similarly, multilevel theories identify the individual-level characteristics, behaviors, attitudes and perceptions that underlie and shape organization-level characteristics and outcomes. (Klein et al., p.243)

From the multilevel perspective, then, neither level is more or less important. Furthermore, individual learning would be seen as an integral part of achieving organizational and individual goals.

Performance Paradigm Assumption 4: Human potential in organizations must be nurtured, respected and developed. Performance advocates believe in the power of learning and the power of people in organizations to accomplish great things. It is important to distinguish between the performance paradigm of HRD and simple performance management. The latter does not necessarily honor human potential in organizations as performance-oriented HRD does. Performance-oriented HRD advocates remain HRD and human advocates at the core. Performance advocates do not believe that emphasizing performance outcomes invalidates their belief in and respect for human potential.

The performance paradigm of HRD recognizes that it is the unleashing of human potential that creates great organizations. While performance advocates emphasize outcomes, they do not demand that outcomes be achieved through control of human potential. Performance advocates fully embrace notions of empowerment and human development because they will also lead to better performance when properly executed (Huselid, 1995; Lam and White, 1998). Furthermore, they see no instances where denying the power of human potential in organizations would lead to better performance. Thus, they see it as completely consistent to emphasize both human potential and performance.

Performance Paradigm Assumption 5: HRD must enhance current performance and build capacity for future performance effectiveness in order to create sustainable high performance. Kaplan and Norton (1996) suggest two categories of performance measures: outcomes and drivers. Unfortunately, they do not offer concise definitions of either. For our purposes, *outcomes* are measures of effectiveness or efficiency relative to core outputs of the system, subsystem, process or individual. The most typical are financial indicators (profit, ROI, etc.) and productivity measures (units of goods or services produced) and are often generic across similar performance systems. According to Kaplan and Norton, these measures tend to be lag indicators in that they reflect what has occurred or has been accomplished in relation to core outcomes.

Drivers measure elements of performance that are expected to sustain or increase system, subsystem, process, or individual ability and capacity to be more effective or efficient in the future. Thus, they are leading indicators of future outcomes and tend to be unique for particular performance systems. Together with outcome measures, they describe the hypothesized cause and effect relationships in the organization's strategy (Kaplan and Norton, 1996).

From this perspective, the views of performance improvement experts who focus solely on actual outcomes, such as profit or units of work produced, are flawed in that they are likely to create short-term improvement but neglect aspects of the organization that will drive future performance outcomes. The views of experts who focus solely on performance drivers such as learning or growth are equally flawed in that they fail to consider the actual outcomes. Only when outcomes and drivers are jointly considered will long-term, sustained performance improvements occur. Neither is more or less important, but both work in an integrated fashion to enhance mission, process, subsystem, and individual performance. Performance-based HRD advocates do not support such "performance at all costs" strategies. Long-term sustainable high performance, which is the goal performance-oriented HRD advocates, requires a careful balance between outcomes and drivers. High short-term performance that cannot be sustained is not really high performance.

Performance Paradigm Assumption 6: HRD professionals have an ethical and moral obligation to ensure that attaining organizational performance goals is not abusive to individual employees. Performance advocates agree that the drive for organizational performance can become abusive and unethical. In no way should performance-oriented HRD support organizational practices that exceed the boundaries of ethical and moral treatment of employees. Clearly, there is ample room for disagreement as to the specifics of what is ethical and moral, but the basic philosophical position is that performance improvement efforts must be ethical. This is not viewed as hard to accomplish because of the assumption described below that effective performance is good for individuals and organizations.

Performance Paradigm Assumption 7: Training/learning activities cannot be separated from other parts of the performance system and are best bundled with other performance improvement interventions. The broadest approach, and the one advocated by performance-based HRD, is the whole systems performance improvement approach. This approach focuses on improving performance outcomes at multiple levels with nonlearning and learning interventions. In most organizations there is no profession or discipline charged with responsibility for assessing, improving, and monitoring performance as a whole system. This void is directly responsible for the proliferation of "quick fixes" and faddish improvement programs, most of which focus on only a single element or a subset of performance variables. Because HRD is grounded in systems theory and the whole systems perspective of organizations, it is the logical discipline to take responsibility for whole system performance improvements in organizations.

Performance Paradigm Assumption 8: Effective performance and performance systems are rewarding to the individual and to the organization. Performance clearly benefits the organization. However, lost in the literature is the recognition that effective performance benefits the individual equally. In many instances, performance is presented as almost antithetical to individual benefits, implying one must choose between them. In fact, a variety of research tells us that people like to perform effectively:

- The goal-setting literature indicates that individuals build self-esteem by accomplishing challenging goals (Katzell and Thompson, 1990).
- Hackman and Oldham's (1980) job characteristics model and the research supporting it have shown that experienced meaningfulness of work and responsibility for work outcomes are two critical psychological states that individuals seek.
- Self-efficacy is built when individuals experience success at task performance that is referred to as *enactive mastery* (Wood and Bandura, 1989).
- The relationship between job satisfaction and performance has been shown to be a reciprocal relationship, with performance enhancing job satisfaction and vice versa (Katzell, Thompson, and Guzzo, 1992; Spector, 1997).
- Success at work is seen as important to an individual's basic adult identity because it helps them see themselves as productive, competent human beings (Whitbourne, 1987). Conversely, failure or frustration threatens an individual's self-concept of competence.
- Work allows the individual to implement his or her self-concept and fulfill their unique goals and interests. Work and life satisfac-

tion depend on the extent to which individuals find outlets for their needs and abilities (Super, Savickas, and Super, 1996)

- Success at work fulfills an individual's innate drive for what has been called *self-actualization* (Maslow, 1970) or the need for achievement (McClelland, 1965).
- Self-determination theory and research suggest that humans have three innate needs that are essential to optimal functioning and well being: The needs for competence, relatedness, and autonomy (Ryan and Deci, 2000). Thus, effective performance will contribute to an individual's sense of well being by enhancing feelings of competence.
- Certain individuals have high levels of a dispositional trait called *conscientiousness* that is a valid predictor of job performance (Barrick and Mount, 1991). For these individuals, failure to perform would be very frustrating.
- Performance also helps individuals achieve instrumental goals. It may lead to more career advancement and career opportunities in organizations as well as valued intrinsic and extrinsic rewards as a result of performance

This list is not offered as a comprehensive presentation of ways that performance benefits individuals. Rather, it is representative enough to conclude safely that performance benefits individuals in a myriad of ways. People do not want to fail to perform in their jobs. Therefore, to the extent that HRD helps them be more successful in their jobs, performance-oriented HRD is just as valuable to the individual as the organization. Effective performance can make a significant contribution to individuals as well as their organizations.

Performance Paradigm Assumption 9: Whole systems performance improvement seeks to enhance the value of learning in an organization. Performance-based HRD actually seeks to increase the value of the individual employee and individual learning in the system, not diminish it. It fully agrees that enhancing the expertise of individual employees is fundamentally important. However, performance-based HRD suggests that individually oriented HRD violates the fundamental principles of systems theory (Bertalanffy, 1968), which tell us that no one element of the system can be viewed separately from other elements. Intervening in only one element of the system without creating congruence in other parts of the system will not lead to systemic change. Furthermore, intervening in the whole system to improve outcomes or drivers alone is also flawed. For example, a company that downsizes drastically may increase profits (outcomes) in the short run, but it will leave itself without any intellectual capital (driver) for future growth. Human performance technologists (Stolovich and Keeps, 1992) and needs assessors (Moore and Dutton, 1978) have understood the need to view the individual domain within the larger organizational system in order to make individual domain performance improvement efforts more effective. Whole systems performance improvement goes a step further to analyze and improve performance of the whole system through a balanced emphasis on outcomes and drivers in the four performance domains.

Performance Paradigm Assumption 10: HRD must partner with functional departments to achieve performance goals. One common lament from HRD practitioners is that the performance approach forces them to deal with organizational variables over which they have no control (e.g., rewards, job design, etc.). Performance-oriented HRD acknowledges this and stresses that HRD must become a partner with functional units in the organization to achieve performance improvement, even through learning. Opponents often suggest that HRD should focus on learning because they can influence learning. Yet, classroom learning is the only variable in the performance system over which HRD professionals have the primary influence. Learning organization advocates stress the fact that much of the really valuable learning that takes place in organizations occurs in the workplace, not the classroom (Watkins and Marsick, 1993). Performance-oriented HRD advocates suggest that if HRD is not willing to be a performance partner, then it is doomed to play only small roles in organizations with minimal impact and with great risk for downsizing and outsourcing.

Performance Paradigm Assumption 11: The transfer of learning into job performance is of primary importance. Because the dependent variable in performance-oriented HRD is not just learning but individual and organizational performance, considerable emphasis is placed on the transfer of learning to job performance. As Holton et al. (2000) point out, researchers are still working to operationalize the organizational dimensions important to enhancing transfer. Nonetheless, there is widespread recognition that the transfer process is not something that occurs by chance or is assured by achieving learning outcomes but rather that it is the result of a complex system of influences (Baldwin and Ford, 1988; Broad, 2000; Ford and Weissbein, 1997; Holton and Baldwin, 2000). Learning is a necessary, but not sufficient, condition for improving job performance through increased expertise (Bates, Holton, and Seyler, 2000; Rouillier and Goldstein, 1993; Tracey, Tannenbaum, and Kavanaugh, 1995).

Expertise has emerged as a construct integrating the performance component of HRD with learning (Swanson and Holton, 1999). Expertise, defined as "human behaviors, having effective results and optimal efficiency, acquired through study and experience within a specialized domain" (p.26), focuses HRD on core outcomes from learning. Performance advocates are known for emphasizing measurement of HRD outcomes to see whether outcomes are achieved. Measuring performance is a common activity in organizations, so it is logical that performance-oriented HRD would also stress measurement. This emphasis stems from two key observations. First, it seems that important performance outcomes in organizations are almost always measured in some manner. Thus, if HRD is to improve performance, then it must measure its outcomes. Second, components of organizational systems that are viewed as contributing to the organization's strategic mission are usually able to demonstrate their contribution through some measurement. Thus, if HRD is to be a strategic partner, it must measure results.

Myths about the Performance Paradigm

It should be apparent that a variety of the criticisms leveled at the performance paradigm are actually myths.

Performance is behavioristic. The performance paradigm is not the same as behaviorism. The performance paradigm is most concerned that performance *outcomes* occur, but in no way are the *strategies and interventions* employed restricted to behavioristic ones. Barrie and Pace's (1998) contention that "improvements in performance are usually achieved through behavioral control and conditioning" is simply wrong. Similarly, Bierema's (1997) view that the performance approach is "mechanistic" and Dirkx's (1997) view that it leads organizations to "transmit to passive workers the knowledge and skills needed" are also wrong. The performance paradigm advocates none of these things, nor must it lead organizations in that direction. This myth probably arose because of the early work in performance technology that indeed grew out of behaviorism (Gilbert, 1978). It may persist for two reasons: (1) the performance paradigm places considerable emphasis on building effective systems, in addition

to individual development, and (2) performance-based HRD sanctions interventions that
change the system in which the individual
works but do not involve the individual.

It is perfectly possible for a performance-
oriented person to take a humanistic approach
to HRD, as long as that approach will lead to
performance outcomes. For example, interventions that attempt to spark more creativity and
innovation in an organization can rarely be
done using a behaviorialistic strategy. Or, a
more spiritual approach to adding meaning to
employees' lives may be quite appropriate, if
it leads to performance outcomes. Furthermore, the performance paradigm would not
restrict learning solely to the objectivist
paradigm (Mezirow, 1996) but would also embrace critical and transformational learning if
needed to improve performance. In fact, many
organizational change interventions to improve
performance encourage employees to think
more critically about their work and the
organization. The performance paradigm can
and does adopt any type of HRD strategy, as
long as outcomes occur which further the
mission of the system.

Performance is deterministic. Another mis-
taken belief is that the performance paradigm
demands that outcomes of HRD interventions
be predetermined before the interventions. If

that were true, then the only interventions that would be acceptable would be those for which outcomes could be determined in advance, thereby leaving out strategies such as the learning organization. In fact, the performance paradigm advocates no such thing. Performance advocates are just as comfortable as learning advocates with less certain outcomes, provided that outcomes do occur at some point. For example, in a learning organization example, an organization does not need to know exactly *where* the performance improvement will occur. However, performance advocates would say that they should expect to see that performance improvements do occur at some point and be able to assess outcomes when they do occur.

Performance ignores individual learning and growth. The performance paradigm honors and promotes individual learning and growth just as much as a learning paradigm does. The key difference is that the performance paradigm expects that learning and growth will benefit the performance system in which it is embedded. That is, learning and growth for the sole benefit of the individual and which will never benefit the organization is not acceptable for organization-sponsored HRD. Note that many performance HRD advocates would honor learning and growth of the individual as a core outcome for other circumstances, but not for organization-sponsored HRD.

Performance is abusive to employees. There is little doubt that a performance approach to HRD *can* be abusive to employee, particularly when organizations use cost-cutting through downsizing as a substitute for sound performance improvement. However, this is a problem of implementation, not one that is inherent in the theoretical framework. Research (e.g., Huselid, 1995; Lau and May, 1998) clearly shows that creating an environment that is supportive and respectful of employees is not only the morally right thing to do, but also results in improved performance. When properly implemented, performance-based HRD is not abusive to employees.

Performance is focused on the short term. Once again, this is a problem of implementation, not theory. It is true that many organizations place too much emphasis on short-term results. However, most organizations have learned that focusing on short-term performance and not building capacity for long-term success simply does not work. There is nothing inherent in performance theory that says it must be short-term. Many long-term interventions have been abused by companies and inappropriately conducted with a short-term perspective (e.g., Total Quality Management). Performance-oriented HRD is no different—some will do it right, and others will not.

FUSING THE TWO PARADIGMS

In recent years more energy has gone into reconciling the two paradigms and finding common ground. It is fair to say that there is now much greater understanding and harmony between groups representing both views.

Runoa (2000) studied the core beliefs of a select group of HRD scholar-leaders. Her findings, profiled in Figure 7.2, summarizes the issues around serving both individuals and organizations. Straddling belief systems that honor both the individual and the organization creates a natural tension that the HRD profession believes is both important and difficult.

In the end, substantial overlap exists between the HRD paradigms. In particular:
- A strong belief in learning and development as avenues to individual growth
- A belief that organizations can be improved through human expertise
- A desire to see people and organizations as healthy and growing
- A commitment to people and human potential
- A passion for learning and productivity

It is this common ground that keeps people within the two paradigms in the field of human resource development. They represent a strong uniting bond that clearly defines the field and separates it from other disciplines.

At the same time, unresolved issues persist between the two paradigms. The differences seem to be deeply held values and philosophical assumptions (Ruona, 1999). Because of that, they are very difficult to resolve, as there are few "right" answers when the differences are defined at the value level. Let's review some key differences.

The issue of organizational control over the learning process and outcomes is a difficult one for those who believe that only the individual should control his or her learning process (Bierema, 2000). It may be the one issue where there can be no agreement because it is a philosophical issue about which people have passionate feelings. The performance paradigm accepts the premise that the organization and the individual should share control of the individual's learning if the organization is the sponsor of the intervention. However, performance advocates would argue that ignoring performance in favor of individual control might ultimately be bad for the individual if the organization is not able to survive or prosper.

Figure 7.2 Serving Individuals versus Serving Organizations: Potential Contrasting Systems of Beliefs for Human Resource Development

	Serving Individuals	Serving Organizations
Core focus for HRD	Defined by its work with people	Defined by its work with organizations
Responsibility for HRD	To and for individuals	To and for organizations and organizational mission and goals
Setting for HRD	Any setting—not limited to the organizational setting	Conducted in some kind of goal-oriented system
Importance of organization	To improve the human condition, help individuals achieve life purpose, and improve society	To achieve organizational mission and goals, and contribute to capitalistic system, thus benefiting individuals and society
People in organizations	Should care for and support people, fostering meaning, and help people connect to something	Have some, but not primary, responsibility for individuals' short and long-term development
Profit	Needs of individuals should be more highly valued than the aims of profit	HRD should enhance performance on multiple dimensions and for short-and long-term value
People	People are inherently valuable	People are valuable to organizations for the resources they provide

	Serving Individuals	Serving Organizations
Humans and learning	Humans are learning beings	Humans are learning beings, however when learning is organizationally sponsored, individuals learn on behalf of the organization (explicitly in full agreement)
Results of development	Growth of the individual and helping people reach their full potential	Changes in job/role and performance, fulfilling organizational needs
Driver to develop systems	To help people achieve their potential within the system	To foster alignment and help organizations achieve their mission and goals
Prioritization between the individual and organization	Put people first, and organizational benefits will follow	Put organizations first, and people benefits will follow

Source: Ruona, 2000, pp. 23–24.

The individual employee presumably needs the benefits of employment (e.g., economic, psychological, instrumental) that will only exist if the organization thrives. Thus, sharing control in order to advance organization performance is viewed as appropriate and beneficial to both parties. Learning advocates would argue that learning is inherently an individual and personal experience that should never be controlled. That is, to control a person's learning is to control the person, which is objectionable.

The other argument for shared control is an economic one. Simply, if the performance system or organization is paying for the HRD efforts, it has a right to derive benefits from it and share control over it. This is one area of criticism that performance advocates truly struggle to understand. It is difficult to understand how organizations can be expected to pay for HRD efforts yet have those efforts focus primarily on what is good for the individual. To performance advocates, this sounds perfectly appropriate for schools and universities in a democratic society, but not for organization-sponsored HRD. In fact, most would wholeheartedly support the individually oriented philosophy for learning activities outside of organizations. Yet, most performance advocates also understand there are deeply held fears about institutional control over individual learning. Nonetheless, they view the situation as different once HRD crosses the organizational boundary and employers fund HRD efforts.

Many of the learning paradigm tenets are best understood by remembering that their roots are in adult education. Adult education is a broader and different field of practice than human resource development, although some would debate this. Adult education is grounded in the idea that education should be used to maintain a democratic society, which is best accomplished by building individuals' power through education and knowledge. When viewing adult learning in a broader societal context, this makes perfect sense. Where the differences arise is when learning is moved inside the boundaries and sponsorship of a purposeful system like an organization. Then performance advocates believe a different set of assumptions is warranted. Learning advocates, on the other hand, believe that a very similar set of assumptions still applies.

We acknowledge that our bias is toward the performance paradigm. Perhaps the best way of thinking about the importance of the performance paradigm is to ask this question: Could HRD sponsored by a performance system survive if it did *not* result in improved performance for the system? Most would agree that the answer is no. Second, will it thrive if it does not contribute in a *substantial* way to the mission of the organization? Again, most would answer no. Like all components of any system or organization, HRD must enhance the organization's effectiveness. The challenge is to consider how performance is incorporated in HRD theory and practice, not whether it will be.

The performance paradigm is the most likely approach to lead to a strategic role for HRD in organizations. HRD will only be perceived as having strategic value to the organization if it has the capability to connect the unique value of employee expertise with the strategic goals of the organization (Torraco and Swanson, 1995; Walton, 1999; Yorks, 2005). Performance advocates see little chance that HRD will gain power and influence in organizations by ignoring the core performance outcomes that organizations wish to achieve. By being *both* human and performance advocates, HRD stands to gain the most influence in the organizational system. If HRD focuses only on learning or individuals, then it is likely to end up marginalized as a staff support group.

CONCLUSION

While it would be naive to think that the performance and learning paradigms would ever converge, it is important to realize that there may be much more common ground than has been stated by learning advocates. Further scholarly research and debate are needed to articulate the similarities as well as the differences more clearly. This chapter is a step in that direction as we have attempted to define core assumptions of each paradigm in order to discuss differences and common ground more accurately. In the end we believe HRD is probably best served by the integration of the two paradigms.

REFLECTION QUESTIONS

1. Which paradigm do you feel most comfortable with and would adopt as your own personal belief system?
2. Do you see the learning and performance paradigms as competing paradigms, or do you see them as mutually reinforcing?
3. How can HRD operate from a performance paradigm and ensure that human development is honored and supported?
4. How can HRD operate from a learning paradigm and play a core strategic role in organizations?
5. How would an employee, an employee's manager, and a corporate CEO each view the preceding issue?

CHAPTER 8

Perspectives on Performance in Human Resource Development

CHAPTER OUTLINE

338

- Gilbert's Human Performance Engineering Model
  The Spoils of Performance
  Conclusion
  Reflection Questions

INTRODUCTION

This chapter examines core theories of performance that inform the performance perspective of HRD. Unlike learning theory that is essentially focused solely on the individual, performance theory is much more diverse. Performance theories address individuals, teams, processes, and organizational systems. Some theories are multilevel.

One of the hallmarks of performance theories is that they all attempt to capture the complexity of organizational systems while still presenting a set of constructs discrete enough to be usable. Given the complexity of organizational systems, it is easy to develop a model so complex that it becomes unwieldy. Thus, most performance theories take a particular perspective so as to define a more limited range of useful performance ideas while maintaining their integrity with systems theory. Imagine picking up a crystal and turning it in the light—each perspective yields a slightly different view. Such is the case with performance theory, where each theory is an attempt to capture adequate complexity but still be useful to the HRD profession.

ORGANIZATIONAL EFFECTIVENESS ASA PRECURSOR TO PERFORMANCE

Figure 8.1 Well-known Models of Organizational Effectiveness

Model	Definition	Appropriateness
	ORGANIZATION EFFECTIVE IF:	**MODEL PREFERRED WHEN:**
Goal	It accomplishes stated goals.	Goals are clear, overt, consensual, time bound, and measurable.
System resource	It acquires needed resources.	Resources and outputs are clearly connected.
Internal processes	It has smooth functioning and an absence of strain.	Processes and outcomes are clearly connected.
Strategic constituencies	All constituencies are at least minimally satisfied.	Constituencies have power over or in the organization.
Human relations	Members are satisfied and collaboration occurs.	Coordinated effort and harmony are directly attached to results.

Source: Adapted from Cameron, 1984.

Figure 8.2 The Competing Values Framework of Organizational Effectiveness: An integration of the five well-known models, with key areas of interest

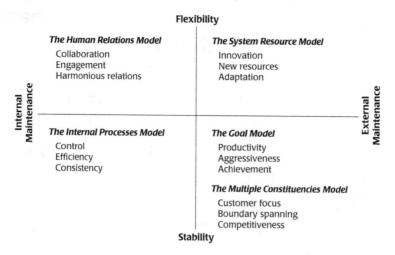

Source: Cameron, 2005, p.309.

Cameron (2005) has provided an important analysis and discussion of the concept of *orga-*

nizational effectiveness that helps in thinking clearly about performance. He notes that organizational effectiveness was once the dominant outcome or dependent variable in organizational studies, and that other variables have taken its place. Examples include customer loyalty, productivity, error rates, financial ratios, and share price (Cameron and Whetten, 1996).

In Figure 8.1, Cameron (2005) summarizes five models of organizational effectiveness along with an encapsulated definition and assessment of appropriateness. For the most part these models are self-explanatory, and it is easy to recognize their presence within any organization or the tension between stakeholders having different positions about their organization. Cameron then places the five models of organizational effectives into a competing values framework (Figure 8.2).

The competing values around organizational effectiveness and performance are positioned into four cells created by the axes of *flexibility-stability* and *internal maintenance-external positioning.* The effectiveness models placed into the four cells represent competitors. Some people in HRD and in organizational leadership positions might see HRD as being totally in the *Human Relations Model* and therefore in the upper left corner of the framework. The extended discussion in this chapter suggests otherwise. In developing and unleashing expertise, HRD has the potential to contribute to performance and organizational effectiveness in all four cells. It is up to HRD professionals to understand, advocate for, and facilitate performance based on professional judgment.

DISCIPLINARY PERSPECTIVES ON PERFORMANCE

HRD is not the only discipline that is interested in performance and performance improvement. It is thus very important to recognize that HRD is advanced, challenged, and judged by these various performance perspectives in business and societal organizations.

To clarify perspectives on performance, it is important to be aware of the performance theories and models in disciplines within HRD and those closely associated with HRD. The results, as discussed here and shown in Figure 8.3, are meant to be representative, not comprehensive.

These models illustrate the diversity of performance perspectives and point to key considerations in performance theory:

- *Performance is a multidisciplinary phenomenon.* It should be apparent from Figure 8.2 that many different disciplines study performance. This search revealed performance models in a wide range of disciplines, including psychology, human resource management, ethics, quality, sociology, economics, strategic management, and industrial engineering. This range of disciplines is consistent with performance improvement competency models that indicate that a performance improvement professional must be proficient in skills drawn from multiple disciplines (Stolovich, Keeps, and Rodriguez, 1995).

- *Performance models have a disciplinary bias.* Each discipline has defined performance to fit its unique needs. For example, psychology, which focuses on individuals, has defined performance through the *individual* lens (Campbell, 1990). The quality movement, which focuses on improving organizational processes, sees performance through a *process* lens (Juran, 1992). Strategic management, which focuses on positioning the organization competitively, sees performance through the *organization* and *industry* lens (Porter, 1980). While nothing is inherently wrong with a disciplinary bias, it does indicate a need for caution when viewing performance models from other disciplines.
- *There is no such thing as a single view of performance.* Each discipline or perspective

has defined performance in a way that fits its purpose. The search for a single model of performance may be a futile search, or at least likely to result in a model so complex as to be unusable. Each discipline has to limit its performance models to focus on aspects of performance appropriate for that discipline. The lesson is that HRD must define performance in a manner that fits its unique role in performance improvement and that acknowledges the legitimate role of other disciplines. It is not essential that HRD's model define every possible view of performance. As professionals responsible for improving performance in predominantly work-related social systems (Dean, 1997), HRD needs to define performance domains that fit that purpose.

- *Types (levels) of performance and indicators of performance are confused in some models.* One persistent source of confusion in the literature is between levels of performance and indicators or metrics of performance. For example, several models include "customer" as a level of performance (Edvinsson and Malone, 1997; Juran, 1992; Kaplan and Norton, 1996). Clearly customer satisfaction is important, but it is an indicator of process and organizational performance, not a level of performance. Similarly, several models define some aspect of employee behavior such as learning (Edvinsson and Malone, 1997; Kaplan and Norton, 1996), demonstrating effort (Campbell,1990), or individual ethics (D.L. Swanson, 1995) as a level of performance. All are really indicators of individual performance but are defined as levels due to disciplinary biases.

Sleezer, Hough, and Gradous (1998) point out that performance is usually not measured directly. What is measured are attributes of performance and their indicators. Performance indicators and metrics are vitally important but must not be confused with performance itself. And, as Sleezer et al. point out, multiple levels of measurement may be involved. For example, customer satisfaction may be an indicator of process performance, but it is also measured in multiple ways. That is, we do not measure all possible dimensions of satisfaction directly but could use a metric such as repeat visits to a store as an indicator of satisfaction.

- Subsystems in the models vary widely. Part of the disciplinary bias is reflected in the subsystems included in the models. Organization development (Cummings and Worley, 1993) defines groups as its primary subsystem because OD focuses on interpersonal dimensions of an organization. Needs assessment (McGehee and Thayer, 1961; Sleezer, 1991) defines work or task as its primary subsystem because it focuses on analyzing work-related learning needs. Others (Rummler and Brache, 1995; Swanson, 1994, 2007) include process as a subsystem, reflecting current emphasis on process improvement. In the case of human capital or strategic management, the organization becomes the subsystem, with society as the larger system. There seems to be little uniformity in terminology.

FINANCIAL PERFORMANCE

For most HRD professionals, assessing the financial benefits of HRD programs is an underdeveloped area of expertise. Much of the activity of HRD is spent on performance drivers versus actual performance. Thus, HRD uses interventions like executive coaching, system redesign, training worker expertise, action research, and valuing diversity as a means to a performance goal, not as a goal in itself.

Figure 8.3 Perspectives on the Domain of Performance

Perspective	Author	Domains of Performance/Analysis
Performance improvement	Brache (2002); Rummler and Brache (1995, 1990)	• Environment
		• Organization

Perspective	Author	Domains of Performance/Analysis
Performance improvement—strategic	Hronec (1993)	• Process • Individual Quantum Performance Matrix Levels • Organization • Process • People Measures • Cost • Quality • Time
HRD and performance improvement	Swanson (2007, 1994)	Levels • Organization • Process • Team • Individual Measures of Outputs • Quantity • Time • Quality features
Human performance technology	Kaufmann, Rojas, and Mayer (1993)	Organizational Elements Model Results • Mega-outcomes • Macro-outputs • Micro-intermediate products Means • Processes • Resources

Perspective	Author	Domains of Performance/Analysis
HRD and microeconomics	Swanson (2001)	• Units of Performance • Performance value calculation • Cost calculation • Benefit calculation
HRM and macro/microeconomics	Fitz-Enz (2000)	• Organizational • Functional • Human capital management
Human performance technology	Silber (1992)	• All organizations in society • All organizations in system • Whole organization • One unit of organization
HRD—training	McGehee and Thayer (1961); Moore and Dutton (1978); Sleezer (1991)	• Organizational • Work/task • Individual
	Ostroff and Ford (1989)	Levels • Organizational • Sub-unit • Individual Content • Organizational • Task

Perspective	Author	Domains of Performance/Analysis
HRD—organization development	Campbell (1990) Cummings and Worley (2001)	• Person • Psychology • Individual level • Organizational
HRD—organization development	Rashford and Coghlan (1994)	• Group • Individual • Organizational • Interdepartmental group • Face-to-face team • Individual
Management—strategy	Kaplan and Norton (1996)	• Financial • Customer • Internal business process • Learning and growth (employee based)
Management—strategy	Porter (1980)	• Society • Industry • Company
Management—strategy	Hitt, Ireland, and Hoskisson (1997)	• Corporate level • Competitive dynamics • Business level
Systems—quality	Juran (1992)	• Customer needs • Product features

Perspective	Author	Domains of Performance/Analysis
Systems—reengineering	Hammer and Champy (1993)	• Processes • Process efficiency
Social responsibility	D.L. Swanson (1995)	• Societal impacts • Organizational ethical performance • Individual ethical performance
HR—performance management	Schneir (1995)	• Company • Work process • Unit • Team • Individual
HRM—general	Lewin and Mitchell (1995)	• Firm • Plant • Individual
Economics—human capital	Becker* (1993)	• Society/economy • Firm • Individual
Economics—macroeconomics	Case and Fair (1996)	• Society/economy • Markets • Firm • Individual
Intellectual capital	Edvinsson and Malone (1997)	• Financial • Customer • Process

Perspective	Author	Domains of Perfor- mance/Analysis
		• Renewal and devel- opment
		• Human focus

[* from analysis of levels discussed in the book.]

Figure 8.3 Perspectives on the Domain of Performance

Perspective	Author	Domains of Perfor- mance/Analysis
Sociology—general	Kammeyer, Ritzer, and Yetman (1997)	• Society
		• Cultures
		• Organizations
		• Groups
		• Individuals
Sociology—industrial	Hodson and Sullivan (1995)	• Workplaces (firm)
		• Occupation
		• Industry
		• Labor force
		• Worker
Sociology—industrial	Ford (1988)	• Macro (society, so- cial systems, culture)
		• Mezzo (organiza- tions and associa- tions)
		• Micro (social groups, roles, and norms/rules)

1Derived from analysis of levels discussed in the book.

A number of value-laden myths have influenced the HRD profession, and a few have been

related to financial analysis of HRD: (1) HRD costs too much, (2) you can't quantify the benefits of HRD, and (3) it is good to give organizations the HRD they want. These myths should be exploded.

Myth: HRD Costs Too Much. Good HRD generally costs a fair amount of money. Most of the worthwhile projects that go on in an organization cost a fair amount of money. Usually management decides to spend available dollars on the equipment, services, and projects that will give it the best return on its investment. Whenever something must be purchased that apparently will have little effect on the business, management will request the one with the lowest price.

The following example will have a familiar ring: If low quality mailing envelopes will do the job, management tends to say, "Get them as cheaply as you can." If these inexpensive envelopes later stick together or will not feed through the postage machine, or if they make the organization look tacky in the eyes of customers, management then will tend to say, "Stop buying such junk." Conversely, if the more expensive envelopes are the kind that seal automatically and thus increase output, or if they catch the attention of potential customers and bring increased sales, management will tend to say,

"Get a good price if you can, but we want the best."

Cost figures by themselves are irrelevant. Reviewing HRD costs without also reviewing the associated benefits is not smart. Analyzing what you get for your money *is* smart. What most HRD managers fail to realize is that organizational decision makers usually focus only on HRD costs. When they lack information about the economic benefits of HRD, many decision makers decide consciously or unconsciously that a proposed HRD program is just another HRD program—just as an envelope is only an envelope. "So get the cheapest one."

Myth: You Cannot Quantify the Benefits of HRD. Listening to people find excuses why something cannot be done is always interesting. Rationalizing that the benefits of HRD cannot be quantified has kept the HRD profession in the dark ages of organizational performance. Do you suppose that management knows how many products it will sell next year? Of course not. If it knew the correct figures ahead of time, it would make exactly that many products. But because management does not know precisely how many products it will sell, it gathers the best estimates it can find and makes its decision without the satisfaction of knowing it is right.

This process takes knowledge of past results, intelligence, and guts—not perfection. Likewise, a record of assessed benefits, a little more intelligence, and a lot more guts on the part of HRD professionals will explode this myth.

There is a strong possibility that these myths have arisen from inside the HRD profession. If decision makers have also learned these HRD myths, they probably learned them from HRD people. Executives, as leaders of change and opportunity, have the right to expect HRD departments to join them in their struggle to achieve performance and profitability. Organizational decision makers are not enemies of HRD. They want to be organizational partners and to reap the added value that HRD can provide to the organization.

Myth: It is good to give organizations the HRD they want. The real pressure for HRD activity will come as the result of identifying critical performance requirements. Good performance analyses are the basis for making financial benefit assessments. A major practical issue in most organizations is how to distinguish between wants and requirements. What managers want is not always what they need or require. Performance variables are critical conditions that organizations must meet in order to achieve their performance goals and mission. The relationship between financial

benefits assessment and performance requirements is important. Wants are not so important. The most important HRD skill is to be
able to work with decision makers to discover
genuine organizational performance requirements and to convince them that they want
what they need. This goal is best accomplished
by working in partnership with managers rather
than by making high-pressure attempts to sell
faddish HRD programs.

The outcome of a particular HRD program
is valuable only if it is connected to an
organizational performance goal and the core
processes designed to achieve those perfor-
mances. A high-cost HRD program does not
always result in a performance gain, while a
low-cost HRD program may result in a large
performance gain. Determining the critical
performance to be attained and its value to
the organization should precede the financial
assessment of an HRD program.

Units of Performance

All human-made organizations are economic
entities. Organizations produce goods and
services for customers and over time they
must have income that equals or exceeds the
costs of operating that system. This is equally
true for multinational corporations, family-

owned businesses, nonprofit arts groups, churches, regional governments, and families.

The goods and services that an organization produces are expressed in terms of units of performance or a clear proxy that makes the most sense. A retail furniture corporation can express its unit of performance simply as total dollar sales in a particular time period. This then could be compared to the total cost of operation during the same time period to determine if there is a profit or loss. In a sales organization, units of sales performance can be tracked to the total organization, each division, each department, each line of products, each sales team, and each salesperson.

Thus, HRD programs aimed at improving sales performance can be financially assessed. Each unit of performance can be monetized. The number of additional units produced following the intervention times the monetary value of each unit gets you to the real financials of an organization and the bottom-line impact of HRD interventions.

Financial Benefit Analysis

A number of scholars have addressed the topic of assessing the financial benefits of investing in human resources (Bassie and

2003; Cascio and Boudreau, 2008; Fitz-Enz, 2000; Swanson, 2001). Financial benefit analysis is a research-based and field-tested methodology for financially assessing HRD programs (Swanson, 2001). Using the microeconomic methodology, assessing financial benefits of HRD interventions is quite easy. The process follows the Basic *Financial Assessment Model* (Swanson, 2001, p.28):

Performance Value (*performance value resulting from the HRD intervention*)
$-$ Cost (cost of the HRD intervention)
Benefit (*benefit is the performance value minus the cost*)

Worksheets are provided for each of the three components of the model. In addition, a framework for assessing financial benefits is presented that identifies three perspectives on assessing the financial benefits of HRD interventions:

- What is the *forecasted financial benefit* resulting from an HRD intervention? (Before-the-fact assessment based on estimated financial data.)
- What is the *actual financial benefit* resulting from an HRD intervention? (During-the-process assessment based on actual financial data.)
- What is the *approximate financial benefit* resulting from an HRD intervention? (After-the-fact assessment based on approximated financial data.)

These three perspectives offer three financial benefit assessment strategies that fit with the financial decision points in an organization.

ROI of Human Capital

Jac Fitz-Enz (2000) presents a research-based and field-tested methodology for determining the return on investment (ROI) of human capital through employee performance. His methodology spans macro and micro-economics. While Swanson (2001) focuses on the ROI of individual HRD interventions, Fitz-Enz provides methodology for assessing human capital performance contributions at the organization-wide level and organization-wide change initiative level. In creating a corporate scorecard, he combines quantitative and perceptual data for organization-level financial assessment. In addition, he provides a methodology that is aimed at assessing processes under human control.

Human capital performance evaluation, according to Fitz-Enz, uses a matrix to acquire and categorize data. The matrix contains four core human resource activities: acquisition, maintenance, development, and retention on one axis. The second axis specifies component performance measures: cost, time, quantity, error, and reaction. Figure 8.4 illustrates the

Human Capital Performance Matrix with examples in the cells.

MULTILEVEL PERFORMANCE MODELS

Scholars of organizational performance have long been frustrated with piecemeal approaches to performance improvement. Systems theory tells us that interventions that focus on only a subset of organizational performance variables are usually doomed to failure unless they are embedded in the context of whole-system performance improvement. Thus, efforts to improve performance using an individual-level model are missing key elements of the organizational context. Fundamentally, this is the reason that the performance-based HRD perspective has developed and become popular. Development is often futile unless it is embedded in a systems approach to organizational performance improvement.

When viewed from a systems perspective, organizations are extremely complex social systems. In fact, they become so complex that the average person has trouble comprehending them, let alone improving them. Thus, various scholars have attempted to reduce the complexity of organizational systems to a more manageable form by creating taxonomic models of key performance variables. These models usually embrace multiple levels of performance and multiple dimensions of performance within those levels. This chapter looks at five multilevel models: Brache's (2002) enterprise model, Rummler and Brache's (1995) performance model, Swanson's (2007) performance diagnosis process and matrix, an OD performance model from Cummings and Worley (2001), and Holton's (1999) integrated taxonomy of performance system domains.

Figure 8.4 Human Capital Performance Matrix and Examples

	Acquiring	Maintaining	Developing	Retaining
Cost	Cost per hire	Cost per paycheck Cost per EAP case*	Cost per trainee	Cost of turnover
Time	Time to fill jobs	Time to respond time to fulfill request	Cost per trainee	Turnover by length service
Quantity	Number mixed	Number of claims processed	Number trained	Voluntary turnover rate
Error	New hire rating	Process error rate	Skills attained	Readiness level
Reaction	Manager satisfaction	Employee satisfaction	Trainee responses	Turnover reasons

Source: Fitz-Enz, 2000, p.109. [* EAP=Employee assistance program]

Brache's Enterprise Model

Brache (2002) presents what he calls a holistic approach to enterprise health. His approach supports the idea that performance improvement professionals need to understand organizational structures and how organizations work. The methodology guides the analysis of the internal and external variables of an organization's environment as a means of diagnosing the overall health of a firm.

Brache presents his Enterprise Model (see Figure 8.5) as a holistic view of the structures of an organization that are categorized into internal and external components. In addressing the integration of the organization as a whole, the importance of each individual variable of the Enterprise Model is described as well as the impact they have on each other. Brache's work is particularly good at providing a clear and not overly technical conceptualization of how organizations work and the key questions required to assess an organization's health.

Rummler and Brache's Performance Model

Rummler and Brache (1995) provide an integrated framework for achieving competitive advantage by learning how to manage organizations, processes, and individuals effectively. The subtitle of their book is *Managing the White Space in Organizations.* From a sociotechnical perspective, the white space represents the essential connection between components and where performance breakdowns most often occur. Beginning with a holistic view of the organization, they set forth a rational, clear, yet simple view of the organizational skeleton, process levels, and interdependencies. Their model hypothesizes that organizational failure is due not to lack of desire or effort, but lack of understanding of the variables that influence organizational, process and individual performance. Rummler and Brache call these variables "performance levers" (p.2). With a complete understanding and holistic management of these variables, high performance should result.

To guide the management of organizations as systems, Rummler and Brache present the nine-cell matrix described here and in Figure 8.6, along with questions each cell raises. They define three levels of performance:

- *Organizational level*—the organization's relationship with its market and the basic skeleton of the major functions that comprise the organization

- *Process*—the work flow, how the work really gets done
- *Job/performer*—the individuals doing various jobs

Within each of these three levels are three performance variables:

- *Goals*—specific standards that reflect customers' expectations for product and service quality, quantity, timeliness, and cost

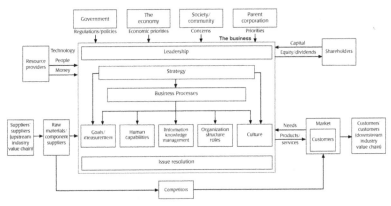

Figure 8.5 The Enterprise Model Source: Brache, 2002, p.5.

Figure 8.6 Rummler and Brache Model and Questions at Each Level

Organization Goals	Organization Design	Organization Management
• Has the organization's strategy/direction been articulated and communicated?	• Are all the relevant functions in place?	• Have appropriate function goals been set?

Organization Goals	Organization Design	Organization Management
• Does the strategy make sense, in terms of the external threats and opportunities and the internal strengths and weaknesses?	• Are all functions necessary?	• Is relevant performance measured?
• Given this strategy, have the required outputs of the organization and the level of performance expected from each output been determined and communicated?	• Is the current flow of inputs and outputs between functions appropriate?	• Are resources appropriately allocated?
	• Does the formal organization structure support the strategy and enhance the efficiency of the system?	• Are the interfaces between functions steps being managed?
Process Goals	Process Design	Process Management
• Are goals for key processes linked to customer and organization requirements?	• Is this the most efficient/effective process for accomplishing process goals?	• Have appropriate process sub goals been set?
		• Is process performance managed?

Organization Goals	Organization Design	Organization Management
		• Are sufficient resources allocated to each process?
		• Are the interfaces between process steps being managed?
Job/Performer Goals	**Job Design**	**Job/Performer Management**
• Are job outputs and standards linked to process requirements (which are in turn linked to customer and organization requirements)?	• Are process requirements reflected in the appropriate jobs?	• Do the performers understand the job goals (outputs they are expected to produce and the standards they are expected to meet)?
	• Are job steps in a logical sequence?	• Do the performers have sufficient resources, clear signals and priorities, and a logical job design?
	• Have supportive policies and procedures been developed?	• Are the performers rewarded for achieving the job goals?
	• Is the job environment ergonomically sound?	• Do the performers know if they are meeting the job goals?

Organization Goals	Organization Design	Organization Management
		• Do the performers have the necessary skills and knowledge to achieve the job goals? • If the performers were in an environment in which the five questions listed above were answered yes, would they have the physical, mental, and emotional capacity to achieve the job goals?

• *Design*—the necessary structural components configured in a way that enables the goals to be efficiently met

• *Management*—management practices that ensure goals are current and being achieved

Organization Level

According to Rummler and Brache (1995), "If executives [leaders] do not manage at the organization level, the best they can expect is modest performance improvement. At worst, efforts at other levels will be counterproductive" (p.33). This "level emphasizes the organization's relationship with its market and the basic 'skeleton' of the major functions that comprise the organization" (p.15). They further suggest that organization-level performance addresses the set of core questions as shown in Figure 8.6.

Process Level

According to Rummler and Brache (1995), an organization is only as good as its processes. Organizational processes describe the actual work of an organization and are responsible for producing goods and services (i.e., outputs) for customers. For the process level, the analyst must go "beyond the cross-functional boundaries that make up the organization chart, we see the work flow—how the work gets done.... At the process level, one must ensure that processes are installed to meet customer needs, that those processes work effectively and efficiently, and that the process goals and measures are driven by the customers' and the organizations' requirement" (p.17).

Rummler and Brache (1995) make these arguments for the importance of focusing on processes in performance systems:

- Process is the least understood and least managed domain of performance.
- A process can be seen as a value chain, with each step adding value to the preceding steps.
- An organization is only as effective as its processes.

- Enhancing organizational and individual effectiveness will improve performance only as much as the processes allow.
- Strong people cannot compensate for a weak process (p.45).

Individual Level

Finally, Rummler and Brache (1995) identify three performance variables at the job/performer level: job/performer goals, design, and management, and they developed the core questions shown in Figure 8.5. "At the individual level it is recognized that processes ... are performed and managed by individuals doing various jobs" (p.17). These performance levels determine effectiveness at the individual job/performer level and contribute to the efficiency of the process and organizational levels.

Swanson's Performance Diagnosis Process and Matrix

In his book, *Analysis for Improving Performance* (2nd Edition), Swanson (2007) advances a process and method of performance diagnosis. His general five-phase process, shown in Figure 8.7, begins with an initial purpose and culminates in a performance improvement proposal.

Within the performance diagnosis process, assessing the performance variables is a critical phase. Swanson provides a matrix similar to Rummler and Brache's matrix, but with changes in categories. Initially advanced as part of his performance analysis system, the core performance diagnosis model also stands alone as one definition of an organizational performance system.

Performance Levels

Four levels are identified and consistently referred to throughout the performance diagnosis phases:

- Organization
- Process
- Team
- Individual

Organizational system levels have been carefully presented by FitzGerald and FitzGerald (1973). Systems theory helps us understand the levels. For example, the cause of a company sending a customer a contract bid containing an inaccurate budget and an incomplete list of services may lie in any or all of the four levels. Even so, the decision maker may be falsely convinced early on that the cause is lodged at a single level. For example:

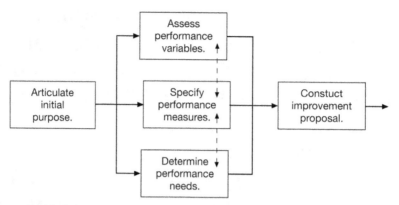

Figure 8.7 Diagnosing Performance Process Source: Swanson, 2007, p.58.

- "There is so much bureaucracy around here that it is a miracle anything even gets done!" or
- "The financial computer program has a glitch in it!" or
- "Our financial analysts are incompetent!"

Performance Variable

The second component of the performance diagnosis is five performance variables that occur at each of the four performance levels:
- Mission/goals
- System design
- Capacity
- Motivation
- Expertise

These performance variables, matrixed with the levels of performance—organization, process, and/or individual—provide a powerful perspective in diagnosing performance. For example, a work process may have an inherent goal built into it that is in conflict with the mission and/or goal of the organization or a person working in the process. The questions presented in the performance variable matrix help the diagnostician sort out the performance overlaps and disconnects (see Figure 8.8).

Like all multilevel models, Swanson emphasizes that bad systems almost always overwhelm good people. This idea was most evident in the World War II performance improvement efforts (Dooley, 1945). How else to explain the failure of workers with high aptitudes? When the work system ties the hands of competent persons behind their backs and then punishes them for doing their best, they either quit and leave—or quit and stay! Likewise, when a well-designed work process is coupled with organizational policies and procedures that hire employees lacking the capacity to perform the work, no reasonable amount of training will get the employees up to required performance standards.

Organization Development Performance Model

Another representative multilevel performance model comes from organization development. Figure 8.9 shows the Cummings and

Figure 8.8 Swanson's Performance Diagnosis Matrix

Performance Variables	Performance Levels			
	ORGANIZATION LEVEL	**PROCESS LEVEL**	**TEAM LEVEL**	**INDIVIDUAL LEVEL**
Mission/Goal	Does the organization mission/goal fit the reality of the economic, political, and cultural forces?	Do the process goals enable the organization to meet organization and individual missions/goals?	Do the team goals provide congruence with the process and individual goals?	Are the professional and personal mission/goals of individuals congruent with the organization's?
System Design	Does the organization system provide structure and policies supporting the desired performance?	Are processes designed in such a way to work as a system?	Do the team dynamics function in such a way to facilitate collaboration and performance?	Does the individual clear obstacles that impede his or her job performance?
Capacity	Does the organization have the leadership, capital, and infrastructure to achieve its mission/goals?	Does the process have the capacity to perform (quantity, quality, and timeliness)?	Does the team have the combined capacity to effectively and efficiently meet the performance goals?	Does the individual have the mental, physical, and emotional capacity to perform?
Motivation	Do the policies, culture, and reward systems support the desired performance?	Does the process provide the information and human factors required to maintain it?	Does the team function in a respectful and supportive manner?	Does the individual want to perform no matter what?
Expertise	Does the organization establish and maintain selection and training policies and resources?	Does the process of developing expertise meet the changing demands of changing processes?	Does the team have the team process expertise to perform?	Does the individual have the knowledge and expertise to perform?

Source: Swanson, 2007, p. 65.

Source: Swanson, 2007, p.65.

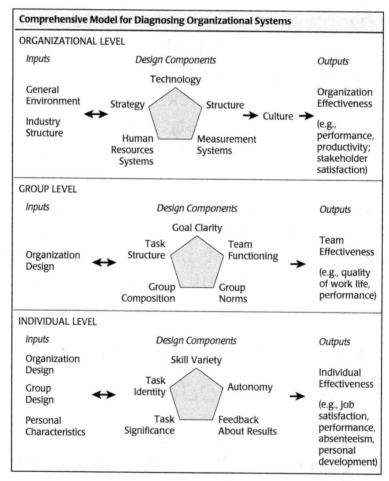

Source: Cummings and Worley, 2001.

Worley (2001) organizational diagnosis model. This model is typical of performance models found in the OD field.

There are several clear differences between the OD model and the Rummler and Brache models. The obvious difference is in the levels defined. Instead of including a process performance level, most OD models include a group or team performance level. Swanson's model includes both. The other two levels—organization and individual—are usually the same in most models. The group/team level reflects a clear difference in values and perspective by OD professionals who place a great deal of emphasis on groups and interpersonal dynamics in organizations.

The other clear difference is in the performance variables included in the model, which are called *design components* in this model. Sixteen variables are included across the three levels, roughly equivalent to the other models. The variables at the organization level are similar, encompassing strategy (goals), design, systems, and management. Notice, however, that one key variable explicitly included is organization culture, another variable of key interest to OD but not as explicit in other models. At the group and individual levels, the variables included represent traditional areas of concern for OD professionals. They emphasize elements that affect the social dynamics in organizations that are likely to enhance quality of work life. In fact, this model explicitly includes quality of work life, job satisfaction, and personal development as outcome variables along with performance.

Holton's Integrated Taxonomy of Performance Domains

Holton (1999) presents an integrated taxonomy of performance system domains in an attempt to reconcile differences between various models (see Figure 8.10). In addition, he wanted to change the language of the model to make it more universal and to address criticisms of other models whose performance was viewed as a short-term phenomenon.

Holton proposed four domains of performance: *mission, process, social subsystem,* and *individual.* It should be noted that he originally called social subsystem "critical performance subsystem" but since changed it.

Mission Domain

The system's mission, and the goals derived from it, specifies the expected outcomes of that system. Every purposefully organized system operates with a mission, either explicitly or implicitly, and the role of the mission is to reflect the system's relationship with its *external* environment. For a business organization, the mission may reflect its relationship with its industry, society, and competitors. For a nonprofit organization, its mission may reflect its relationship with the community and society. It is not necessary to specify in the taxonomy what the possible levels of impact outside the system are, because the mission will reflect that system's understanding of its responsibilities to the external environment.

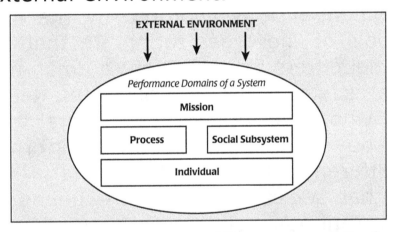

Figure 8.10 Holton's Integrated Taxonomy of Performance Domains Source: Holton, 1999.

It is important to note that the concept of "performance system" was used instead of "organization." A mission may be defined for any system organized to accomplish some purpose. If the system has a purpose then it also has desired outputs, so performance theory is applicable. In many instances, the mission domain will be the same as the organization domain, particularly in for-profit firms. However, for a trade association, the mission domain may focus on an entire industry, or an entire profession for a professional association. For example, the Academy of Human Resource Development's mission is the advancement of the HRD profession through research. In other situations, the mission may include community outcomes, or societal outcomes.

The particular system's definition of its performance relationship with the external environment is fully captured by the mission and goals of the organization. In that sense, his model differs from that of Kaufman and his associates (see Kaufman et al., 1998; Kaufman, 1987), who have argued that societal benefits should be included as a level of performance. This difference should not be interpreted to mean that societal benefits are unimportant. Rather, Kaufman believes that the mission of that system most appropriately captures the relationship between the performance system and society. The degree to which the performance system targets societal outcomes will be incorporated in its mission. The actual level of societal performance targeted will vary greatly, depending on the performance system.

For business organizations, the mission-level metrics are likely to be dominated by traditional business outcome measures, including economic outcomes. However, the mission domain for a government organization may be dominated by metrics assessing societal benefits first and the economic effectiveness second. The notion that the performance perspective only embraces economic returns as the system's mission (Bierema, 1997; Dirkx, 1997) is fundamentally flawed. Performance metrics are defined by and depend on the mission of the organization.

Process Domain

The process domain in Holton's model is identical to Rummler and Brache's and Swanson's. Holton notes that one of the positive outcomes of the quality and reengineering movements is the realization that managing and designing effective processes is an essential part of performance improvement. A number of performance experts have clearly articulated the need for including the process domain of performance (Davies, 1994; Hammer and Champy, 1993; Harbour, 1993; Hronec, 1993; Juran, 1992; Kaplan and Norton, 1996; Rummler and Brache, 1995; Swanson, 1994, 2007). Readers desiring a deeper understanding of the importance of process to performance improvement should consult these sources.

Social Subsystem

This taxonomy includes a domain for social subsystems, defined as an *internal* social entity (group, team, department, etc.) for which performance goals have been set that are derived from, and contribute to, the mission of the overall system. Thus, the core difference between this domain and the mission domain is that the mission domain defines performance outcomes relative to the external environment, while this domain defines internal performance subsystems that do not always directly connect with the external environment. Social subsystem is a more general construct than "group" or "team" although it encompasses both of these terms. In the case of structural subunits, it is easier to see how the "organization" domain can be redefined to be "department" or "division" than for team performance that has unique components.

The social subsystem is an important point of analysis. For example, the following questions may have to be answered:

- What are the social subsystems that are critical to accomplishing the system's mission?
- What are the explicit social subsystems? The implicit ones?
- Are the explicit and implicit subsystems congruent?
- Are the social subsystems appropriate for the mission of the system?
- Are the relationships between social subsystems optimal?

- Do organizational factors help or hinder subsystem performance?
- Are appropriate metrics in place?

Drivers and Outcomes in Each Performance Domain

Kaplan and Norton (1996) suggest two categories of performance measures: outcomes and drivers. Unfortunately, they do not offer concise definitions of either. For our purposes, *outcomes* are measures of effectiveness or efficiency relative to core outputs of the system, subsystem, process or individual. The most typical are financial indicators (profit, ROI, etc.) and productivity measures (units of goods or services produced), and they are often generic across similar performance systems. According to Kaplan and Norton, these measures tend to be lag indicators in that they reflect what has occurred or has been accomplished in relation to core outcomes.

Drivers measure elements of performance that are expected to sustain or increase system, subsystem, process, or individual ability and capacity to be more effective or efficient in the future. Thus, they are leading indicators of future outcomes and tend to be unique for particular performance systems. Together with outcome measures, they describe the hypothesized cause-and-effect relationships in the organization's strategy (Kaplan and Norton, 1996).

Thus, drivers should predict future outcomes. For example, for a particular company, return on investment might be the appropriate outcome measure, which might be driven by customer loyalty and on-time delivery, which in turn might be driven by employee learning so internal processes are optimized. In a state government department of revenue, an outcome measure might be the percentage of tax returns processed correctly within two weeks of receipt. A performance driver for that outcome might be the number of quality improvement initiatives successfully implemented.

Kaplan and Norton (1996) go on to say:

> Outcome measures without performance drivers do not communicate how the outcomes are to be achieved.... Conversely, performance drivers without outcome measures may enable the business unit to achieve short-term operational improvements, but will fail to reveal whether the operational improvements have been translated into expanded business with existing and new customers, and, eventually, to enhanced financial performance. A good balanced scorecard should have an appropriate mix of outcomes (lagging indicators) and performance drivers (leading indicators) of the business unit's strategy. (pp.31–32)

From this perspective, performance improvement models that focus solely on actual outcomes, such as profit or units of work produced, are flawed in that they are likely to create short-term improvement but neglect aspects of the organization that will drive future performance outcomes. Models that focus solely on performance drivers such as learning or growth are equally flawed in that they fail to consider the actual outcomes. Only when outcomes and drivers are jointly considered will long-term sustained performance improvement occur.

The correct perspective is that performance drivers and performance outcomes should be linked within each performance domain. Both work in an integrated manner to enhance mission, process, subsystem, and individual performance.

PROCESS AND TEAM-LEVEL PERFORMANCE MODELS

Performance perspectives at the process and team levels functionally fall between the organizational and individual levels. Much of the organization and individual-level thinking and many of the tools are equally useful in these middle levels. Yet, there are some unique differences.

There are two major views of process performance improvement. One is incremental and the other is radical. *Reengineering* is a radical approach to performance improvement. Impatient with standard process improvement, reengineering is willing to scrap an entire process for one that is projected to be more efficient and more effective. The criticisms of reengineering are that it takes a narrow systems view without seriously considering human beings as part of the equation.

Incremental *process improvement* is focused on measuring processes at each step and assessing the process steps and the process as a whole as being under control (within quality range limits). Once under control, additional process improvement actions are taken and performance measures track the results. The mantra for process improvement is the relentless pursuit of quality.

W. Edwards Deming (1986) and Joseph Juran (1992) are considered the gurus of quality and total quality management. Six Sigma methodology is simply upping the bar for the performance expectations. Six Sigma is a quality process improvement method developed by Motorola Corporation. Quality methods embrace the following:

1. Continuous efforts to reduce variation in process outputs is key to business success.
2. Manufacturing and business processes can be measured, analyzed, improved and controlled.
3. Succeeding at achieving sustained quality improvement requires commitment from the entire organization, particularly from top-level management.

Some process performance efforts rely heavily on the use of statistical analysis of process data (2 above) while others rely more heavily on team building and managerial support (3 above).

Team performance is often pursued as a part of process performance. The core idea that teams oversee processes and that teams can cooperatively make sound judgments is central to process improvement efforts.

To a larger extent, pursuit of team development takes place outside the *process performance* banner by organizations wanting to simply improve workteam performance. As team work increases and individual work wanes, the performance measures that once were attributable to individuals are now attributable to teams.

INDIVIDUAL-LEVEL PERFORMANCE MODELS

Because HRD has its roots in individual learning, it was logical that individual-level performance models would be the first to develop. These models are now known collectively as *human performance technology* (Stolovich and Keeps, 1999) models. The common characteristic of these models is that they attempt to define individual performance and key factors that impact upon individual performance. Two representative models are John Campbell's taxonomy of individual performance and Thomas Gilbert's human performance engineering model.

Campbell's Model of Individual Performance

Campbell's (1990) model of individual performance is considered one of the few performance models in industrial psychology. Campbell developed it because he noted that psychologists had paid little attention to the dependent variable (performance) focusing most of their energy on the independent variables. As he said, "The literature pertaining to the structure and content of performance is a virtual desert. We essentially have no theories of performance" (1990, p.704).

Campbell's theory has three key parts: performance *components,* performance *determinants,* and *predictors* of performance determinants. First, he suggests that the predictors of performance fall into three groups (see Figure 8.11). Predictors of declarative and procedural knowledge include ability, personality, interests, education, training, experience, and the interaction of these components. Predictors of motivation vary depending on which theory of motivation one uses.

Campbell (1990) then proposed eight components that are hypothesized to be collectively sufficient to describe job performance in all listings in the *Dictionary of Occupational Titles.* They are as follows:

1. *Job-specific task proficiency*—the degree to which an individual can perform the core substantive or technical tasks central to his or her job.

2. *Non-job-specific task proficiency*—the degree to which an individual can perform the tasks or execute behaviors that are not specific to his or her particular job

3. *Written and oral communication*—the proficiency with which an individual can write or speak, independent of the correctness of the subject matter

4. *Demonstrating effort*—the consistency of an individual's effort day by day, the de-

gree to which he or she will expend extra effort when required, and the willingness to work under adverse conditions

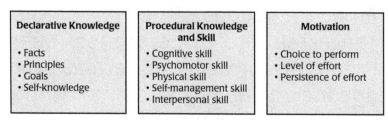

Declarative Knowledge	Procedural Knowledge and Skill	Motivation
• Facts • Principles • Goals • Self-knowledge	• Cognitive skill • Psychomotor skill • Physical skill • Self-management skill • Interpersonal skill	• Choice to perform • Level of effort • Persistence of effort

Figure 8.11 Campbell's Job Performance Components
Source: Campbell, 1990.

5. *Maintaining personal discipline*—the degree to which negative behaviors are avoided (e.g., abusing alcohol, breaking laws and rules, etc.)

6. *Facilitating peer and team performance*—the degree to which the individual supports his or her peers, helps them with job problems, and helps train them

7. *Supervision*—proficiency in the supervisory component includes all the behaviors directed at influencing the performance of supervisees through face-to-face interpersonal interaction and influence

8. *Management/administration* —includes the major elements in management that are independent of direct supervision

Gilbert's Human Performance Engineering Model

Tom Gilbert's 1978 book *Human Competence: Engineering Worthy Performance* is regarded as one of the classics in human performance technology. While the more recent multilevel performance models discussed in the next section are more comprehensive, Gilbert's work remains as an important benchmark in individual-level performance improvement.

Gilbert presented his work in a series of theorems which he called "Leisurely Theorems." His first theorem states:

Human competence is a function of worthy performance *(W),* which is a function of the ratio of valuable accomplishments *(A)* to costly behavior *(B).* Mathematically this is stated as:

$$W = \frac{A}{B}$$

According to Gilbert, this theorem tells us that having large amounts of work, knowledge, and outcomes without accomplishment is not worthy performance. Performance, he points out, is not the same as activity, but rather is a function of the worth of the accomplishment for a given unit of effort (similar to return on investment). Thus, systems that reward people for effort, not worthy accomplishments, encourage incompetence, according to Gilbert. Similarly, rewarding accomplishment without examining the relative worth of those accomplishments squanders people's energies.

Measuring performance alone does not give us a measure of competence, according to Gilbert. To measure competence, Gilbert proposed his second theorem:

Typical performance is inversely proportional to the potential for improving performance (the PIP), which is the ratio of exemplary performance to typical performance. The ratio, to be meaningful, must be stated for an identifiable accomplishment, because there is no "general quality of competence." (1978, p.30)

Mathematically this is stated as:

$$PIP = \frac{W_{ex}}{w^t}$$

The PIP tells us how much competence we have and how much potential we have for improving it. For example, simply knowing that a person can produce ten widgets a day tells us little about competence. If the best performance possible is ten widgets, then this person is an exemplary performer. On the other hand, if the best performance is twenty widgets, then this person is only at 50 percent of exemplary performance and has a high potential for improving performance.

The third theorem deals directly with engineering human behaviors to create the accomplishments. It states:

> For any given accomplishment, a deficiency in performance always has at its immediate cause a deficiency in a behavior repertory *(P)*, or in the environment that supports the repertory *(E)*, or in both. But its ultimate cause will be found in a deficiency of the management system *(M)*.

Gilbert (1978, p.88) then provides what may be the most well-known part of this model, the behavior engineering model (see Figure 8.12).

Gilbert's notion of human performance was clearly grounded in behavioral psychology. The strength of his framework is that he focused on both the individual and the individual's environment, unlike Campbell's model that focuses solely on the individual. While modern conceptualizations of performance encompass more than just behaviorist notions of human behavior, Gilbert's emphasis on the environmental influences on behavior are fundamental to performance improvement. In addition, his emphasis on the worth of behavior as a measure of wise investments in competence remains fundamental to performance-based HRD. Gilbert's emphasis on behaviorism is viewed by some as its weakness. These criticisms suggest that his work is mechanistic and dehumanizing. The irony is that he believed in human beings and their capacity to perform, in human potential, and in providing people what they needed to successfully perform.

THE SPOILS OF PERFORMANCE

Getting to performance is no small accomplishment. It is important to note that attaining ethical performance goals is worthy and important to individual contributors, top executives, and society. In the big picture, it is important and discouraging to note that HRD tools and techniques can be and are being used for evil purposes. These applications are generally quite obvious and should be shunned and reported.

Figure 8.12 Gilbert's Behavior Engineering Model

	S^D Instrumentation	R Instrumentation	ST Motivation
E	Data	Instruments	Incentives
Environmental supports	1. Relevant and frequent feedback about the adequacy of performance	1. Tools and materials of work designed scientifically to match human factors	1. Adequate financial incentives made contingent upon performance

	S^D Instrumentation	R Instrumentation	ST Motivation
	2. Descriptions of what is expected of performance		2. Nonmonetary incentives made available
	3. Clear and relevant guides to adequate performance		3. Career development opportunities
P	Knowledge	Capacity	Motives
Person's repertory of behavior	1. Scientifically designed training that matches the requirements of exemplary performance	1. Flexible scheduling of performance to match peak capacity	1. Assessment of people's motives to work
	2. Placement	2. Prosthesis	2. Recruitment of people to match the realities of the situation
		3. Physical shaping	
		4. Adaptation	
		5. Selection	

Source: Gilbert, 1978.

At a more subtle level, questions of exploitation, inequity, and unfairness in the distribution of the spoils of performance are deeply disturbing. These questions go beyond the performance paradigms and into the realms of ethics, human decency, morality, abuse of power, and the law. While the field of HRD should and must be a partner in pursuing performance, HRD professionals should avoid being duped into facilitating conditions of exploitation, inequity, and unfairness in the distribution of the spoils of performance. This warning is particularly important in applying the group process tools within organization development when used to placate workers or to provide the illusion of meaningful participation instead of their true purposes.

CONCLUSION

The integration of performance models into HRD has introduced an entirely new perspective to HRD thinking, research, and practice. Their primary contribution is that they all remind us that the individual is embedded in a performance system that has a major effect on the individual's performance. Even if one believes that the primary purpose of HRD is to enhance individual development, the individual is embedded in an organizational system and so HRD professionals must understand the system and its effects on the individual. A broader view suggests that enhancing human performance means working on the system as well as developing individuals. The broadest application of these models suggests that HRD professionals should work to improve all aspects of the performance system.

REFLECTION QUESTIONS

1. Which performance model do you think best represents performance constructs of concern to HRD? Explain why.
2. What are the implications of multilevel, multiattribute performance models for HRD practice?
3. Do performance models enhance or diminish the value of learning in organizations?
4. Performance models are often seen as useful to management, but not as tools to benefit employees. What is your position on this?
5. How can HRD lead change in each of the performance variables?
6. What do you believe is the future of performance-oriented HRD and why?

CHAPRER 9

Perspectives on Learning in Human Resource Development

CHAPRER OUTLINE

Introduction
Basic Theories of Learning
- Behaviorism
- Cognitivism (Gestalt)
- Humanism
- Social Learning
- Constructivism
- Holistic Learning
- Summary
Learning Models at the Individual Level
- Andragogy: The Adult Learning Perspective
- Experiential Learning Model
- Informal and Incidental Workplace Learning
- Transformational Learning
Learning Models at the Organizational Level
- The Learning Organization Strategy
- Learning Organization and Performance Outcomes
Conclusion

Reflection Questions

INTRODUCTION

Learning is at the heart of HRD and continues to be a core part of all paradigms of HRD. Whatever the debates about paradigms of HRD, nobody has ever suggested that HRD not embrace learning as an organizing construct for the field. This chapter takes a closer look at some representative theories and research on learning in HRD. First, six core theories of learning are discussed. Then, representative learning models at the individual and organizational level are reviewed. The purpose of this chapter is to provide key foundational perspectives on learning, but not a comprehensive review.

BASIC THEORIES OF LEARNING

A summary of six basic theories of learning including humanism, social learning, constructivism, and holistic learning as well as behaviorism and cognitivism are summarized in Figure 9.1. These are six theoretical perspectives that can apply to learning in all settings, for all age groups, and for all types of learning events. In this section, each theory is described along with its primary contribution to HRD. Each has been the subject of extensive thinking, writing and research.

Figure 9.1 helps to shows that each approach represents a fundamentally different view of learning. Each would define learning differently, prescribe different roles for the teacher, and seek different outcomes from learning. Each has made a substantial contribution to learning and will continue to inform HRD practice. This section provides only a brief summary of each. Readers interested in a more thorough presentation are encouraged to consult Ormond (1999), Hergenhahn and Olson (1997), or Merriam, Caffarella, and Baumgartner (2006).

It is important to realize that very few HRD professionals or HRD interventions utilize only one of these metatheories. Most are quite eclectic, using a combination of approaches that fit the particular situation. Thus, these six approaches should not be read as either-or choices but rather as five different approaches to be drawn upon as appropriate to one's particular needs. They are presented here in their more pure form to enhance the understanding of each. However, in practice they are usually adapted and blended to accomplish specific objectives. The challenge for the HRD professional is to understand them and be able to make sound judgments about which approach to utilize in a given situation. It is important not to reject any single theory, for each has its strengths and weaknesses.

Behaviorism

Figure 9.1 Six Orientations to Learning

Aspect	Behaviorist	Cognitivist (Gestalt)	Humanist	Social Learning	Constructivist	Holistic
Learning theorists	Thorndike, Pavlov, Watson, Guthrie, Hull, Tolman, Skinner	Koffka, Kohler, Lewin, Piaget, Ausubel, Bruner, Tolman, Gagne	Maslow, Rogers, Knowles	Bandura, Rotter	Candy, Dewey, Lave, Piaget, Rogoff, von Glaserfeld, Vygotsky	Yang, Jarvis & Parker
View of the learning process	Change in behavior	Internal mental process (including insight, information processing, memory, perception)	A personal act to fulfill potential	Interaction with and observation of others in a social context	Construction of meaning from experience	Involves facets of explicit, implicit, and emancipatory knowledge
Locus of learning	Stimuli in the environment	Internal cognitive structuring	Affective and cognitive needs	Interaction of person, behavior and environment	Internal construction of reality by individual	Occurs as a result of interactions with and between knowledge facets
Purpose of education	Produce behavioral change in desired direction	Develop capacity and skills to learn better	Become self-actualized, autonomous	Model new roles and behavior	Construct knowledge	Systematization, participation, and transformation
Teacher's role	Arranges environment to elicit desired response	Structures content of learning activity	Facilitates development of whole person	Models and guides new roles and behavior	Facilitates and negotiates meaning with learner	Facilitator
Manifestation in adult learning	■ Behavioral objectives ■ Competency-based education ■ Skill development ■ Skill development	■ Cognitive development ■ Intelligence, learning, and memory as function of age ■ Learning how to learn	■ Andragogy ■ Self-directed learning	■ Socialization ■ Social roles ■ Mentoring ■ Locus of control	■ Experiential learning ■ Self-directed learning ■ Perspective transformation ■ Reflective practice	■ Holistic and dialectical perspective ■ Dynamic

Source: Adapted from Merriam, Caffarella, and Baumgartner, 2006, p. 264.

Source: Adapted from Merriam, Caffarella, and Baumgartner, 2006, p.264.

Behaviorists are primarily concerned with changes in behavior as a result of learning. Behaviorism has a long and rich history, having been originally developed by John B. Watson, who introduced the term in 1913 and developed it in the early twentieth century (Ormond, 1999). Six prominent learning theorists are mostly commonly included in this school: Ivan Pavlov, Edward L. Thorndike, John B. Watson, Edwin R. Guthrie, Clark L. Hull, and B.F. Skinner. Pavlov and Skinner are the best-known contributors, with Pavlov having developed the classical conditioning model and Skinner the operant conditioning model. While each of these six men scholars had different views of behaviorism, Ormond (1999) identified seven core assumptions that they share:

1. Principles of learning apply equally to different behaviors and to different species of animals.
2. Learning processes can be studied most objectively when the focus of study is on stimulus and response.
3. Internal cognitive processes are largely excluded from scientific study.
4. Learning involves a behavior change.
5. Organisms are born as blank slates.
6. Learning is largely the result of environmental events.
7. The most useful theories tend to be parsimonious ones.

As discussed earlier, behaviorists put primary emphasis on how the external environment influences a person's behavior and learning. Rewards and incentives play a key role in building motivation to learn. In classic behaviorism, the role of the learning facilitator is to structure the environment to elicit the desired response from the learner.

Behaviorism has played a central role in human resource development. Its key contributions include the following:

- *Focus on behavior.* The focus on behavior is important because performance change does not occur without changing behavior. Although behavior change alone without internal cognitive changes is usually not desirable, neither is cognitive change alone. Thus, behaviorism has led to popular practices such as behavioral objectives and competency-based education.

- *Focus on the environment.* Behaviorism reminds us of the central role the external environment plays in shaping human learning and performance. Individuals in an organization are subjected to a number of factors (e.g., rewards and incentives, supports, etc.) that will influence their performance. As discussed in chapter 6, behaviorism thus provides the link between psychology and economics in HRD.
- *Foundation for transfer of learning.* Behaviorism also provides part of the foundation for transfer of learning research. Transfer of learning is concerned with how the environment impacts the use of learning on the job. Transfer research (e.g., Rouiller and Goldstein, 1993) shows that the environment is at least as important, if not more important, than learning in predicting use of learning on the job.
- *Foundation for skill development training. As* indicated in Figure 9.1, behaviorism has provided much of the foundation for skill or

competency-oriented training and development. Behavioral objectives are another contribution from behaviorists.

Behaviorism has also been heavily criticized, primarily by adult educators who prefer a more humanistic and constructivist perspective. The chief criticism is that behaviorism views the learner as passive and dependent. In addition, behaviorism does not account for the role of personal insight and meaning in learning. These are legitimate criticisms and explain why behaviorism is rarely the only learning theory employed. On the other hand, there are training interventions that are appropriately taught in a behavioral approach. For example, teaching police officers how to respond when attacked is an appropriate use of behavioral methods because officers have to respond instinctively.

Behavioristic interventions are also objectionable to some HRD professionals because they find it offensive at a values level. This is particularly true of those who favor an adult learning perspective that abhors external control over a person's learning process. Most believe that there are legitimate uses of behaviorism when the situation warrants this type of learning. We question the objections in training such as the police example or in situations where certification of skills externally mandated is essential for safety. For example, airplane pilots, chemical plant operators, and nuclear plant operators all must pass rigorous certification programs that are behavioristic but which few of us would want changed.

Cognitivism (Gestalt)

Gestalt psychology (cognitivism) arose as a direct response to the limits of behaviorism, particularly the "thoughtless" approach to human learning. The early roots can be traced back to the 1920s and 1930s through the work of Edward Tolman, the Gestalt psychologists of Germany, Jean Piaget, and Lev Vygotsky (Ormond 1999). However, contemporary cognitivism did not begin to appear until the 1950s and 1960s. Ormond (1999) identifies seven core assumptions of contemporary cognitivism:

1. Some learning processes may be unique to human beings.
2. Cognitive processes are the focus of study.
3. Objective, systematic observations of people's behavior should be the focus of scientific inquiry; however, inferences about unobservable mental processes can often be drawn from such behavior.
4. Individuals are actively involved in the learning process.

5. Learning involves the formation of mental associations that are not necessarily reflected in overt behavior changes.
6. Knowledge is organized.
7. Learning is a process of relating new information to previously learned information.

Cognitivists are primarily concerned with insight and understanding. They see people not as passive and shaped by their environment but instead as capable of actively shaping the environment themselves. Furthermore, they focus on the internal process of acquiring, understanding, and retaining learning. Because of that, they suggest that the focus of the learning facilitator should be on structuring the content and the learning activity so learners can acquire information optimally.

Gestalt theory is one type of, and the first form of, cognitivist theory. Some very well-known names within HRD fit under this umbrella, including Kurt Lewin (organization development), Jean Piaget (cognitive development), Jerome Bruner (discovery learning), and Robert Gagne (instructional design). Contemporary cognitivism can be thought of as having three perspectives: information-processing theory, constructivism, and contextual views (situated cognition).

404

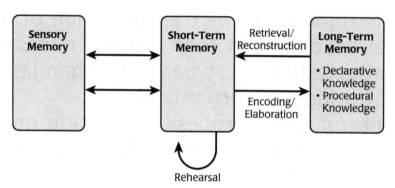

Figure 9.2 The Information-Processing Model Source: Bruning, Schraw, and Ronning, 1999, p.16. Used with permission.

Cognitivism has made significant contributions to HRD and adult learning. Some key ones include the following:

- *Information processing.* Central to cognitivism is the concept of the human mind as an information processor. Figure 9.2 shows a basic schematic view of the human information-processing system. Notice that there are three key components: sensory memory, short-term memory, and long-term memory. Cognitivists are particularly concerned with the processes shown by arrows in this schematic. These arrows represent the mental processes of moving information from sensory memory to short-term memory, and from short-term memory to long-term memory, and retrieving information from long-term memory.
- *Metacognition.* Along with these basic information-processing components, cognitivism

also focuses on how individuals control their cognitive processes, which is called *metacognition.* This concept is more commonly known in HRD and adult learning as "learning how to learn."

- *Cognitive development.* Another important contribution has been the focus on how cognition develops over the life span. It is now generally accepted that cognitive development continues throughout adulthood. Chapter 13 will discuss adult cognitive development in more detail.

Cognitivism has not received the same degree of criticism that behaviorism has. For the most part, cognitivism has made important contributions and is widely utilized in HRD. At the same time, it is viewed in some circles as incomplete because it views the human mind as too mechanical. Cognitivism is also seen as the stimulant for more recent trends of brain research. Byrnes (2001) argues that several "trends have created an atmosphere on increased (though certainly not universal) acceptance of the idea that neuroscientific research could provide answers to important questions about learning and cognition. But I must underscore my use of the term 'could' here. Most scholars believe that the available neuroscientific evidence is provocative and interesting, but far from conclusive" (p.2).

Humanism

Humanism did not emerge as a learning theory but rather as a general approach to psychology. The work of Abraham Maslow (1968, 1970) and Carl Rogers (1961) provides the core of humanistic psychology. Buhler (1971), a leading humanistic psychologist (Lundin, 1991), suggests that the core assumptions of humanism are as follows:

- The person as a *whole* is the main subject of humanistic psychology.
- Humanistic psychology is concerned with the knowledge of a person's entire life history.
- Human existence and intention are also of great importance.
- Life goals are of equal importance.
- Human creativity has a primary place.
- Humanistic psychology is frequently applied to psychotherapy.

Rogers (1980) puts forth his principles of significant learning by saying that such learning must have the following characteristics:

- Personal involvement: The affective and cognitive aspects must come from within.
- Self-initiated: A sense of discovery must come from within.

- Pervasive: The learning makes a difference in the behavior, the attitudes, perhaps even the personality of the learner.
- Evaluated by the learner: The learner can best determine whether the learning experience is meeting a need.
- Essence is meaning: When experiential learning takes place, its meaning to the learner becomes incorporated into the total experience.

Humanism adds yet another dimension to learning and has dominated much of adult learning. It is most concerned with development by the whole person and places a great deal of emphasis on the affective component of the learning process largely overlooked by other learning theories. The learning facilitator has to take into account the whole person and his or her life situation in planning the learning experience. Humanists view individuals as seeking self-actualization through learning and of being capable of controlling their own learning process. Adult learning theories, particularly andragogy, best represent it in HRD. In addition, self-directed learning and much of career development are grounded in humanism. (Andragogy will be discussed in much more detail in the next section.)

In many respects, humanism is absolutely central to the field of human resource development. If humans are not viewed as motivated to develop and improve, then at least part of the core premise of HRD disappears. At the same time, humanism is also a primary source of debate within the field because the performance paradigm is viewed by some as violating the humanistic tenets of the field. As we have stated, we do not believe they are contradictory. However, if a person believes completely in the humanistic view of learning, then allowing for behavioral components in the learning process is disconcerting. We prefer to see them coexist.

Social Learning

Social learning focuses on how people learn by interacting with and observing other people. This type of learning focuses on the social context in which learning occurs. Some people view social learning as a special type of behaviorism because it reflects how individuals learn from people in their environment. Others view it as a separate metatheory because the learner is also actively making meaning of the interactions.

A foundational contribution of social learning is that people can learn vicariously by imitating others. Thus, central to social learning processes is that people learn from role models. This was in direct contradiction to behaviorists who said that learners had to perform themselves and be reinforced for learning to occur. Thus, the facilitator must model new behaviors and guide learners in learning from others. Albert Bandura is probably the best-known name is this area. It was his works in the 1960s and extending through the 1980s that fully developed social learning theory.

Ormond (1999) lists four core assumptions of social learning theory: people can learn by observing the behaviors of others and the outcomes of those behaviors; learning can occur without a change in behavior; the consequences of behavior play a role in learning; and cognition plays a role in learning.

Social learning also occupies a central place in HRD. One contribution is in classroom learning in which social learning focuses on the role of the facilitator as a model for behaviors to be learned. Facilitators often underestimate their influence as a role model and forget to utilize role modeling as part of their instructional plan.

Social learning may make its biggest contribution through non-classroom learning. One area is in new employee development, where socialization processes account for the largest portion of new employee development (Holton, 1996c; Holton and Russell, 1999; Korte, 2007). *Socialization* is the process by which organizations pass on the culture of the organization to new employees and teach them how to be effective in the organization. It is an informal process that occurs through social interactions between new employees and organizational members. Another key area is mentoring, a primary means of on-the-job development in many organizations. It is often used to develop new managers. This is clearly a social learning process as mentors teach and coach protégés. Yet another key area is on-the-job training whereby newcomers learn their jobs from job incumbents, in part by direct instruction but also by observing the incumbent and using the incumbent as a role model.

There are few critics of social learning as it mostly contributes to learning theory in HRD without inciting any sharp arguments. Social learning is widely accepted as an effective and important learning process. When properly applied, it enhances learning and contributes learning that often cannot occur in the classroom.

Constructivism

While controversial, especially in its more radical versions, constructivism is emerging as a useful perspective for some adult learning situations (Wiswell and Ward, 1987). Constructivism stresses that all knowledge is context bound and that individuals make personal meaning of their learning experiences. Thus, learning cannot be separated from the context in which it is used. They also stress the cumulative nature of learning. That is, new information must be related to other existing information in order for learners to retain and utilize it. For adults, experience might be conceptualized as creating a giant funnel of previous knowledge, whereby new information that enters the top of the funnel cascades downward and eventually falls out unless it "sticks" to some element of prior knowledge. The role of the facilitator is to help learners make meaning of new information.

Many learning theorists, including Ormond (1999), do not view constructivism as a separate metatheory but rather as a special type of cognitivism. Adult learning theorists (e.g., Merriam and Caffarella, 1999) are more inclined to differentiate it from cognitivism because of its importance for adult learning.

The contributions of constructivism to HRD are still emerging. The emphasis on how adults make meaning of new information by relating it to previous experience largely supports the andragogical view of learning (Knowles, Holton, and Swanson, 2005). In fact, the parallels between moderate views of constructivism and andragogy are rather striking. Both stress ownership of the learning process by learners, experiential learning, and problem-solving approaches to learning. However, andragogy and the more extreme views of constructivism are not compatible. Constuctivism plays an important role in understanding informal and incidental learning, self-directed learning, and perspective transformation.

Holistic Learning

Figure 9.3 Holistic Theory of Knowledge and Learning: Indications of Three Knowledge Facts and Three Knowledge Layers

Knowledge Layers	Knowledge Facets		
	EXPLICIT	IMPLICIT	EMANCIPATORY
Foundations	Axioms, assumptions, beliefs, hypotheses	Habits, social norms, traditions, routines	Values, aspirations, vision
Manifestations	Theories, principles, models, conceptual frameworks, formulas	Tacit understandings, know-how, intuition, mental models	Attitudes, motivations, learning needs, equity, ethics, moral standards
Orientations	Rational	Practical	Freedom

Source: Yang, 2003.

More recently, the *Holistic Theory of Knowledge and Adult Learning* has been advanced by Baiyin Yang (2003; 2004a; 2004b). His theory plays a unique role in integrating so many of the rival learning theories that distinguish themselves by their differences, rather than their commonalities. Yang's holistic theory conceptualizes knowledge into three indivisible facets—implicit, explicit, and emancipatory. Furthermore, each of these has three layers—foundation, manifestation, and orientation. The interactions between the facets and layers are shown in Figure 9.3.

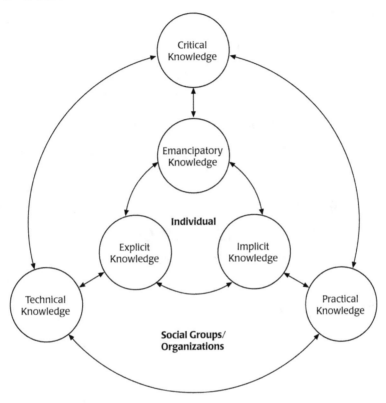

Source: Yang, 2003.

Figure 9.4 Holistic Theory of Knowledge and Learning: Dynamic Relationships between Individual, Organization, and Social/Cultural Contexts

It is important to note that most perspectives on learning are focused on the individual level, and that the holistic theory embraces the individual, group, and organizational learning challenges facing HRD. Figure 9.4 visually arranges the knowledge facets and knowledge layers in an individual and social group/organization relationship.

Another feature of the holistic theory is its attempt to harness the best of three major views on the nature of knowledge and learning put forth by Mezirow (1996). They include: (1) the empirical/analytic paradigm (objective interpretation), (2) the interpretist paradigm (subjective interpretation), and (3) the critical paradigm (power interpretation).

The value of the holistic theory is in making connections between seemingly disparate streams of philosophy and research related to knowledge and learning (Jarvis and Parker, 2005; Nafukho, 2006). Critics would argue that such connections are tenuous.

Summary

Most learning theories in HRD can be embedded in one or a blend of these six general theories of learning. Each general theory makes unique contributions and adds power to learning practice in HRD. Readers are advised to understand each so that they can be employed in appropriate situations. We reiterate that no single approach is best, but in any given situation one or a combination of approaches is likely to be most powerful.

LEARNING MODELS AT THE INDIVIDUAL LEVEL

In this section, four middle-range models of learning are reviewed. First, andragogy is discussed as a core adult learning model that has played a central role in adult learning within HRD. Also, the andragogy in practice model (Knowles et al., 1998; Holton, Swanson, and Naquin, 2001) is presented as a more comprehensive elaboration of andragogy. Next, Kolb's experiential learning model is considered, followed by informal and incidental learning. Last, transformational learning is discussed.

Andragogy: The Adult Learning Perspective

In the late 1960s when Knowles introduced andragogy in the United States, the idea broke new ground and sparked much subsequent research and controversy. Since the earliest days, adult educators have debated what andragogy really is (Henschke, 1998). Spurred in part by the need for a defining theory within the field of adult education, andragogy has been extensively analyzed and critiqued. It has been alternately described as a set of guidelines (Merriam,

1993), a philosophy (Pratt, 1993), and a set of assumptions (Brookfield, 1986). Davenport and Davenport (1985) note that andragogy has been called a theory of adult learning/education, a method or technique of adult education, and a set of assumptions about adult learners. The disparity of these positions is indicative of the perplexing nature of andragogy. But regardless of what it is called, "it is an honest attempt to focus on the learner. In this sense, it does provide an alternative to the methodology-centered instructional design perspective" (Feur and Gerber, 1988).

Despite years of critique, debate and challenge, the core principles of adult learning advanced by andragogy have endured (Davenport and Davenport, 1985; Hartree, 1984; Pratt, 1988), and few adult learning scholars would disagree with the observation that Knowles's ideas sparked a revolution in adult education and training (Feur and Gerber, 1988). Brookfield (1986), positing a similar view, asserts that andragogy is the "single most popular idea in the education and training of adults."(p.91). Adult educators and human resource development professionals, particularly beginning ones, find them invaluable in shaping the learning process to be more effective with adults.

The Core Andragogical Model

Popularized by Knowles (1968), the original andragogical model presents core principles of adult learning and important assumptions about adult learners. These core principles of adult learning are believed to enable those designing and conducting adult learning to create more effective learning processes for adults. The model is a transactional model (Brookfield, 1986) in that it speaks to the characteristics of the learning transaction. As such, it is applicable to any adult learning transaction, from community education to human resource development in organizations.

Depending on which resource is consulted, various authors present andragogy in different ways. Accordingly, it has often been difficult to ascertain both the number and content of the core principles of andragogy. This difficulty stems from the fact that the number of andragogical principles has grown from four to six over the years as Knowles refined his thinking (Knowles, 1989). The addition of assumptions and the discrepancy in the number cited in the literature has led to some confusion (see Holton, Swanson, and Naquin, 2001 for a complete review of the history of the andragogical assumptions). The current six core assumptions or principles of andragogy (Knowles, Holton, and Swanson, 2005) are as follows:

1. Adults need to know why they need to learn something before learning it.
2. The self-concept of adults is heavily dependent on a move toward self-direction.
3. Prior experiences of the learner provide a rich resource for learning.
4. Adults typically become ready to learn when they experience a need to cope with a life situation or perform a task.
5. Adults' orientation to learning is life centered, and they see education as a process of developing increased competency levels to achieve their full potential.
6. The motivation for adult learners is internal rather than external.

These core principles provide a sound foundation for planning adult learning experiences. Absent any other information, they offer an effective approach to adult learning.

The second part of the andragogical model is what Knowles (1995, 1984) called the *andragogical process design* for creating adult learning experiences. Originally, Knowles presented this as seven steps (Knowles 1984, 1990). Later, he added a new first step, preparing learners for the program, which brought the total to eight steps (Knowles, 1995): (1) preparing learners for the program, (2) establishing a climate conducive to learning, (3) involving learners in mutual planning, (4) involving participants in diagnosing their learning needs, (5) involving learners in forming their learning objectives, (6) involving learners in designing learning plans, (7) helping learners carry out their learning plans, and (8) involving learners in evaluating their learning outcomes.

Figure 9.5 shows the andragogical process elements and andragogical approaches as presented and updated by Knowles (1992, 1995).

Figure 9.5 Process Elements of Andragogy

Element	Andragogical Approach
Preparing learners	Provide information
	Prepare for participation
	Help develop realistic expectations
	Begin thinking about content
Climate	Relaxed, trusting
	Mutually respectful
	Informal, warm
	Collaborative, supportive
Planning	Mutually by learners and facilitator
Diagnosis of needs	By mutual assessment
Setting of objectives	By mutual negotiation
Designing learning plans	Learning contracts

Element	Andragogical Approach
Learning activities	Learning projects
	Sequenced by readiness
	Inquiry projects
	Independent study
	Experiential techniques
Evaluation	Learner-collected evidence validated by peers, facilitators, and experts.
	Criterion referenced.

Source: Developed from Knowles (1992, 1995).

Integrated System or Flexible Assumptions?

In early works Knowles presented andragogy as an integrated set of assumptions. However, following the period of experimentation, it now seems that the power of andragogy lies in its potential for more flexible application. As others have noted (Brookfield, 1986; Feur and Gerber, 1988; Pratt, 1998), over the years the assumptions became viewed by some practitioners as somewhat of a recipe implying that all adult educators should facilitate the same way in all situations. Clear evidence indicates that Knowles intended for them to be viewed as flexible assumptions to be altered depending on the situation. Knowles (1984) reiterated this point in the conclusion to his casebook examining thirty-six applications of andragogy. He noted that he had spent two decades experimenting with andragogy and had reached certain conclusions, including these:

- The andragogical model is a system of elements that can be adopted or adapted in whole or in part. It is not an ideology that must be applied totally and without modification. In fact, an essential feature of andragogy is flexibility.
- The appropriate starting point and strategies for applying the andragogical model depend on the situation (p.418).

More recently, Knowles (1989) stated in his autobiography, "So I accept (and glory in) the criticism that I am a philosophical eclectic or situationalist who applies his philosophical beliefs differentially to different situations. I see myself as being free from any single ideological dogma, and so I don't fit neatly into any of the categories philosophers often want to box people in" (p.112). He further stated that "what this means in practice is that we educators now have the responsibility to check out which assumptions are realistic in a given situation" (Knowles, 1990, p.64).

It seems clear that Knowles always knew, and then confirmed through use, that andragogy could be utilized in many different ways and would have to be adapted to fit individual situations. Unfortunately, he never offered a systematic framework of factors that should be considered when determining which assumptions are realistic in order to adapt andragogy to the situation. As a result, the andragogical assumptions about adults have been criticized for appearing to claim to fit all situations or persons (Davenport, 1987; Davenport and Davenport, 1985; Day and Baskett, 1982; Elias, 1979; Hartree, 1984; Tennant, 1986). While a more careful read of Knowles's work shows he did not believe this, andragogy is nonetheless open to this criticism because it fails to account for the differences explicitly.

The Andragogy in Practice Model

Andragogy in practice, the framework depicted in Figure 9.6, is an enhanced conceptual framework to apply andragogy more systematically across multiple domains of adult learning practice (Knowles, Holton, and Swanson, 2005). The three dimensions of andragogy in practice, shown as rings in the figure, are (1) goals and purposes for learning, (2) individual and situational differences, and (3) andragogy (core adult learning principles).

In contrast to the traditional model of andragogy, this approach conceptually integrates the additional influences with the core adult learning principles. The three rings of the model interact, allowing the model to offer a three-dimensional process for adult learning situations. The result is a model that recognizes the lack of homogeneity among learners and learning situations and illustrates that the learning transaction is a multifaceted activity. This approach is entirely consistent with most of the program development literature in adult education that in some manner incorporates contextual analysis as a step in developing programs (e.g., Houle, 1972; Knox, 1986; Boone, 1985).

Goals and purposes for learning, the outer ring of the model, are portrayed as developmental outcomes. The goals and purposes of adult learning serve to shape and mold the learning experience. In this model, goals for adult learning events may fit into three general categories: *individual, institutional,* or *societal.* Knowles (1970, 1980) used these three categories to describe the missions of adult education, though he did not directly link them to the andragogical assumptions. Beder (1989) also used a similar approach to describe the purposes of adult education as facilitating change in society and supporting and maintaining good social order (societal), promoting productivity (institutional), and enhancing personal growth (individual).

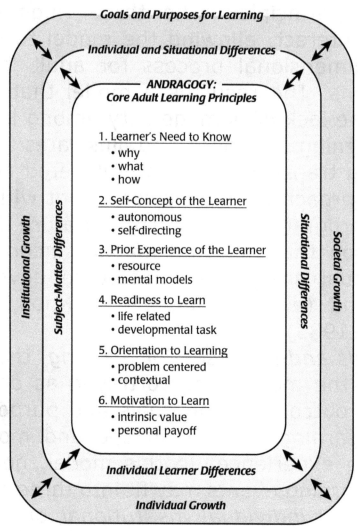

Figure 9.6 Andragogy in Practice Model Source: Knowles, Holton, and Swanson, 2005, p.4.

Merriam and Brockett (1997) discuss seven content-purpose typologies (Bryson, 1936; Grattan, 1955; Liveright, 1968; Darkenwald and Merriam, 1982; Apps, 1985; Rachal, 1988; Beder, 1989), using Bryson's (1936) five-part typology (liberal, occupational, relational, remedial, and political), noting that the purposes for adult learning have changed little since then. Bryson's (1936) typology would also fit into Knowles's three-part typology with liberal, relational, and remedial fitting into the individual category; occupational fitting into the institutional category; and political fitting into the societal category. Thus, Knowles's three category typology can be seen as also encompassing all of the categories found in other major typologies of purposes for adult learning.

Individual Growth

The traditional view among most scholars and practitioners of adult learning is to think exclusively of individual growth. Representative researchers in this group might include some mentioned earlier such as Mezirow (1991) and Brookfield (1987, 1984). Others advocate an individual development approach to workplace adult learning programs (Bierema, 1997; Dirkx, 1997). At first glance, andragogy would appear to fit best with individual development goals because of its focus on the individual learner.

Institutional Growth

Adult learning is equally powerful in developing better institutions, as well as individuals. Human resource development, for example, embraces organizational performance as one of its core goals (Brethower and Smalley, 1998; Swanson and Arnold, 1996), which andragogy does not explicitly embrace, either. From this view of human resource development, the ultimate goal of learning activities is to improve the institution sponsoring the learning activity. Thus, control of the goals and purposes is shared between the organization and the individual. The adult learning transaction in an HRD setting still fits nicely within the andragogical framework, although the different goals require adjustments to be made in how the andragogical assumptions are applied.

Societal Growth

Societal goals and purposes that can be associated with the learning experience are illustrated through Paulo Freire's work (1970). This Brazilian educator sees the goals and purposes of adult education as societal transformation, contending that education is a consciousness-raising process. He says that the aim of education is to help participants put knowledge into practice and that the outcome of education is societal transformation. Freire is clearly concerned with creating a better world and the development and liberation of people. As such, the goals and purposes within this learning context are oriented to societal as well as individual improvement.

Individual and situational differences, the middle ring of the andragogy in practice model, are portrayed as variables. We continue to learn more about the differences that impact adult learning and which act as filters that shape the practice of andragogy. These variables are grouped into the categories of individual *learner differences, subject-matter differences,* and *situational differences.*

Subject-matter differences may require different learning strategies. For example, individuals may be less likely to learn complex technical subject matter in a self-directed manner. Or, as Knowles stated in the earlier quote, introducing unfamiliar content to a learner will require a different teaching/learning strategy. Simply, not all subject matter can be taught or learned in the same way.

Situational differences captures any unique factors that could arise in a particular learning situation and incorporates several sets of influences. At the micro-level, different local situations may dictate different teaching/learning strategies. For example, learners in remote locations may be forced to be more self-directed, or perhaps less so. At a broader level, this group of factors connects andragogy with the sociocultural influences now accepted as a core part of each learning situation. This is one area of past criticism that seems particularly appropriate.

Jarvis (1987) sees all adult learning as occurring within a social context through life experiences. In his model, the social context may include social influences prior to the learning event that affect the learning experience, as well as the social milieu within which the actual learning occurs. Thus, situational influences prior to the learning event could include anything from cultural influences to learning history. Similarly, situational influences during learning can be seen as including the full range of social, cultural and situation-specific factors that may alter the learning transaction.

Individual differences is a result of a surge of interest in linking the adult education literature with psychology to advance our understanding of how individual differences affect adult learning. Analyzing psychological theories from an adult learning perspective, Tennant (1997) argues for psychology as a foundation discipline of adult education. Interestingly, a group of educational psychologists has recently argued for building a bridge between educational psychology and adult learning, calling for creation of a new subfield of adult educational psychology (Cecil and Pourchot, 1998).

This may be the area in which our understanding of adult learning has advanced the most since Knowles first introduced andragogy. A number of researchers have expounded on a host of individual differences affecting the learning process (e.g., Dirkx and Prenger, 1997; Kidd, 1978; Merriam, Caffarella, and Baumgartner, 2006). This increased emphasis on linking adult learning and psychological research is indicative of an increasing focus on how individual differences affect adult learning. From this perspective, there is no reason to expect all adults to behave the same, but rather our understanding of individual differences should help shape and tailor the andragogical approach to fit the uniqueness of the learners.

An understanding of individual differences helps make andragogy more effective in practice. Effective adult learning professionals use their understanding of individual differences to devise adult learning experiences in several ways. First, they tailor the manner in which they apply the core principles to fit adult learners' cognitive abilities and learning style preferences. Second, they use them to know which of the core principles are most salient to a specific group of learners. For example, if learners do not have strong cognitive controls, they may not initially emphasize self-directed learning. Third, they use individual differences to expand the goals of learning experiences. For example, one goal might be to expand learners' cognitive controls and styles to enhance future learning ability. This flexible approach explains why andragogy is applied in so many different ways (Knowles, 1984).

Applying the Andragogy in Practice Framework

The andragogy in practice framework is an expanded conceptualization of andragogy that incorporates domains of factors that will influence the application of core andragogical principles. We suggest a three-part process for analyzing adult learners:

1. The core principles of andragogy provide a sound foundation for planning adult learning experiences. Without any other information, they reflect the sound approach to effective adult learning.
2. Analysis should be conducted to understand (a) the particular adult learners and their individual characteristics, (b) the characteristics of the subject matter, and (c) the characteristics of the particular situation in which adult learning is being used. Adjustments necessary to the core principles should be anticipated.
3. The goals and purposes for which the adult learning is conducted provide a frame that puts shape to the learning experience. They should be clearly identified and possible effects on adult learning defined.

This framework should be used in advance to conduct what we call *andragogical learner analysis.* As part of the needs assessment for program development, andragogical learner analysis is used to determine the extent to which andragogical principles fit a particular situation.

Experiential Learning Model

Kolb (1984) has been a leader in advancing the practice of experiential learning for adults that we most associate with John Dewey (1910; 1938). Kolb defines learning as "the process whereby knowledge is created through transformation of experience" (p.38). For him, learning is not so much the acquisition or transmission of content as the interaction between content and experience, whereby each transforms the other. The educator's job, he says, is not only to transmit or implant new ideas but also to modify old ones that may get in the way of new ones.

Kolb bases his model of experiential learning on Lewin's problem-solving model of action research, which is widely used in organization development (Cummings and Worley, 2001). He argues that it is very similar to Dewey and Piaget's as well and specifies four steps in the experiential learning cycle (see Figure 9.7): (1) *concrete experience*—being fully involved in here-and-now experiences; (2) *observations and reflection*—reflecting on and observing their experiences from many perspectives; (3) *formation of abstract concepts and generalizations* —creating concepts that integrate their observations into logically sound theories; and (4) *testing implications of new concepts in new situations*—using these theories to make decisions and solve problems.

Kolb goes on to suggest that these four modes combine to create four distinct learning styles.

Kolb's model has made a major contribution to the experiential learning literature by providing (1) a theoretical basis for experiential learning research and (2) a practical model for experiential learning practice. The four steps in his model are an invaluable framework for designing learning experiences for adults. At a macrolevel, programs and classes can be structured to include all four components, as well as at a microlevel, units or lessons. Shown below are examples of learning strategies that may be useful in each step:

Kolb's Stage	Example Learning/Teaching Strategy
Concrete experience	Simulation, case study, field trip, real experience, demonstrations
Observe and reflect	Discussion, small groups, buzz groups, designated observers

Kolb's Stage	Example Learning/Teaching Strategy
Abstract conceptualization	Sharing content
Active experimentation	Laboratory experiences, on-the-job experience, intern-ships, practice sessions

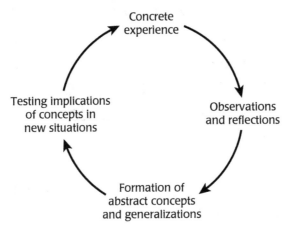

Figure 9.7 Kolb's Experiential Learning Model

Research on Kolb's model has focused mostly on learning styles he proposes. Unfortunately, research has done little to validate his theory, due in large part to methodological concerns about his instrument (Cornwell and Manfredo, 1994; Freedman and Stumpf, 1980; Kolb, 1981; Stumpf and Freedman, 1981).

Human resource development practitioners, while always valuing experience, are increasingly emphasizing experiential learning as a means to improve performance. Action reflection learning is one technique developed to focus on the learner's experiences and integrate experience into the learning process. Transfer of learning researchers are also focusing on experiential learning as a means to enhance transfer of learning into performance (Holton, Bates, Seyler, and Carvalho, 1997; Bates, Holton, and Seyler, 2000) and to increase motivation to learn (Seyler, Holton, and Bates, 1997). Structured on-the-job training (Jacobs, 2003) has emerged as a core method to capitalize more systematically on the value of experiential learning in organizations and as a tool to more effectively develop new employees through the use of experienced coworkers (Holton, 1996c). Experiential learning approaches have the dual benefit of appealing to the adult learner's experience base, as well as increasing the likelihood of performance change after training.

Informal and Incidental Workplace Learning

While many people think first of formal training in HRD, much of the learning that occurs in organizations happens outside formal training or learning events. Informal and incidental learning has deep roots in the work of Lindeman (1926) and Dewey's (1938) notion of learning from experience, although it was

Knowles (1950) who introduced the term *informal learning.*

Watkins and Marsick (1990, 1992, 1997) and their associates have advanced inquiry on informal and incidental learning. They define the constructs in this way:

> *Formal learning* is typically institutionally-sponsored, classroom-based, and highly structured. *Informal learning,* a category which includes incidental learning, may occur in institutions, but is not typically classroom-based or highly structured, and control of learning rests primarily in the hands of the learner. *Incidental learning* is defined as a byproduct of some other activity, such as task accomplishment, interpersonal interaction, sensing the organizational culture, trial-and-error experimentation, or even formal learning. Informal learning can be deliberately encouraged by an organization or it can take place despite an environment not highly conducive to learning. Incidental learning, on the other hand, almost always takes place although people are not always conscious of it. (Watkins and Marsick, 1990, p.12, emphasis added)

Thus, informal learning can be either intentional or incidental. Examples of informal learning include self-directed learning, mentoring, coaching, networking, learning from mistakes, trial and error, etc. Incidental learning can also lead to embedded assumptions, beliefs and attributions that can later become barriers to other learning. Argyris (1982) and Schon (1987) refer to *double loop learning* (or *reflection in action)* as the learning process required to challenge the implicit or tacit knowledge that arises from incidental learning. Tacit knowledge is increasingly recognized as an important source of knowledge for experts and innovation (Glynn, 1996).

Watkins and Marsick (1990, 1992; Cseh, et al., 1999) have developed a model of informal and incidental learning where learning is embedded within the individual's daily work and is highly contextual. Furthermore, they contend that learning occurs as a result of some trigger (internal or external) and an experience. This is in sharp contrast to the planned learning approach of formal learning events.

The question of whether informal or incidental learning can and should be facilitated is unsettled. On the one hand, it seems that there are efforts HRD organizations should use to facilitate the process. For example, Raelin (2000) suggests using action learning, communities of practice, action science, and learning teams in management development to encourage informal work-based learning. Piskurich (1993) takes a similar approach to self-directed learning, while Jacobs (2003) and Rothwell and Kasanas (1994) advocate a structured approach to on-the-job training. Realistically, attempting to over-facilitate informal and incidental learning gets to the point that they become formal learning.

Nijhof and Nieuwenhuis (2008) have published the most up-to-date analysis of workplace learning related to HRD in their book titled *The Potential of Workplace Learning.* They note, "Learning is becoming a constituent part of work. Anthropologists would smile, because it is their main belief that lifelong learning in context is the essence of mankind, and therefore an integral part of what people do, including work" (p.4). Yet, one conclusion is that there are misconceptions about learning in the workplace and that the workplace is not always an effective learning environment (Nijhof, 2006). Figure 9.8 profiles learning functions as being most appropriate in a classroom or workplace setting.

Figure 9.8 Functions of Schooling and Learning Settings

Functions	Formal Learning (generic)	Workplace (job-specific)
Socialization		X
Innovation		X
Maintenance		X
Cognitive acquisition	X	
Skills acquisition	X	X

438

Functions	Formal Learning (generic)	Workplace (job-specific)
Personal development	X	
Career development		X
Lifelong learning	X	X
Vocational studies	X	
Job performance		X

Source: Nijhof and Nieuwenhuis, 2008, p.5. Used with permission.

Throughout this discussion of informal workplace learning, it is important to highlight the ideas of unstructured and structured on-the-job learning. Unstructured is equivalent to informal workplace learning and structured on-the-job training uses the actual workplace as a learning setting.

"The learning potential of the workplace should be proved by evidence that students and employees learn something that changes their behavior with durable results—cognitive, affective, technical, and social. While the workplace is a place to work and perform, learning is an intermediate condition, and the learning potential of the workplace therefore lies in its condition to support or stimulate learning" (Nijhof and Nieuwenhuis, 2008, p.5).

Transformational Learning

Transformational learning has gained increasing attention in HRD. The fundamental premise is that people, just like organizations, may engage in incremental learning or in deeper learning that requires them to challenge fundamental assumptions and meaning schema they have about the world. This concept has appeared in a variety of forms in the literature.

Rumelhart and Norman (1978) propose three different modes of learning in relation to mental schema: *accretion, tuning,* and *restructuring.* Accretion and tuning involves no change or only incremental changes to a person's schemata. Restructuring involves the creation of new schema and is the hardest learning for most adults.

Argyris (1982) labels learning as either "single-" or "double-loop" learning. *Single-loop learning* is learning that fits prior experiences and existing values, enabling the learner to respond in an automatic way. *Double-loop learning* is learning that does not fit the learner's prior experiences or schema and generally requires learners to change their mental schema in a fundamental way. Similarly, Schon (1987) discusses "knowing in action" and "reflection in action." *Knowing in action* refers to the somewhat automatic responses based on our existing mental schema that enable us to perform efficiently in daily actions. *Reflection in action* is the process of reflecting while performing, to discover when existing schema are no longer appropriate and changing those schema when appropriate.

Mezirow (1991) and Brookfield (1986, 1987) are leading advocates for transformational learning in the adult learning literature. Mezirow (1991) calls this *perspective transformation,* which he defines as "the process of becoming critically aware of how and why our assumptions have come to constrain the way we perceive, understand, and feel about our world; changing these structures of habitual expectation to make possible a more inclusive, discriminating, and integrative perspective; and finally, making choices or otherwise acting upon these new understandings" (p.167).

The concept of deep transformational change is found throughout the HRD literature. Many believe that transformational change at the organization level (discussed in chapter 14) is not likely to happen unless transformational change occurs at the individual level through some process of critically challenging and changing internal cognitive structures. Furthermore, without engaging in deep learning through a double-loop or perspective transformation process, individuals will remain trapped in their existing mental models or schemata. It is only through critical reflection that emancipatory learning occurs and enables people to change their lives at a deep level. Thus, transformational change processes are important to HRD.

LEARNING MODELS AT THE ORGANIZATIONAL LEVEL

While individual learning has long dominated HRD practice, in the 1980s and particularly the 1990s, increased attention turned to learning at the organizational level. The literature refers to two related but different concepts: Organizational learning and learning organizations. A *learning organization* is a prescribed set of strategies that can be enacted to enable organizational learning. It is important to recognize that *organizational learning* is different, and that the terms are not interchangeable.

Organizational learning is learning occurring at the system level rather than at the individual level (Dixon, 1992). It does not exclude the learning that occurs at the individual level. But, it is greater than the sum of the learning at the individual level (Fiol and Lyles, 1985; Kim,

1993; Lundberg, 1989). Organizational learning is more specifically defined as "the intentional use of learning processes at the individual, group and system level to continuously transform the organization in a direction that is increasingly satisfying to its stakeholders" (Dixon, 1994). It is learning keenly perceived at the system level, and it arises from processes surrounding the sharing of insights, knowledge, and mental models (Strata, 1989).

According to Kim (1993), the key element differentiating individual and organizational learning revolves around mental models. When individuals make their mental models explicit and organizational members develop and take on shared mental models, organizational learning is enabled. Learning becomes organizational learning when these cognitive outcomes, the new and shared mental models, are "embedded in members' minds, and in ... artifacts ... in the organizational environment" (Argyris and Schon, 1996). Organizational learning is embedded in the culture, organizational systems, and work procedures and processes.

The Learning Organization Strategy

The learning organization became a focus of attention in the organizational literature in the 1990s. Interest in this organization development (OD) intervention has been spurred by the constantly changing work and business environments, which have been prompted by technological advances, increased levels of competition, and globalization of industries. Senge and other researchers have described the characteristics of the learning organization and made suggestions for organizational implementation (Kline and Saunders, 1993; Marquardt, 2002; Pedler, Bourgoyne, and Boydell, 1991; Senge, 1990; Watkins and Marsick, 1993).

The dimensions commonly described in the literature as being associated with a learning organization are not new concepts, but their coordination into a system focused on organizational learning is. However, there is no single definition of what the learning organization is. Senge (1990) defines a learning organization as "a place where people are continually discovering how they create their reality" (p.13). Watkins and Marsick (1993) define it as "one that learns continuously and transforms itself" (p.8). A comprehensive definition of a learning organization is offered by Marquardt (1996): "an organization which learns powerfully and collectively and is continually transforming itself to better collect, manage, and use knowledge for corporate success. It empowers people within and outside the company to learn as they work. Technology is utilized to optimize both learning and productivity" (p.19).

There appears to be some common recognition and agreement about the core characteristics of a learning organization. Researchers suggest that individuals and teams work toward the attainment of linked and shared goals, communication is open, information is available and shared, systems thinking is the norm, leaders are champions of learning, management practices support learning, learning is encouraged and rewarded, and new ideas are welcome (Marquardt, 2002; Senge, 1990; Watkins and Marsick, 1993). The learning outcomes found in a learning organization are expected to include experiential learning, team learning, second-loop learning, and shared meaning (Argyris, 1977; Argyris and Schon, 1978; Dodgson, 1993; Senge, 1990). As a result of this learning, organizations are believed to be capable of new ways of thinking.

Senge's Learning Organization Theory

Peter Senge (1990) is credited with popularizing the learning organization, even though considerable work was done on it in the 1980s. In laying out the foundation for his model of the learning organization, Senge (1992, 1993) speaks about the three levels of work required of organizations. The first level focused on the development, production, and marketing of products and services. This organizational task is dependent on the second level of work: the designing and development of the systems and processes for production. The third task undertaken by organizations centers around thinking and interacting. Senge (1993) claims that the first two levels of organizational work are affected by the quality of this third level. That is, the quality of the organizational thinking and interacting affects the organizational systems and processes, and the production and delivery of products and services. This belief places organizational thinking in a pivotal position affecting the ability of an organization to accomplish goals and perform effectively.

It is the third level of organizational work that Senge addresses with his concept of learning organizations. In defining a learning organization, he states, "We can build learning organizations, where people continually expand their capacity to create the results they truly desire, where new and expansive patterns of thinking are nurtured, where collective aspiration is set free, and where people are continually learning how to learn together" (1990, p.3).

Senge (1990) suggests that organizations need to develop five core disciplines or capabilities to accomplish the following defined goals of a learning organization:

- Personal mastery
- Mental models
- Shared vision
- Team learning
- Systems thinking

Systems thinking, the fifth discipline, acts to integrate the other four disciplines. It is described as the ability to take a systems perspective of organizational reality. Senge (1990) discusses strategies that organizations can implement to develop and encourage the five core disciplines of a learning organization. The recommended strategies involve the following organizational variables: climate, leadership, management, human resource practices, organization mission, job attitudes, organizational culture, and organizational structure.

Watkins and Marsick (1993) suggest that learning is a constant process and results in changes in knowledge, beliefs, and behaviors.

They also believe that, in a learning organization, the learning process is a social one and takes place at the individual, group, and organizational levels. They propose six imperatives that form the basis for the organizational strategies recommended to promote learning:

1. Create continuous learning opportunities.
2. Promote inquiry and dialogue.
3. Encourage collaboration and team learning.
4. Establish systems to capture and share learning.
5. Empower people toward a collective vision.
6. Connect the organization to its environment.

Figure 9.9 shows the interrelationship of these six imperatives across the individual, team and organizational levels.

These six imperatives are similar to the disciplines suggested by Senge (1990, 1994). Marquardt (1996) similarly focuses on a learning system composed of five linked and interrelated subsystems related to learning: the organization, people, knowledge, technology, and learning. Most theories of a learning organization appear to focus on the values of continuous learning, knowledge creation and sharing, systemic thinking, a culture of learning, flexibility and experimentation, and finally a people-centered view (Gephart et al., 1996).

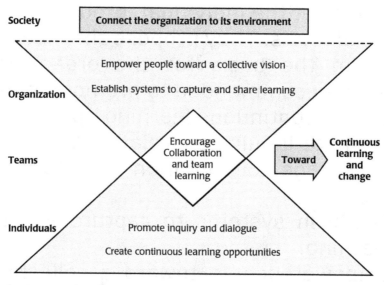

Figure 9.9 Watkins and Marsick's Learning Organization Action Imperatives Source: Watkins and Marsick, 1993, p.10. Used with permission.

Learning Organization and Performance Outcomes

Much of the learning organization literature is conceptual and descriptive. While there are numerous descriptive accounts and suggestions about why the process works, there are limited concrete descriptions about *how* it works to achieve performance improvement. Learning organizations perceive learning as the means to long-term performance improvement (Guns, 1996). However, there is little data supporting the claim that performance improvement is directly related to adoption of the learning organization's suggested behaviors or policies. One exception is recent evidence that firm performance is associated with those strategies (Ellinger, Ellinger, Yang, and Holton, 2000) and that learning organization strategies are related to perceived innovation (Holton and Kaiser, 2000).

Kaiser and Holton (1999) suggest that innovation provides the critical link between learning organization strategies and performance. The learning organization and the innovating organization are both dependent on the acquisition of information, the interpretation of information, the creation of meaning, and the creation of organizational knowledge. The stated end goal of both the learning system and the innovating system is improved organizational performance. The similarities between the two literatures are striking: the linking pin for both is knowledge; the goal in both is performance improvement.

A comparison of both literatures (Kaiser and Holton, 1999) suggests that the organizational strategies engaged to support the learning and innovating endeavors are similar and suggest parallel strategies. Innovation appears to be affected by culture, climate, leadership, management practices, dynamics of information processing, organizational

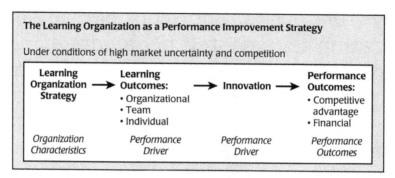

Figure 9.10 Learning Organization Performance Model
Source: Kaiser and Holton, 1999.

structure, organizational systems, and the environment.

Kaiser and Holton (1999) propose the conceptual model in Figure 9.10 based on their review of the learning organization and innovation literature and on the parallel sets of variables and theorized relationships to performance improvement. This model hypothesizes that learning organization strategies increase learning and innovation (performance drivers), which in turn improve performance outcomes.

This hypothesized model of the learning organization as a performance improvement strategy results in the following conclusions:

- Learning—in particular, improved learning at the team and organizational levels—leads to increased organization innovation.
- The adoption of learning organization strategies is appropriate for organizations in markets where innovation is a key performance driver.

- Innovation in expected to result in improved performance outcomes, leading to competitive advantage for the organization.

CONCLUSION

The good news for HRD is that learning has never been as highly regarded in organizations as it is today. HRD is entrusted with developing the knowledge and expertise in organizations to enable them to be competitive and effective in a challenging global economy. HRD must continue to research and define effective learning processes. While much is known about learning, much remains to be discovered about learning in the workplace.

REFLECTION QUESTIONS

1. Think about the six learning theories discussed in this chapter. Which is most attractive to you and why?
2. Think about the four learning models at the individual level presented in this chapter. Which is most attractive to you and why?
3. How can the andragogy in practice model be applied to enhance the learning that takes place through HRD?
4. Do you believe that organizations can learn? Or, are organizations merely the

sum of individual learning? Take a position and explain.

5. If learning is a defining construct for the HRD discipline and field of practice, how can learning be made more powerful in organizations?

PART FOUR

Developing Expertise through Training and Development

This section captures the essence of the training and development component of HRD as well as the nature of expertise. Illustrations of training and development practice that exist in host organizations are presented along with variations in core thinking, processes, interventions, and tools.

CHAPTERS
10   Overview of Training and Development
11   The Nature of Expertise
12   Training and Development Practices

CHAPTER 10

Overview of Training and Development

CHAPTER OUTLINE

- Organizational Learning
  Training Roles and Responsibilities
  Conclusion
  Reflection Questions

INTRODUCTION

Training and development constitutes the largest realm of HRD activity. *Training and development* (T&D) is defined as a process of systematically developing work-related knowledge and expertise for the purpose of improving performance. Training is not *education-light*— it is more than knowledge. People experiencing T&D should end up with new knowledge and be able to do things well after they complete a training program (Zemke, 1990). New knowledge by itself generally is not enough.

Within T&D, more effort is focused on *training* than on *development.* Also, *training* is more likely focused on new employees and those entering new job roles in contrast to long-term *development.* To be clear, the *development* portion of training and development is seen as "the planned growth and expansion of knowledge and expertise of people beyond the present job requirements" (Swanson, 2002, p.6). In the majority of instances, *development* opportunities are provided to people who have a strong potential to contribute to the organization. Indeed, development often comes under the banner of management development and leadership development. In every case, people at all levels in all organizations need to know how to do their work (expertise) and generally need help with their learning. Davis and Davis (1998) provide an explanation that helps to frame this chapter:

> Training is the process through which skills are developed, information is provided, and attributes are nurtured, in order to help individuals who work in organizations to become more effective and efficient in their work. Training helps the organization to fulfill its purposes and goals, while contributing to the overall development of workers. Training is necessary to help workers qualify for a job, do the job, or advance, but it is also essential for enhancing and transforming the job, so that the job actually adds value to the enterprise. Training facilitates learning, but learning is not only a formal activity designed and encouraged by specially prepared trainers to generate specific performance improvements. Learning is also a more universal activity, designed to increase capability and capacity and is facilitated formally and informally by many types of people at different levels of the organization. Training should always hold forth the promise of maximizing learning. (p.44)

T&D as defined here often appears under other names. Organizations will often title T&D functions to match their communication goals.

Beyond T&D, some carry broader names such as Executive Development or Corporate University. Others are very specific, such as Flight Safety School or Sales Training Department. Whatever the title, it is good to look beyond the name to see what actually is taking place.

VIEWS OF TRAINING AND DEVELOPMENT

Fortunately, no single view of T&D exists. There is so much variety in the nature of organizations, the people who work in them, the conditions surrounding the need for human expertise, and the process of learning that a single lens would be inadequate. Alternative views are useful. Three models that help in understanding T&D include the education-training dichotomy, the taxonomy for performance (Swanson, 2007), and the informal and incidental learning model (Marsick and Watkins, 1997).

Education-Training Dichotomy

The role of general knowledge versus specific job-related knowledge and expertise is an ongoing issue within organizational systems that sponsor T&D (Buckley and Caple, 2007). General knowledge that an individual has is marketable throughout the workplace. For example, the ability to read, write, and do math is not specific to any one organization. Thus, employers generally do not want to pay for programs that do not directly benefit them. Most organizations view high school programs and many college degree programs as providing general knowledge. They hire graduates of these programs understanding that they will need to learn the specific job knowledge and skills required by the employing organization.

Companies resist paying the bill for general knowledge learning programs, and governments resist paying the bill for organization-specific learning programs. Having said this, it is even messier in practice. Companies requiring entry-level workers in a tight labor market can find themselves providing basic education (reading, writing, etc.) as well as job-specific training. They will often appeal to government agencies for assistance in terms of funding for these efforts or for gaining access to public sector adult education resources to help them. Conversely, public sector economic development agencies often proactively fund job-specific T&D programs to maintain or to attract new business and industry in their geographic area.

The politics and pressures surrounding the development of human capital, within and between organizational systems, influences T&D decisions and programming. Questions of survival, competitive advantage, and the pursuit of defined strategies directly influence T&D decisions. For example, employing organizations may decide to support tuition reimbursement for employees who desire more general learning as long as they go about it on their own time. Tepid organizational support of tuition reimbursement programs may have as much to do with providing competitive employee benefits (holding on to good employees) as it does from expecting any direct return on their expenditures.

Taxonomy of Performance

One way of gaining perspective of the expertise required of organizations to function is through the taxonomy of performance (Swanson, 2007; see Figure 10.1). The taxonomy first illustrates the two large challenges that every organization faces that T&D is expected to address: *maintaining the system* and *changing the system.* Keeping any system up and running is hard work. Workplace systems erode in many ways. For example: information is less readily available, equipment wears out, customers demand more than the work processes can produce, and expert workers leave their employment for a variety of reasons.

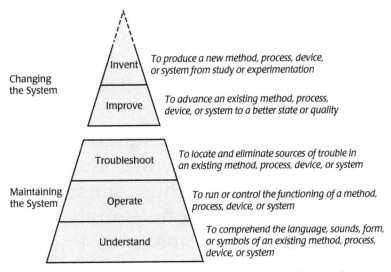

Figure 10.1 Swanson's Taxonomy of Performance
Source: Swanson, 2007, p.24.

Even though a work system is mature and reasonably predictable, conditions can change and things can go wrong. A variety of forces cause systems to erode. Thus, managers and workers have the continuing pressure of "maintaining" their work systems. When there is inadequate expertise, training can be applied. Furthermore, the "Maintaining the System" subcategories of understanding, operation, and troubleshooting of work systems allow for clearer specification of the performance required and what it takes to achieve it. You could not expect a person trained only to "understand" the work system to be able to go into the workplace with the expertise required to "operate" and "troubleshoot" in that system. A fundamental error in HRD practice would be to provide training to employees at one lower level and expect them to demonstrate expertise at a higher level.

It is generally assumed, either through on-the-job experience or through formal training, that people who have designed and worked successfully in a system are subject-matter experts on that system. Thus, these people are key resources to T&D professionals wanting to analyze what a person needs to know and be able to do to maintain the system. In addition, supporting documentation about the existing system is usually available that can also be used to put together sound training.

In contrast to the challenge of "maintaining systems," the challenge of "changing systems" is presented by the taxonomy of performance. Changing the system can mean either *improving* it or *inventing* a whole new system. Changing the system strikes another chord. What a person needs to know and be able to do in order to change a system is to engage in activity that is primarily outside the maintaining realm. A person needs expertise in problem identification and problem-solving methods. For example, training in human-factors design, process redesign, and statistical process control are specific strategies for *improving the system* that must be learned in order to apply them to an existing work system. A person can be an expert in this *improvement* work without being an expert in the system he or she wishes to improve. This individual typically partners with people having system-specific expertise. In other situations, organizations train people who are experts in existing systems on tools for *improving the system* with the expectation that they can apply those tools to change the very system in which they work. Thus, they are expecting the same people to be able to *maintain* and *improve* systems. Leading teams in carrying out improvement efforts falls in the realm of organization development, the natural partner of T&D.

The *invention* level of "changing the system" has little regard for the existing system. Totally new ways of thinking and doing work are entertained. One mea-sure of success is that the existing system goes away as a result of being replaced by the new system and that the next challenge is to maintain the new system. This cycle of renewal is fed by HRD interventions and ends up requiring still more HRD interventions. Two examples include T&D experiences in scenario planning (see Chermack and Burt, 2008) and antecedents to creativity (Robinson and Stern, 1997). It is part of the dynamic of the HRD profession that both these demands of *maintaining* the system and *changing* the system go on—go on simultaneously in organizations and go on simultaneously within individual contributors.

Experts on changing the system (see Brache, 2002; Deming, 1986; Rummler and Brache, 1995) provide us fair warning about the realms of maintaining the system and changing the system in organizations. An organization in crisis first needs to focus itself on the core issue of *maintaining the system* before it goes about *improving the system.* While improving the system may be more appealing, it would be analogous to rearranging the chairs on the deck of the *Titanic.* More than once we have started with a "changing the system" project only to discover that there was a frantic need to develop core expertise in order to get the system functioning at an acceptable level (maintain)—to the point that *changes to the system* could then be entertained.

The learning and performance paradigms discussed in chapters 7 and 8 play an important role in meeting the challenges posed by the taxonomy of performance. With learning viewed as a driver of performance, it is easy to make a short-term connection between learning and performance when there are system maintenance issues. In comparison, it is not as easy to make the long-term learning-to-performance   connection when

T&D is involved in system change issues. The extended time required to change a work system makes it more difficult to claim system performance gains and suggests that intermediate evidence of learning and new work behaviors are legitimate short-term goals until the change takes full effect.

The traditional lines drawn between those people working in a system who are responsible for maintaining it and those responsible for changing the system have been blurred. Some of the traditional thoughts about hourly workers getting short-term training versus salaried workers getting longer-term development experiences have also been blurred. Strategies must be thought through for each setting based on accurate analysis of the expertise required to function in specific jobs.

Informal and Incidental Learning

While it has been known all along, T&D professionals have only recently written formally about the unstructured dimensions of workplace learning. Most T&D professionals had been advocating their structured training view of the world only and not acknowledging the unstructured or trial-and-error role of learning in the organization. The classic rival

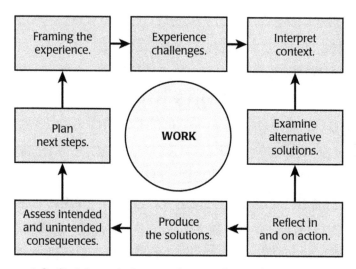

Figure 10.2 Marsick and Watkins's Informal and Incidental Learning Model Source: Marsick and Watkins, 1997, p.299. Used with permission.

to structured T&D has been unstructured T&D, which has not been viewed formally. Swanson and Sawzin (1976) define each, noting that the difference was whether or not there was a plan for learning coming from the organization—structured or unstructured training. Planning was at the heart of the argument. Jacobs is credited with consciously differentiating on-the-job training as being either structured or unstructured (see Jacobs and McGriffen,1987). The conscious acknowledgment and study of informal and incidental workplace learning has continued to be of interest in recent years. These studies are based on the reality that the majority of what people actually learn related to their work performance is not planned in the way T&D professionals have traditionally thought about work-related learning.

Marsick and Watkins (1997) have provided an "informal and incidental learning model" to understand this phenomenon (see Figure 10.2). Their model is based on a core premise that the behavior of individuals is a function of their interaction with their environment (Lewin, 1951). Work and the workplace context are at the core of informal and incidental workplace learning (Nijhof and Nieuwenhuis, 2008). One could argue that the moment an organization begins planning and taking actions to encourage informal and incidental learning, the process is no longer informal or incidental. Such an argument would shortchange the confidence in the capability and integrity of workers as learners that the informal and incidental learning perspective offers. They highlight power of the context—the organization and the work—both to ignite the learning process and to serve as the primary learning aid. The work provides the challenge to learn, to define problems, to solve problems, and there is usually not time to reflect. In this vein, Nijhof (2006) cautions the profession as to the limitations of the learning potential of work settings that demand ongoing performance.

As a middle ground, it is no wonder that organizational leaders are interested in ideas that embrace *action learning* and *team problem solving*. *Action learning* results in learning and possible solutions to real contextual problems. *Team problem solving* results in solving a specific organization-specific problem with learning as a vehicle or side benefit. Both action learning and team problem solving rely on the power of work and context in their structured T&D experience.

KEY TRAINING AND DEVELOPMENTTERMS AND STRATEGIES

Key training and development terms and concepts provide a basis of understanding the profession. *Expertise,* a human state, is acquired through a combination of knowledge and experience. It enables individuals to consistently achieve performance outcomes that meet or exceed the performance requirements (see chapter 11 for a full discussion of expertise). *Training* is the process of developing knowledge and expertise in people. Development is the planned growth and expansion of the knowledge and expertise of people beyond the present job requirements. This is accomplished through systematic training, learning experiences, work assignments, and assessment efforts.

T&D interventions vary in the amount of their structure. It is typical for T&D programs focused on life and death matters—such as medicine, flight operation, and nuclear power plant operation—to be highly structured. This is especially true in managing the experiential portion of the T&D program and verifying attainment of the required expertise.

T&D can take place on the job or off the job. On-the-job programs take advantage of the resources of the workplace and actual conditions in which the person will be expected to perform. Off-the-job offerings allow learners to disconnect from the pressures of the workplace so in order to entertain new information and new ways of doing things better.

Individual T&D program titles are generally derived from a job title, job task, work concept, work system, work process, or hardware/software. T&D programs can be custom produced or purchased off the shelf. Custom-produced programs are designed to match the performance, learning, and expertise requirements of a specific group of people in a specific organization. Off-the-shelf programs are generic, generally cost much less, and are less likely to address the specific learning or performance needs. Organizations sometimes buy off-the-shelf programs from external providers and then customize portions of the program to establish a better fit.

Subject Matter Focus of T&D

Technical T&D programs are generally thought of as people – thing, people – procedure, or people – process focused. They are often classified and administered under varying banners within the same organization. For example, a large corporation with multiple divisions producing unique products or services can have division-level skill and technical training functions that are focused on the substance of the division-level technology.

In contrast, management and leadership T&D is almost always held constant across an organization. These programs focus on people – people and people – idea expertise that mirrors organizational culture and strategy that transcend specific divisions. Manager and supervisor tasks T&D primarily focuses on getting the work done—maintaining the system—with a lesser concern for improving and changing the system. In comparison, leadership tasks are more focused on concerns about the future state of the system, while not losing sight of the present.

Motivational T&D is a smaller segment of programming that focuses on attitudinal content in the form of values and beliefs. It is generally pursued through intense structured experiences. Emotional presentations by role model facilitators and placing people in unfamiliar settings, such as wilderness or survival situations (that are actually quite safe) are two familiar strategies. Motivational T&D programs are often used to create readiness for change, followed by either technical or management programs aimed at developing the expertise required to carry out the change.

Career T&D is an extended view of the learning and expertise development journey. A simple example would be to plan and construct a purposeful pattern of T&D experiences with an eye toward long-term development of one's career.

A significant shift took place in the 1980s. Firms were sponsoring career development programs that groomed people to move up in their stable organizational system. Once the realization hit that firms were changing at such a rapid rate, organizations cut back on their career development programs, and the locus of control for career development moved from the firm to the individual. Thus, when a person is asked today, "Who is in charge of your career development?" the answer is most likely—"I am." The void that presently exists results from individuals inadequately prepared to manage their own career development working in organizations that are tenuous about their own futures.

THE GENERAL TRAINING AND DEVELOPMENT PROCESS

We have defined HRD as essentially a problem-defining and problem-solving method. For those who react negatively to the notion of problems, we suggest they use a positive word of their choice (e.g., *opportunity, improvement,* etc). We also characterize T&D as a five-phase process. We use variations in the wording for the HRD, T&D, and OD processes to capture the common thread and varying elements. Here are all three variations:

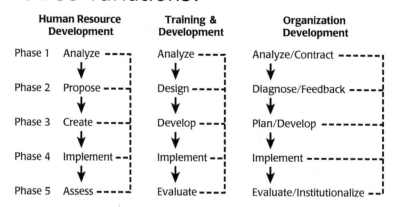

	Human Resource Development	Training & Development	Organization Development
Phase 1	Analyze	Analyze	Analyze/Contract
Phase 2	Propose	Design	Diagnose/Feedback
Phase 3	Create	Develop	Plan/Develop
Phase 4	Implement	Implement	Implement
Phase 5	Assess	Evaluate	Evaluate/Institutionalize

T&D professionals within HRD almost universally talk about their work in terms of the ADDIE process (analyze, design, develop, implement, and evaluate). It is the most widely used methodology for developing systematic training (Allen, 2006). The origins of the ADDIE process are rooted in the four-step Training Method and the Instructional Systems Development model. The WWI and WWII Training Within Industry Project (Dooley, 1945) laid out the Four-Step Training Method:

1. Prepare the learner
2. Present instruction
3. Try out performance
4. Follow up

The instructional systems development (ISD) model was developed by the United States military in 1969 (United States, 1969; Campbell, 1984). Many contemporary training models are rooted in these early systematic training efforts.

INSTRUCTIONAL SYSTEMS DEVELOPMENT (ISD)

The instructional system development (ISD) model of procedures was developed by the U.S. military for the purpose of going about training in a systematic and effective manner in the context of an enormous military training enterprise. Furthermore, it was meant to provide a common language and process that transcended the various branches of the military service.

The ISD model is illustrated in Figure 10.3. The first level of the graphic shows the five phases of the training process in its original form as analysis, design, develop, implement and control. The *control* phase was later changed to *evaluation* in most adaptations of the original work. The second tier of the graphic specifies the numerous steps within the phases.

In that the original ISD was designed for the military, it is best suited to the following conditions:

- Large numbers of learners must be trained.
- A long lifetime is expected for the program.
- Standard training requirements must be maintained.
- High mastery levels are required because of criticality, such as safety or high cost of errors.
- Economic value is placed on learner's time.
- Training is valued in the organizational culture (Gagne and Medsker, 1996).

The original IDS model began with the assumption that training is needed. Thus, the beginning point of the analysis phase was to analyze the job and its tasks. The ending points were to assess trainee behaviors and to revise programs as needed. The sheer size of the military and the degree of standardization in personnel and equipment helped shape the original ISD model with features that were incompatible with most business and industry training requirements.

Allen (2006) offers the following reflections on the ADDIE training model: "The ADDIE process is an adaptation of the systems engineering process to problems of workplace training and instruction. The process assumes that alternative solutions to instructional problems will be more or less cost efficient depending on the instructional need and environmental constraints, and that a systems approach intelligently choosing among alternative solutions will produce the most effective results" (p.431).

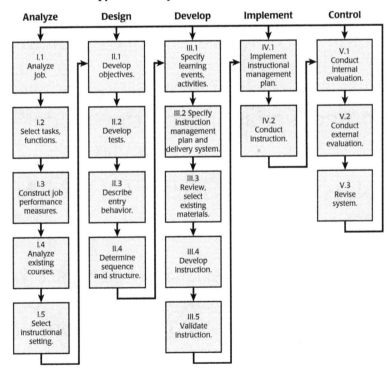

Figure 10.3 The Model of Interservice Procedures for Instructional Systems Development (ISD)

"In practice beyond the military context, the ADDIE process was found to be too rigid and did not account for the different situations and applications for which it had to be used. To account for the situational differences, the external control of the system (i.e., the boxes and arrows) gave way to phases of ADDIE that could be manipulated in any order by the training professional. This third generation model assumed that ADDIE was an interactive process that could be entered at any point depending on the current situation. Although behavioral learning theory was still dominant, cognitive theory was beginning to have an impact, such as in the use of simulations for acquisition of cognitive expertise in decision-making" (Allen, 2006, p.431). The estimates on the evolution of ADDIE suggest that over one hundred variations of the model are in existence.

TRAINING FOR PERFORMANCE SYSTEM

The training for performance system (TPS) is a process for developing human expertise for the purpose of improving organization, process, and individual performance. The TPS was originally developed in 1978 by Richard A. Swanson for a major United States manufacturing firm.

The firm wanted a comprehensive training process that would embrace all training at all levels (corporate, division, and plant; management, technical, and motivational), thus allowing for a common systematic approach and common language for personnel training throughout the company. The system was originally called the "training technology system" and can be viewed as a major adaptation of the earlier ADDIE model more appropriate for dynamic organizations. The name was changed to reflect the true purpose of the training system better and eliminate the misinterpretations that were given to the word *technology* (Swanson, 1980).

When the TPS was developed in the late 1970s, the sponsoring firm raised several issues about the existing state of the training profession. First, there was a concern about the inadequacy of the dominant ISD model to connect up with core business performance requirements at the analysis phase. Second, the firm pointed out the inadequacy of the tools and processes being used in management training and development in getting at the substance of knowledge work. Third, it was similarly concerned about the inadequacy of the tools and processes being used in technical T&D in getting to the heart of systems/process work. And fourth, there was a concern about the inadequacy of the dominant instructional systems development (ISD) model to connect up with core business performance outcomes at the evaluation phase. The TPS embraces the titles of the traditional five phases of training presented in most models (Swanson, 1996; see richardswanson.com): Analyze, design, develop, implement, and evaluate; the model is generally referred to as the "ADDIE" model as well as "TPS." In addition, the critical overarching task of "leading the training and development process" is added to the ADDIE process.

TPS Model

The TPS model is illustrated in two forms in Figures 10.4 and 10.5. Figure 10.4 shows the five phases of the training process being integrated and supported through leadership. The second graphic of the TPS model, Figure 10.5, specifies the major steps within the phases and the leadership component.

It is important to note that the systematic process of the TPS has integrity and can be maintained even in the simplest of situations (severe time and budget constraints) or can be disregarded in the most luxurious situations (generous time and budget allocations). Professional expertise—training process knowledge and experience—is what is necessary to maintain training integrity.

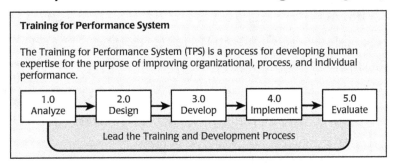

Figure 10.4 Training for Performance System Source: Swanson, 2002.

Steps within the Process Phases of the Training for Performance System

1.0 Analyze	2.0 Design	3.0 Develop	4.0 Implement	5.0 Evaluate
1.1 Diagnose Performance and Propose Intervention	2.1 Design Training Program	3.1 Develop Training Materials	4.1 Manage Training Program	5.1 Evaluate Training Effective-ness
1.2 Document Expertise	2.2 Design and Plan Lessons	3.2 Pilot-test Training Program	4.2 Deliver Training	5.2 Report Training Effective-ness

Lead the Training and Development Process:
• Champion T&D Mission/Goals • Manage the Process • Improve the Process

Figure 10.5 Steps within the Process Phases of the Training for Performance

Phases of the TPS

The TPS is a process for developing human expertise for the purpose of improving organization, process, and individual performance. A closer look at its five phases and the overarching concern for leading the process:

Phase 1: Analyze

Diagnose the performance requirements of the organization that can be improved through training, and document the expertise required to perform in the workplace. The integrity of the TPS is in its connection to important performance goals and in answering one or more of the following questions positively after the program: (1) Did the organization perform better? (2) Did the work process perform better? (3) Did the individuals (group) perform better?

The front-end organizational diagnosis is essential in clarifying the goal and in determining the performance variables that work together to achieve the goal. It requires the analyst to step back from T&D and to think more holistically about performance. This diagnosis culminates with a performance improvement proposal having the likely need of human expertise being a part of the improvement effort. The overall process is portrayed in Figure 10.6.

Given the need for human expertise, the documentation of what a person needs to know and be able to do (expertise) is the second part of the analysis phase. The TPS addresses job and task analysis with special tools for documenting procedural, system, and knowledge work. Task analysis invariably requires close careful study and generally spending time with a subject matter expert in his or her work setting. The process is portrayed in Figure 10.7.

Phase 2: Design

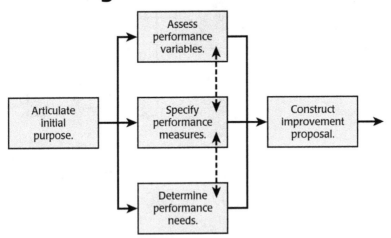

Figure 10.6 Diagnosing Performance Source: Swanson, 2007, p.58.

Create and/or acquire general and specific strategies for people to develop workplace expertise. T&D design is at the program and lesson/session levels. At the program design level, the overall design strategy must be economically, systemically, and psychologically sound. Critical information that will influence the design is gathered. The "Training Strategy Model" depicted in Figure 10.8 allows the program designer to consider the critical interaction between the stability of the content, the number of trainees, and the primary method used to develop the required knowledge and expertise.

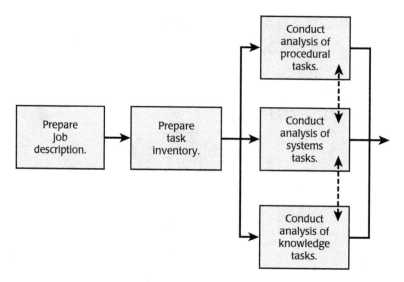

Figure 10.7 Documenting Expertise Source: Swanson, 2007, p.130.

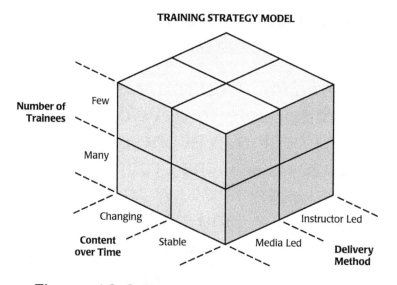

Figure 10.8 Training Strategy Model

General Whole-Part-Whole Model

Whole-Part
1.   •   Whole
2.   • Part
3.   •   Whole

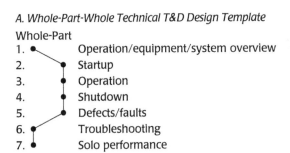

A. Whole-Part-Whole Technical T&D Design Template

Whole-Part
1. Operation/equipment/system overview
2. Startup
3. Operation
4. Shutdown
5. Defects/faults
6. Troubleshooting
7. Solo performance

In thinking about delivery methods one can plan using about the continuum of training being "Media-led" through "Instructor-led." All would likely use media; the dividing point is when the locus of delivery control is in the instructor or within the media itself.

Media-led includes such alternatives as interactive video, computer-based training/performance support programmed instruction (video/audio/paper), and programmed instruction/job aid (paper). In contrast, instructor-led involves off-site classrooms, on-site classrooms, structured on-the-job, and learning team settings.

T&D Design Templates The "Whole-Part-Whole Learning Model" (Swanson and Law, 1993) serves as the basis for T&D design templates. The basic human psychological need for the "whole" (as explained by Gestalt psychology) and the need for the "parts" (as explained by behavioral psychology) are utilized to structure whole-part-whole (W-P-W) learning templates. The W-P-W model can be applied at

484

both the program design and individual lesson/session design levels.

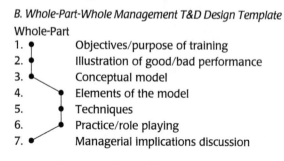

B. Whole-Part-Whole Management T&D Design Template
Whole-Part
1. Objectives/purpose of training
2. Illustration of good/bad performance
3. Conceptual model
4. Elements of the model
5. Techniques
6. Practice/role playing
7. Managerial implications discussion

C. Whole-Part-Whole Motivational T&D Design Template
Whole-Part
1. Acceptance of group/individuals
2. Problem/opportunity
3. Fear/greed illustrations (with role models)
4. The solution
5. Solicit commitment to solution
6. Vision success

Lesson/Session Plan Design The lesson/session plan is the final and official document in the design phase. It brings together the original performance requirement, the documentation of expertise, and the resulting training objectives into the "artful" articulation of content and method. The lesson/session plan is not a private document. It is the property of the sponsoring organization, and it should be detailed to the point that another knowledgeable trainer could take the lesson/session plan and the supporting materials and teach essentially the same content via the same method in the same period of time.

Phase 3: Develop

Develop and/or acquire participant and instructor training materials needed to execute the training design. There is an almost unlimited range of instructor- and media-based T&D materials and media options available to the T&D profession.

The development of training materials is a paradox. While the range of creative options is enormous, most training programs actually utilize planned materials such as those portrayed in level 2 of the following five-level portrayal:

Level 1: No planned instructor materials; no planned participant materials.

Level 2: Projected slides; paper copies of the transparencies or slides for the participants.

Level 3: Projected slides; trainee's print materials in the form of a structured trainee notebook (including paper copies of the transparencies or slides for the participants).

Level 4: Projected slides; trainees print materials in the form of a structured trainee notebook (paper copies of the transparencies or slides for the participants included); workplace objects and artifacts from the tasks to be learned; dynamic or interactive support materials such as video, interactive video, in-basket case, and simulation.

Level 5: Materials are designed to the level that they can mediate the development of knowledge and expertise *without* the need of a trainer.

There are practical reasons for producing materials at level 2. It is easy to visualize a situation in which only one to two trainees are participating and the content is unstable. In such an instance, structured on-the-job training would likely be the best method utilizing inexpensive level 2 training materials (see Sisson, 2001). In a similar vein, practical considerations are the primary basis for choosing any of the levels.

Once materials are developed, the critical issue emerges of testing T&D programs prior to program implementation. Organizations can approach pilot-testing of training programs in five ways:

1. Conduct a full pilot test of the program with a representative sample of participants.
2. Conduct a full pilot test of the program with a group of available participants.
3. Utilize the first offering of the program as the pilot test, being sure to inform the participants of this fact and gain their support in providing improvement information.

4. Conduct a "walk-through" of the entire program with a selected group of professional colleagues and potential recipients.
5. Presenter of the program conducts a dry run by him-or herself.

Most organizations rely on 5, 4, *and* 3 to meet the pilot test requirements. For programs with limited offerings, options 4 and 5 are used.

Phase 4: Implement

Manage individual training programs and their delivery to participants. The issues around managing and delivering T&D to participants suggests that the strategies for both have been thought through and planned into program materials.

Managing individual T&D programs should not be confused with leading or managing a T&D department. The focus here is on managing individual programs that will most likely be offered on numerous occasions by a variety of presenters. Managing T&D programs should be thought of as those activities (things, conditions, and decisions) necessary to implement a particular training program. They can also be thought of as generally taking place before, during, or after the training event with time specifications recorded in weeks (or days) for the "before" and "after" time periods and hours (or minutes) on the lesson plans for the "during" period of the training event.

Either a simple paper-or computer-based project management system is typically used. It requires specification of the activity, activity details, initial and completion dates, and the responsible party for each. These data can be matrixed into a management chart or placed in a simple computer database for assignments and follow-ups.

Delivery of T&D to participants is the pressure point in the T&D process. Presenters want to succeed, and participants want high-quality interaction. Critics of T&D bemoan the fact that this often causes presenters to digress to gimmicks and entertainment instead of facing and managing delivery problems. One study identified the following twelve most common delivery problems of beginning trainers and the general tactics used by expert trainers in addressing those problems (Swanson and Falkman, 1997):

Delivery Problems and Expert solutions (in brackets)
1. Fear *(Be well prepared; Use ice breakers; Acknowledge fear).*
2. Credibility *(Don't apologize; Have an attitude of an expert; Share personal background).*
3. Personal experiences *(Report personal experiences; Report experiences of others; Use analogies, movies, famous people).*

4. Difficult learners *(Confront problem behavior; Circumvent dominating behavior; Use small groups for timid behavior)*.

5. Participation *(Ask open-ended questions; Plan small group activities; Invite participation)*.

6. Timing *(Plan well; Practice, practice, practice)*.

7. Adjust instruction *(Know group needs; Request feedback; Redesign during breaks)*.

8. Questions *(Answering: Anticipate questions; Paraphrase learners' questions; "I don't know" is OK). (Asking: Ask concise questions; Defer to participants)*.

9. Feedback *(Solicit informal feedback; Do summative evaluations)*.

10. Media, materials, facilities *(Media: Know equipment; Have back-ups; Enlist assistance). (Material: Be prepared) (Facilities: Visit facility beforehand; Arrive early)*.

11. Openings and closings *(Openings: Develop an "Openings" file; Memorize; Relax trainees; Clarify expectations). (Closings: Summarize concisely; Thank participants)*.

12. Dependence on notes *(Notes are necessary; Use cards; Use visuals; Practice)*.

Phase 5: Evaluate

Determine and report training and development effectiveness in terms of performance, learning, and satisfaction. The TPS draws upon a results assessment system (Swanson and Holton, 1999) that is conceptually connected to the first phase—analysis. In effect, it is first and foremost a checkup on those three goal-focused questions from the analysis phase: (1) Does the organization perform better? (2) Does the work process perform better? (3) Do the individuals (group) perform better? With learning being an important performance variable, assessing learning in terms of knowledge and expertise is seen as an essential intermediate goal. To a lesser extent, the perception of T&D participants and program stakeholders is viewed as important.

Based on an analysis of actual T&D practices, traditionally there have been three domains of expected outcomes: performance (individual to organizational), learning (knowledge to expertise), and perception (participant and stakeholder). To focus on a single realm changes the purpose, strategy, and techniques of an intervention. If an intervention is expected to result in highly satisfied participant-learners, T&D professionals will engage in very different activities than if the expected outcome were to increase organizational performance. With organizational performance as the desired outcome, T&D professionals will spend time with managers, decision makers, and subject-matter experts close to the performance setting throughout the T&D process. If the outcome is satisfied learner-participants, T&D people will likely spend time asking potential participants what kind of T&D experience they like, will focus on "fun-filled" group processes, and will have facilities with pleasing amenities.

It is not always rational to think that every T&D program will promise and assess performance, learning, and perception outcomes. Furthermore, it is irrational to think that a singular focus on one domain (performance, learning, or perception) will result in gains in the others. For example:

- An overly demanding T&D program could leave participants less than thrilled with their experience.
- Participants may gain new knowledge and expertise that cannot be used in their work setting.
- Participants can thoroughly enjoy a T&D program but actually learn little or nothing.

Being clear about the expected outcomes from T&D is essential for good practice. As the saying goes, "If you do not know where you are going, you will likely end up someplace else" (Mager, 1966).

Leading the Training and Development Process

Lead and maintain the integrity of the training and development process. The leadership task is the most important task within the T&D effort. The training process requires strong individuals to champion the mission, goals, process, and specific efforts of training in context of the organization. To do this, the champion must clearly articulate to all parties the outputs of training and their connection to the organization, the process by which the work is done, and the roles and responsibilities of the training stakeholders.

Outputs of Training

The output of the TPS is human expertise for the purpose of improving performance. Such a decision radically affects the training process and the training stakeholders. The TPS acknowledges that training by itself can develop expertise and that workplace performance is beyond the training experience alone. Thus:

- Obtaining workplace performance almost always requires line manager actions as well as training.
- Managers must be fully responsible partners in performance improvement interventions that rely on training.

Other common, *and less effective,* outputs of training have been

- clock hours of training or the number of people trained;
- meeting compliance requirements from external or internal source of authority;
- management and/or participant satisfaction apart from measures of knowledge, expertise, and performance;
- knowledge gains that are marginally connected to performance requirements; and
- expertise gains that are marginally connected to performance requirements.

Process of Training

Training leaders must have expertise in a defined training process. The TPS is one such process. Training leaders must advocate for the training process based on findings from research and experience.

Training Stakeholders

Training Stakeholders Expertise among the stakeholders is required to carry out the defined training process. Leaders select or develop the professional training expertise required by the defined training process. Roles and responsibilities of those working in the process—the stakeholders—must also be defined and managed (see the next section).

INDIVIDUAL-FOCUSED TRAINING AND DEVELOPMENT

Most traditional structured classroom T&D is organized for groups of 12–24. In the same organizations, workplaces are generally filled with ongoing delivery of one-on-one training involving a trainer and a trainee. Two well-documented systems provide strategies for this work that typically is provided just in time (at the time the worker needs the knowledge and expertise) and is narrow in scope (task focused). The first strategy, *Hands-On Training* (Sisson, 2001) involves using fellow workers to be trainers of realms in which they are subject-matter experts. The second is *Structured On-the-Job Training* (Jacobs, 2003) and involves a professional trainer engaging and preparing subject-matter experts to deliver task level training one-on-one in the workplace.

Employee to Employee T&D

Sisson (2001) describes Hands-on Training (HOT) as a way of organizational life and not really a training program in the traditional sense. He sees it as a tool that can become part of the natural work setting, yet still dependent on following a step-by-step system, trainees learning the right way of doing the job, and an instructor competent in using HOT.

Sisson presents HOT as including six steps, under the acronym POPPER, to be followed by the trainer/worker/subject-matter expert:

1. Prepare *for training.*
2. Open *the session.*
3. Present *the subject.*
4. Practice *the skills*
5. Evaluate *the performance*
6. Review *the subject*

Sisson's one-hundred-page book describing HOT POPPER can be put directly into the hands of workers taking on the role of training others efficiently and effectively in tasks they have mastered. The core arguments supporting HOT POPPER include it having (1) low costs and high returns, (2) simplicity, and (3) the belief that it adds basic order to something that is going to happen anyway—learning from each other in the workplace.

Trainer to Employee TD

Jacobs (2003) defines structured on-the-job training (S-OJT) as "The planned process of developing competencies on units of work by having an experienced employee train a novice employee at the work setting or a location that closely resembles the work setting" (p.29). He estimates that 90 percent of job-specific

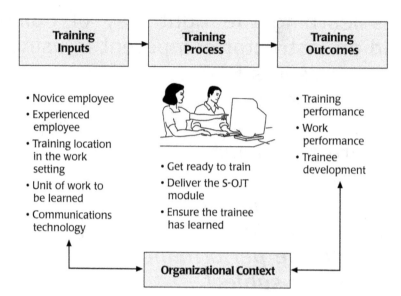

Figure 10.9 The Structured On-the-Job Training System
Source: Jacobs, 2003, p.31.

knowledge is learned on the job (trial and error), and that more money is spent indirectly by organizations on OJT than is spent directly on structured training that takes place off the job. Furthermore, Jacobs (2003) estimates that the costs on unstructured OJT job training (trial and error) consumes up to one third of the salary paid to an employee in the first year.

The S-OJT system is illustrated in Figure 10.9. The four major elements include: Training Inputs, Training Process, Training Outputs, and Organizational Context.

S-OJT relies on T&D professionals to oversee and carry out programs. Subject-matter experts are called upon as team members for content input, development, and delivery while under the direction of a T&D specialist. This level of professional oversight distinguishes it from the HOT POPPER methodology that can be placed totally in the hands of the subject-matter expert.

TEAM/GROUP-FOCUSED T&D

Team/group-focused T&D is a relatively new phenomenon compared to groups of individuals experiencing a T&D program together. Various titles are used—such as action learning, organizational learning, and the learning organization—and they are rooted in two thought streams. One has to do with the power of group learning, versus individual learning and the second is related to the anticipated gains from creating an organizational culture that values and captures the fruits of continuous learning. These T&D options are typically pursued outside the demand for immediate performance results and in anticipation of future demands. Two well-documented strategies include action learning (Yorks, 2005) and the learning organization (Marquardt, 2002).

Action Learning

Yorks (2005) defines action learning as "an approach to working with, and developing people, on an actual project or problem as a way to learn. Participants work in small groups

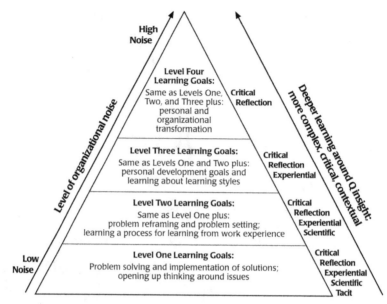

Figure 10.10 Work-based Learning Pyramid Source: Yorks, 2005, p.189.

to take action to solve their problem and to learn from that action. Often a learning coach works with the group in order to help members learn how to balance their work with the learning from that work" (p.185).

Yorks provides a *Work-based Learning Pyramid* (see Figure 10.10) to help practition-ers make one of four program design choices based on the outcomes desired.

The pyramid illustrates learning experiences that increase in depth and complexity as action learning moves up from its base from level one to level four. The interplay with the intensity of the dynamics with the host organization also increases as the levels increase. He calls this factor organizational noise.

Yorks (2005) goes on to say that design decisions are important and that they must be in alignment with the purpose of the program, the adequacy of the support for the learning goals, and organizational culture readiness to support the action learning program.

Organizational Learning

Marquardt (2002) bluntly states that "organizations must learn faster and adapt faster to changes in the environment or they will simply not survive. As in any transitional period, the dominant but dying species (nonlearning organizations) and the emerging, more adaptive species (learning organizations) presently exist side by side. Within the next ten years, I predict that only learning organizations will be left" (pp.xi-xii). Marquardt goes on to list sixteen general steps in building a learning organization and the extensive cultural shift it demands:

1. Commit to becoming a learning organization
2. Form a powerful coalition for change.
3. Connect learning with business operations.
4. Access the organization's capabilities on each subsystem of the Systems Learning Organization model.
5. Communicate the vision of a learning organization.

6. Recognize the importance of systems thinking and action.
7. Leaders demonstrate and model commitment to learning.
8. Transform the organizational culture to one of continuous learning and improvement.
9. Establish corporate-wide strategies for learning.
10. Reduce bureaucracy and streamline the structure.
11. Extend learning to the entire business chain.
12. Capture learning and release knowledge.
13. Acquire and apply best technology to the best learning.
14. Create short-term wins.
15. Measure learning and demonstrate learning successes.
16. Adapt, improve, and learn continuously (p.211).

TRAINING ROLES AND RESPONSIBILITIES

T&D leaders manage and improve the training process. Having a defined process, such as the Training for Performance System (TPS), is a critical first step. Having people with adequate expertise to function in their assigned training process roles is another critical component. Even with these conditions in place, the training process will not necessarily work or work smoothly, let alone improve.

It is therefore important to identify the specific stakeholder roles in the training process, their responsibilities, and the process quality standards. The TPS phases and steps constitute the process. The roles, responsibilities, and process quality standard decisions could vary with specific organizations, but generally they would include the following:

Roles:

Upper management; Line manager; T&D manager; Program leader; Program evaluator; T&D specialist; Subject-matter expert; Support staff; External consultant; and External provider.

Responsibilities:

Leads program; manages program; produces outputs per program, phase, and/or step; determines whether phase/step level outputs meet quality standard; provides information about program, phase, and/or step; and gets information about program, phase, and/or step.

T&D Process Quality Standards Categories (applied to each TPS phase or step outputs):

Quality features; timeliness; and quantity.

Best decisions as to the specifics on how the three sets of data above interact should be made, recorded, and communicated as a means of further defining the training process for the purpose of ensuring the highest quality of training. These training roles, responsibilities, and quality standards decisions would approximate (or actually become) training policy. Once they are stabilized and adhered to, improvements to the training process can be based on solid data and experience.

CONCLUSION

Training and development (T&D) is a process that has the potential of developing human expertise required to maintain and change organizations. As such, T&D can be strategically aligned to its host organization system strategy and performance goals. T&D also has the potential of developing the expertise required to create new strategic directions for the host organizational system.

REFLECTION QUESTIONS

1. How would you define T&D and describe its relationship to HRD?
2. What is the role of informal and incidental learning in T&D?
3. What are the unique aspects of the training and development component of HRD?
4. What is the purpose of each of the five phases of T&D and the relationship between the phases?
5. How does T&D help with organizational challenges of managing the system and changing the system?

CHAPTER 11

The Nature of Expertise

CHAPTER OUTLINE

Introduction

Knowledge versus Expertise

- Insights from Military Training Research and Practice
- Documenting Workplace Expertise
- Learning Strategies for Realms of Expertise
- Expertise and Expert Performance

Operational Definitions of Expertise and Competence

Contributed by Richard W. Herling

- The Need for an Operational Understanding of
  Expertise
- Theoretical Perspectives on Expertise
- Forming an Operational Definition of Expertise
- Implications of Expertise for HRD

Conclusion

Reflection Questions

INTRODUCTION

The concept of expertise lies at the core of human resource development (HRD). The definition of HRD posited by this book describes it as a process of developing and unleashing expertise for the purpose of improving performance, with training and development (T&D) on the developing side and organization development (OD) on the unleashing side. "Workplace expertise is the fuel of an organization. Expertise can be thought of as the level at which a person is able to perform within a specialized realm of activity" (Swanson, 2007, p.125).

Expertise is more than just knowing. Pfeffer and Sutton (2000) make the extended and documented case that "knowing what to do is not enough" (p.1). They go on to report: "One of the main reasons that knowledge management efforts are often divorced from day-to-day activities is that managers, consulting firms, and information technologists who design and build systems for collecting, storing, and retrieving knowledge have limited, often inaccurate, views of how people actually use knowledge in their jobs" (Pfeffer and Sutton, 2000, p.18). Expertise, not just knowledge, addresses the serious issue of the knowing-doing gap. Groopman's book on *How Doctors*

Think magnifies the issue when he cites studies of doctors' diagnoses being wrong 15–20 percent of the time (2000, p.24). These are errors at the diagnosis stage, with treatment errors posing additional risks.

The success of an HRD intervention, regardless of the philosophy on which it is based—learning or performance—is achieved through the development and utilization of an organization's human resources. The development of human resources for the purpose of improving performance requires an ability to understand expertise. While expertise is a complex human state, a basic grasp of the characteristics of expertise makes it possible to formulate an operational definition of expertise and its prerequisites that are applicable to HRD. A solid understanding of the nature of expertise is required of HRD professionals that desire to develop varying levels of expertise in others.

KNOWLEDGE VERSUS EXPERTISE

There are important considerations related to HRD programs sponsored by organizations with particular goals in mind. These considerations specifically influence the T&D role as it relates to developing expertise and its prerequisite knowledge.

Insights from Military Training Research and Practice

The disciplines of psychology and education have a long history of studying the learning process, what happens inside the learner, and the external conditions that bear upon the learning process. These extensive studies have resulted in countless learning principles and learning theories.

Learning psychologist Robert Gagne had a long and distinguished career working in the military as a researcher and as a university faculty member in both psychology and education. His presidential address to the American Psychological Association resulted in an article titled, "Military Training and the Principles of Learning" (Gagne, 1962). Addressing those with an orientation to studying the learner and the learning process, he presented a simple countertheory to effective training. He concluded from his years of research and practice that it was more important to analyze the detailed substance of the task to be learned than it was to analyze the learner. Furthermore, he advanced three principles (Gagne, 1962):

1. Provide instruction on a set of component tasks that build toward a final task.
2. Ensure that each component task is mastered.
3. Sequence the component tasks to ensure optimal transfer to the final task.

All three principles are predicated on a detailed analysis of the task expertise to be learned. As for trial-and-error experience, Gagne went on to illustrate its ineffectiveness. Assessment and feedback to the learners on their task experience while learning was found to be essential.

Documenting Workplace Expertise

Documenting required workplace expertise is a core activity in T&D. If it is done properly, this documentation has many uses. Documentation of workplace expertise clarifies the individual performance goals, provides invaluable information regarding the amount of effort needed to acquire the expertise, provides insights to select the best methods for developing the expertise, and provides the performance standards useful for creating learning goals and the criteria for assessing learner attainment of expertise. The overall process of documenting workplace expertise is illustrated in Figure 11.1.

The true substance of this process of analyzing expertise, as described earlier by Gagne, is in the detailed analysis of tasks (see Swanson, 2007). Three categories of tasks, each with a unique analysis process, are presented: Procedural Tasks, System Tasks, and Knowledge Tasks.

Learning Strategies for Realms of Expertise

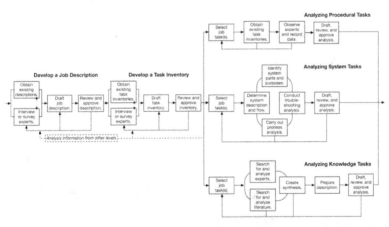

Figure 11.1 Overall Process of Documenting Workplace Expertise Source: Swanson, 2007, p.132.

The looming worry is that "T&D may become a kind of ritual, full of important-sounding terms and acronyms, trendy techniques, and clever activities, all supported by the latest technology but devoid of real learning" (Davis and Davis, 1998, p.2). Davis and Davis, educational psychologists, have created T&D strategies that embrace Gagne's view that studying

510

the task to be learned is more important than studying the learner in creating the desired expertise.

Based on extensive field research of the learning needs in organizations, they created specific learning strategies organized around general areas of expertise required in contemporary organizations. Their approach is to start from the identified realm of expertise and then go to the selection of an appropriate training strategy, providing complete details related to the conduct of the strategy based on learning research. The seven training strategies proposed by Davis and Davis (1998) include:

- The Behavioral Strategy: *Skill Development and Coaching*
- The Cognitive Strategy: *Presentations and Explanations*
- The Inquiry Strategy: *Critical, Creative, and Dialogical Thinking*
- The Mental Models Strategy: *Problem Solving and Decision Making*
- The Group Dynamics Strategy: *Human Relations and Teamwork*
- The Virtual Reality Strategy: *Role Play, Dramatic Scenarios, and Simulation*
- The Holistic Strategy: *Mentoring and Counseling*

The intent of these strategies is to bridge the desired expertise needs of an organization and provide efficient and effective learning methods for achieving them.

Expertise and Expert Performance

The Cambridge Handbook of Expertise and Expert Performance (Ericsson, Charness, Feltovich, and Hoffman, Eds., 2006) provides a voluminous account of the quest for understanding expertise. From a psychological perspective, the handbook pro vides the following generalizable characteristics of expertise (Ericsson, Charness, Feltovich, and Hoffman, Eds., 2006, pp.47–60):

Expertise is limited in its scope and elite performance does not transfer. People hardly ever reach the highest level in more than one domain. Even when domains are seemingly very similar, there is very little transfer in proficiency from one domain to another (Ericsson, Charness, Feltovich, and Hoffman, Eds., 2006).

Knowledge and content matter are important to expertise. Problem solving and expert performance in a specific realm are primarily a function of knowledge, patterns, and associated actions within that specific realm (Newell and Simon, 1972). Identifying the tasks and substance of expert performance gets beyond the general ability factors that are used to describe novices.

Expertise involves larger and more integrated cognitive units. The working environment of experts increases as they gain additional experience (Glaser and Chi, 1988). Experts chunk their knowledge and increase the size of those chunks for ready access.

Expertise involves functional, abstracted representations of presented information. While experts chunk their knowledge and can readily access and integrate it, novices get caught up in trying to impose organization and meaning to their tasks. "Experts see and represent a problem in their domain at a deeper (more principled) level than novices; novices tend to represent a problem at a superficial level" (Glaser and Chi, 1988, p.xviii).

Expertise involves automated basic strokes. Experts with great experience perform faster, smoother, and with less cognitive effort. Thus, they have additional reserve for reflection and added tasks (Ericsson, Charness, Feltovich, and Hoffman, Eds., 2006). Research has shown that automaticity is central to the development of expertise and that it is gained through practice.

Expertise involves selective access to relevant information. Experts demonstrate a selectivity in sorting through information that is very useful versus tangential (Patel and Groen, 1991). Experts demonstrate capacity to invert knowledge as illustrated in understanding a normal functional process versus thinking backwards when troubleshooting that same process when it is failing (Swanson, 2007).

Expertise involves reflection. Experts have the cognitive capacity to perform, as well as the capacity to reflect on their thinking and their methods (Glaser and Chi, 1988). Experts reflecting have the capacity to backtrack through information and evaluate, often withholding decisions until they are satisfied with their conclusion.

Expertise is an adaptation. "The development of expertise is largely a matter of amassing considerable skills, knowledge, and mechanisms that monitor and control cognitive processes to perform a delimited set of tasks efficiently and effectively. Experts restructure, reorganize, and refine their representation of knowledge and procedures for efficient application to their work a day environments" (Ericsson, Charness, Feltovich, and Hoffman, Eds., 2006, p.57).

Simple experience is not sufficient for the development of expertise. "Reviews of the relation between the amount of experience and the attained level of performance show consistently that once an acceptable level of performance is attained, there are hardly any benefits from the common kind of additional experience (Ericsson, Charness, Feltovich, and Hoffman, Eds., 2006, p.60). To improve performance, opportunities for reflection, exploration of alternatives, and problem solving in a protected environment and the help of other experts is required.

Understanding expert performance provides insights as to those who perform higher than most others up through those who attain the highest possible levels of human performance. In addition, understanding expert performance also provides insights as to the steps, stages, and process of attaining expertise.

The following contribution by Richard W. Herling is a distillation of related ideas related to expertise, not a meta-analysis of the literature. The purpose is to present a basic conceptual understanding of expertise as it applies to individual performance within the context of HRD. This understanding can then be used to formulate an *operational definition* of human expertise applicable to the theory and practice of HRD.

OPERATIONAL DEFINITIONS OFEXPERTISE AND COMPETENCE

Contributed by Richard W. Herling

When discussing the concept of human performance, there is a natural tendency to interchange the terms expert and expertise. Several assumptions should be made in developing an operational definition of expertise. The first assumption is that expertise represents a journey, not just a destination. Therefore the term "expertise" characterizes an active process from which experts emerge. The second assumption is that every person, because of his or her acquired experiences, possesses some level of expertise. The final assumption is that human expertise and its development is of primary interest and importance to HRD.

The Need for an Operational Understanding of Expertise

After decades of downsizing, right-sizing, restructuring, reorganizing, and reengineering (various perceived methods of attaining organizational effectiveness), organizations are beginning to realize that their expensive workforce can be thought of as one resource at their disposal which has the greatest potential for attaining and maintaining long-term profitability and growth, not simply a cost to be reduced. In many organizations, human resources are widely recognized as a significant competitive advantage (Pfeffer, 1994; Reichheld, 1996). As noted by Torraco and Swanson (1995), "business success increasingly hinges on an organization's ability to use its employee's expertise as a factor in the shaping of its business strategy" (p.11). Stated another way, it is the combined knowledge, experience, and expertise of the organization's human resources that has become the new competitive edge in the marketplace.

Competence May No Longer Be Enough

As a result of recognizing the workforce as a competitive advantage, caring about their human competence base, and how it is developed, business organizations and governments now realize that their market value increasingly relies on the knowledge and expertise of their employees (McLagan, 2002). Fortunately, a competent workforce is well within the grasp of any organization, but competence is not enough.

The potential to use specific sets of knowledge and skills is what Jacobs (2002) defines as employee competence, noting "employee competence should be viewed within its proper performance context" (p.281). In the context of most organizations, being competent only indicates that an employee has an ability to do something (one's job) at a satisfactory level and not necessarily at a level that would be considered as outstanding, exceeding expectations, or even above average. In open and adaptive systems, change is inevitable, and therefore the "proper performance context" is constantly being redefined. As represented by Swanson's taxonomy of performance (2007, p.24), the expertise required to maintain a system is significantly different from the expertise required to change the system.

This constant change and redefining serves to highlight the limitations of competence. To remain competitive, business organizations and the individuals within those organizations must be able to adapt to the "constantly changing world of new strategies, memberships on multiple teams, customer requirements, and competitive maneuvers" (McLagan, 1997, p.45). They must become top performers, not satisfactory performers.

Thus, to gain competitive advantage, it is the development of workplace expertise, not minimal competence, which is vital to optimal individual and organizational performance. HRD processes, at their best, provide the methods and the means for "improving performance through the development and unleashing of human expertise."

The Context for Understanding of Expertise
In the context of individual performance and human resource development, expertise is defined as "the optimal level at which a person is able and/or expected to perform within a specialized realm of human activity" (Swanson, 2007, p.125). As a descriptive definition of expertise, this provides clarity and focus as expertise is generally thought of as the possession of superior skills or knowledge in a particular area of study. Expertise is also generally recognized as implying proficiency, which is based on a common understanding that an individual gains expertise, and thus proficiency, only through experience and training.

Although an actual measurement of expertness remains illusive, the importance of quantifying expertise has long been recognized. The general level of expertise an individual possesses is readily observable through his or her actions. The need to quantify and the ease of recognizing various levels of expertness has resulted in the classification of different levels of human expertise using myriad terms, typically ranging from novice to expert (Jacobs, 2002; Hoffman, Shadbolt, Burton, and Klein, 1995; Bereiter and Scardamalia, 1993). Unfortunately, the classification of different levels of human expertise, without the ability to quantitatively measure expertise, has limited utility.

Linking Expertise to Performance through Measurement

It is well accepted that the performance of an organization can be evaluated and addressed at three levels: organization, process, and individual job performer (Rummler and Brache, 1995; Swanson, 2007), and that in regard to initiating performance improvement actions, the primary tool for linking the three levels of performance together is measurement. In fact, Rummler and Brache (1995) argue, "without measures we don't get the desired performance" (p.135), that "measurement is the foundation for managing organizations as systems" (p.134), and that it is only through measurement that performance can be monitored, managed, and improved. Swanson (2007), in a more direct manner, simply notes "it is foolhardy to talk about development, change, and performance improvement without specifying the measure of performance" (p.67).

This perspective establishes a clear need for the measurement of expertise—for a definition of the term that will support the efforts of an organization to improve its performance by enabling the performance levels of its human resources to be quantified. Current descriptive definitions of expertise do not meet this need because they do not operationally define what expertise is.

Theoretical Perspectives on Expertise

In the past thirty years entire books, complete chapters, and numerous papers have been written in response to the question: What is expertise? (Chi, Glaser, and Farr, 1988; Slatter, 1990; Ericcson and Smith, 1991; Bereiter and Scardamalia, 1993; Swanson, 2007). For the purpose of developing a basic conceptual understanding of expertise, an in-depth review of the past literature is not necessary; instead it can be derived from a brief examination of several theoretical perspectives.

Cognitive Theories of Expertise

The focused research efforts on the topic of experts and expertise began with the study of expert chess players by deGoot and his published findings in 1965. The flurry of research activity that immediately followed this initial event studied the differences in performance between experts and nonexperts (Johnson, 1988).

After researchers studied expert and nonexpert differences in various human domains, the focus shifted to exploring basic information-processing capabilities inside individuals. These studies resulted in "theories of problem-solving being stated in terms of the human information-processing system" (Kuchinke, 1997). These theories provided the basis for second generation theories that focused on the expert's ability to solve complex problems. The outcome of this refocused research effort, as summarized by Glaser and Chi (1988) and included in Kuchinke's (1997) update of the current theories and literature, was the identification of several key characteristics of experts related to how they solve problems and how they acquire, process, and retrieve information. This combined research indicated that experts (1) know more, (2) use the information they have differently, (3) have better recall, (4) solve problems faster, (5) see problems at a deeper level, (6) analyze problems qualitatively, and (7) are more aware of their ability to make mistakes.

Research on expertise theory is still evolving. Based on a realization that there may be no single *expert way,* current theory and research work is examining expertise as an "ability to rapidly organize and process small bits of information into meaningful and creative solutions to specific problems" (Kuchinke, 1997).

Overview of the Knowledge Engineering Theories of Expertise

While the cognitive psychologists attempted to discover what was required to be an expert, knowledge engineering, another area of study highly interested in human expertise, took a different approach and focused on the replication of human expertise.

Through their attempts to create artificial intelligence, the work of knowledge engineers focused on how an expert thinks. Their results and findings closely paralleled the work of the cognitive psychologists. Over the decades, the knowledge engineers theorized expertise as a thinking process and formulated five major model classifications of human expertise: heuristic models, deep models, implicit models, competence models, and distributed models (Slatter, 1990).

In the beginning, the heuristic models loosely defined expertise as the acquisition of lots of information, including heuristic knowledge—knowledge about a specific domain. Heuristic knowledge, the problem-solving rules of thumb of a specific domain, was seen as the *shallow knowledge.*

The *deep knowledge* models advanced the general theory of expertise by suggesting that experts use "hierarchical relationships, causal models and specialist representation of domain objects ... capturing the temporal, spatial, and/or analogical properties" of the domain to solve complex problems (Slatter, 1990, p.138).

The implicit models that followed this initial work of the knowledge engineers, attempted to explain expertise by differentiating between implicit knowledge and explicit knowledge. In this context, explicit knowledge was seen to encompass the known facts of a specific domain, while implicit knowledge represented the "non-articulable experience-base knowledge that enables a skilled expert to solve a task in an effortless, seemingly intuitive fashion" (Slatter, 1990, p.141).

The competence models made a distinction between domain knowledge (static knowledge) and task knowledge (action knowledge). The implication is that expertise is a competence-level term denoting the potential for *doing something.* These models of expertise recognize that experts know a great deal about a specific domain and that experts use this knowledge to effectively solve problems. The task knowledge, which is gained from the practice of domain-specific behaviors, is compiled by the expert within his or her domain of knowledge in an ongoing search for better ways to do things, including problem solving.

The underlying assumption of the fifth class of expertise models, the distributed models, is that the expertise required to solve complex problems may be distributed among many individuals. The distributed models explain expertise as being a combination of domain knowledge, task knowledge, and cooperative knowledge (knowledge about how one communicates and interacts with others). Consequently, these models are more concerned with what an expert must know to cooperatively solve problems.

The Elements of Expertise

Although a large body of knowledge has been, and continues to be, added to our understanding of the nature of expertise by the cognitive psychologists, cognitive scientists, and knowledge engineers, after thirty years of advancing research on this topic have not been able to agree on what expertise is. In fact, Kuchinke's (1997) review of the expertise theories and Slatter's (1990) summary explanation of the expertise models have shown, through a lack of consensus, that human expertise cannot be operationally defined by its processes. However, the combined summaries of the two reviewers have brought to light several commonly shared elements in the various theories of expertise: (1) Expertise is a dynamic state; (2) expertise is domain specific; and (3) the basic components of expertise are knowledge and associated skills, experience, and problem-solving heuristics. Figure 11.2 is presented as a representation of the relationship of these three foundational concepts of expertise.

Working from this perspective, the most important concept of expertise is that it is a dynamic state—an internal process of continuous learning by the individual characterized by the constant acquisition of knowledge, reorganization of information, and progressive solving of problems. The importance of recognizing expertise as a dynamic state lies in the realization that a person never stops acquiring expertise. Bereiter and Scardamalia (1993) summarized the dynamic characteristic of expertise in their descriptive comparison of experts and nonexperts. The "career of the expert is one of progressively advancing on problems constituting a field of work, whereas the career of the nonexpert is one of gradually constricting the field of work so that it more closely conforms to the routines the nonexpert is prepared to execute" (p.11).

526

The second shared element, that of expertise being domain-specific, may have the most impact on the future creation of programs designed to develop expertise in individuals. The majority of research suggests that extensive, specialized knowledge is "required for excellence in most fields" (Gleespen, 1996, p.502). Research also indicates that "there is little evidence that a person highly skilled in one domain can transfer the skill to another" (Glaser and Chi, 1988, p.xvii). Cognitive psychologists have theorized that "there are some domains where nearly everyone becomes an expert, like reading English words" (Posner, 1988, p.xxxi), but note that the demonstration of expertise in one domain is no guarantee of expertise in other areas (Glaser, 1985, p.7).

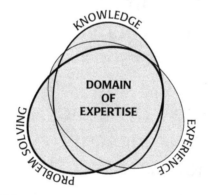

Figure 11.2 The Basic Components of Expertise

The third foundational concept highlighted by the earlier review of the expertise models and theories is that expertise is composed of a few basic components. Although there was not always agreement among the researchers as to which component took precedence, all identified in some manner knowledge, experience, and problem-solving heuristics as the distinguishing points of difference between experts and nonexperts. These three common elements can be viewed as the fundamental components of human expertise. Each one is clearly measurable, and therefore it is reasonable to expect that an operational definition of expertise can be developed from them.

To validate the proposed definition, a closer examination of each of the three components is required.

The Knowledge Component of Expertise

Knowledge appeared in every reviewed theory and model of expertise, and in almost every case it was either descriptively different, or multiple types of knowledge were specified.

Depending upon the theories or models being examined, the knowledge required for expertise could be implicit or explicit, shallow or deep, task specific or heuristic. Bereiter and Scardamalia (1993), in their inquiry into the nature of expertise, noted that "every kind of knowledge has a part in expertise" (p.74). Their definition for every kind of knowledge included what they classified as the obvious kinds of knowledge—procedural knowledge and formal knowledge—as well as what they referred to as the less obvious kinds—informal knowledge, impressionistic knowledge, and self-regulatory knowledge.

Although there may be some disagreement among the theories and models regarding the specific type of knowledge required for expertise, the theorists are in agreement on two points. First, that for the purposes of expertise, knowledge is, and has to be, domain-specific. Second, that knowledge is an interactive component of expertise, one of the requirements for expertise, but not expertise in and of itself. As noted by Bereiter and Scardamalia (1993), nonexperts, as well as experts, have knowledge, "the difference is in how much they have, how well integrated it is, and how effectively it is geared to performance" (p.74).

The Experience Component of Expertise

Just as it is recognized that all experts are knowledgeable, it is also understood that all experts are experienced. Based on their studies of master's-level chess players, Chase and Simon (1973), as cited in Posner (1988), "reasoned that to achieve a master level of expertise a player had to spend between 10,000 and 20,000 hours staring at chess positions" (p.xxxi). A number of years later, through the studied biographies of experts in many fields, it was generalized that 10,000 hours was the minimum amount of time required to gain expert experience (Bereiter and Scardamalia, 1993, p.17). Thus it has been hypothesized from the research, but not verified, that to become an expert one must have the equivalent of ten years of combined studies and related work experience.

Unfortunately, the term experience, like that of expertise, is a term of varied meanings currently lacking qualifying and quantifying boundaries. When specifically related to the development of human expertise, experience is an interactive component that is heavily dependent upon the type and quality, as well as the quantity, of the events experienced by the individual. As Bereiter and Scardamalia (1993) observed in the performance of equally experienced schoolteachers, based on the training received and the number of years worked, experience in this context "distinguishes old-timers from beginners, but does not distinguish experts from experienced non-experts" (p.81).

The Problem-Solving Component of Expertise

The key to expertise thus appears to lie in the third component, an individual's propensity to solve problems. The knowledge engineers, in attempting to replicate the process of applying expertise, have viewed problem solving as the core concept of expertise, and like the concept of knowledge, have ended up describing and identifying a multitude of problem-solving processes.

The concept of problem solving as the primary component of expertise has also been heavily supported by the research of cognitive psychologists and scientists, as summarized by Glaser in his *Thoughts on Expertise* (Glaser, 1987, as cited by Chi, Glaser, and Farr, 1988). Bereiter and Scardamalia (1993) took the emphasis on this concept one step further by describing problem solving as the dynamic element in the growth of expertise.

Problem solving, as the term is currently used in cognitive psychology, constitutes some amount of searching and/or deliberation in order to find a way to achieve a goal, defining a problem as any nonroutine purposeful activity (Bereiter and Scardamalia, 1993).

Wertheimer, an early Gestalt psychologist whose studies and research centered on insightful learning, focused on the abilities required by the individual to solve problems effectively. In his book *Productive Thinking* (1945), Wertheimer placed the emphasis on the type of solution used for solving a problem rather than on the problem itself. Wertheimer believed that problem solutions depended upon the previous experience of the problem solver, noting that "the prime difference was in the originality used by the problem solver to organize information," (Hill, 1971, p.102). Wertheimer also believed that true problem solving involved a "real understanding" of both the problem and the environment in which the problem was framed, which in turn would lead to an insightful solution.

Wertheimer's concepts of real understanding and insightful solutions can also be seen at the core of Bereiter and Scardamalia's (1993) description of expert and nonexpert problem solving. Bereiter and Scardamalia see problem solving as the single dynamic element in the growth of expertise and experts as being progressive problem solvers, while "the problem-solving efforts of the nonexpert is taken over by well learned routines ... aimed at eliminating still more problems thus reducing the activity even further" (p.81).

Forming an Operational Definition of Expertise

From the preceeding examination of the foundational components of expertise, it can be seen that nonexperts can have vast amounts of knowledge, can have many years of experience, and can also solve problems. Thus, a definition of expertise based simply on combining the elements of knowledge, experience, and problem solving would have very little value.

It is generally agreed that the presence of expertise is readily recognized in an individual's actions and that we know expertise when we see it. Basing an operational definition on the characteristics of displayed behavior does carry a degree of practicality.

Experts are capable of doing things at a higher level; they have more knowledge, a greater skill level, and better solutions (VanLehn, 1989). The expert-novice research of different occupations (domains) has verified that this is true (Glaser and Chi, 1988; Van-Lehn, 1989; Ericcson and Smith, 1991). The fundamental basis of expert research has been based on the fact that there are observed differences in the displayed behavior of individuals engaged in the same activities. Thus, the concept of "demonstrated behavior" is essential in formulating an operational definition of expertise.

Behavior, as applied to the discussion of expertise, implies an intended behavior, or action, on the part of the individual, and an action has a consequence, it terminates with a result. Results, and the actions which lead to them, are measurable. Gilbert (1996), equating individual performance to a relationship involving both a behavior and its resulting consequence, believed that the result of behavior should be viewed in the context of value, "the consequence as a valuable accomplishment," a "valuable performance" (Gilbert, 1996, p.17). Thus, individual performance can be quantified by comparing the value of the result of the performance to a predetermined standard assessed in terms of time, quality, quantity, or cost. From this perspective, individual performance is representative of the effectiveness of the consequences of an individual's intended behavior.

Competence is related to expertise. Barrie and Pace (1997) identify this "capacity to think about performance and also to perform" (p.337) as competence, which concurs with Morf's (1986) much earlier definition. Morf defined competence as the product of "the worker's motivational dispositions and abilities that are relevant in the context of work" (p.15).

Morf (1986) attempted to operationalize this relationship of individual performance to competence by stating that it is "a function of the interaction of the person and the work environment" (p.113). Based on the premise that "the aspect of the worker most frequently influenced by performance is ability levels," Morf equated competence to the "new skills developed and new knowledge acquired in the very process of doing a job" (p.14). In other words, the key element in Morf's formula for performance was expertise.

Unlike Morf, Gilbert (1996) saw competence not as a *component* of performance, but as a *function* of "worthy performance" expressed as "the ratio of valuable accomplishments to costly behavior" (p.18). Gilbert believed worthy performance was a product of both the work environment and an individual's repertoire of behavior, or the specialized responses, knowledge, and understanding of a specific area (domain). In Gilbert's mind, competent people were those individuals who could create valuable results without using excessively costly behavior, and his standard of competence was exemplary performance, which he qualified as the "historically best instance of performance" (p.30).

Competence can thus be seen as a displayed characteristic of expertise and measurable subsets within an individual's domain of expertise (Figure 11.3).

From this examination of the characteristics of individual performance and competence, as displayed behavior which is effective, efficient and thus measurable, the remaining pieces of an operational definition of human expertise have been uncovered. As previously stated, we recognize expertise in others by their demonstrated actions. Expanding upon this observation, we recognize experts as those individuals who do things better than anyone else. Experts, in their area of expertise, demonstrate their acquired expertise through outstanding performance, and this means that they can consistently do things more effectively and efficiently than nonexperts.

Expertise can thus be operationally defined by these two desired characteristics of displayed behavior—*the consistent demonstrated actions of an individual which are (1) efficient in their execution and (2) effective in their results.*

Figure 11.3 Competence of a Subset of Expertise

Implications of Expertise for HRD

As a general premise, HRD exists to serve the organization. While the activity of learning can contribute to performance, from the organization's perspective it is only those activities which clearly improve performance that will be seen as value-added. Optimal performance has precedence over minimal performance, and in this context the ability to quantify expertise—efficient and effective behavior—can be seen as having significant implications to HRD.

One could argue that defining expertise adds no value because performance is reflective of only the lowest level of responsive behavior, and that it is competence which promotes efficiency (Barrie and Pace, 1997). Such an argument lacks merit, for although expertise and competence are clearly linked and unquestionably similar in nature, they are distinctly different. Figure 11.3 illustrates, by the relationship to expertise, the limitations of competence as the ultimate desired outcome.

Competence can be visualized as subsets of expertise. In other words, competence reflects very task-specific actions and is therefore found within an individual's domain of expertise, not encircling it. In addition, competence, with its primary goal being efficient action, can be seen as both narrowing in its nature and static, unlike expertise which is dynamic and expanding. Competence is seen and described as an outcome (McLagan, 1997), a destination, while expertise is clearly a process (Bereiter and Scardamalia, 1993), a journey. Finally, competence is limited to a specific domain of knowledge or expertise, while the individual's area of expertise, while also recognized as domain specific, is not limited to a single domain but often extends into several related domains. As shown by the example in Figure 11.4, the competencies are tasks specific to selling houses, but the specific domain of expertise—Selling Houses—overlaps the related, but more general, domains of Selling, Marketing, and Real Estate. With the support of this example it should be evident that HRD must look past competence and focus on the development of expertise as a desired outcome in the process of improving performance.

This is not to say that the need or importance of learning, and the competencies that it supports, is diminished. It has always been generally understood that the acquisition of expertise requires study, practice, and experience, although it has never been clear as to how much of each is needed. The result of this lack of understanding has often been a "more-is-better" approach to providing training. Equipped with an operational definition of expertise, the HRD professional is positioned to gain a better understanding of the requirements for improving performance through the development of the organization's human resources.

The proposed operational definition of expertise allows the actions of exemplary performers within an organization to be benchmarked in qualitative and quantitative terms. This provides HRD the opportunity to focus on the development and implementation of training interventions designed to accelerate both the acquisition of specific knowledge and skills and the transfer of this expertise. However, even in this focused activity there is a potential danger should the goal of these activities be misconstrued by HRD to be the development of experts instead of expertise. As Rummler and Brache (1995) have emphasized, while failure to measure the right things results in no performance improvement, choosing to measure the wrong things (or measuring the right things for the wrong reasons) results in a loss of performance.

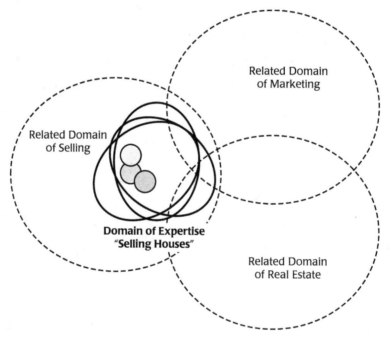

Figure 11.4 The Limitations of Competence

CONCLUSION

Based on Herling's prior analysis, human expertise is clearly a complex, multi-faceted phenomenon, but by the means of an operational definition, expertise can be expressed in measurable terms. He defines *expertise* as

> displayed behavior within a specialized domain and/or related domain in the form of consistently demonstrated actions of an individual which are both optimally efficient in their execution and effective in their results.

Competence, a related construct and component of expertise, can also be expressed in measurable terms and defined as

> displayed behavior within a specialized domain in the form of consistently demonstrated actions of an individual which are both minimally efficient in their execution and effective in their results.

Through the use of an operational definition of expertise and the recognition of domain specific (1) knowledge, (2) experience, and (3) problem solving as being the core elements of expertise, the HRD profession gains conceptual access to one of the most powerful tools for improving performance. Without the capacity to think and deal with substantive issues of the expertise required by organizations, HRD interventions will be limited to low-level programs like new employee orientation training and general team-building exercises.

REFLECTION QUESTIONS

1. What exactly is expertise and why is it important to HRD?
2. Cite a personal experience that illustrates the concept of expertise.
3. What is the difference between knowledge, competence, and expertise?
4. How would HRD/T&D differ if it were committed to developing *knowledge* versus *expertise?*
5. How would HRD/T&D differ if it were committed to *competence* versus *expertise?*
6. What challenges to the profession arise from focusing on expertise as an outcome of T&D? How could they be overcome?

Books For ALL Kinds of Readers

At ReadHowYouWant we understand that one size does not fit all types of readers. Our innovative, patent pending technology allows us to design new formats to make reading easier and more enjoyable for you. This helps improve your speed of reading and your comprehension. Our EasyRead printed books have been optimized to improve word recognition, ease eye tracking by adjusting word and line spacing as well as minimizing hyphenation. Our EasyRead SuperLarge editions have been developed to make reading easier and more accessible for vision-impaired readers. We offer Braille and DAISY formats of our books and all popular E-Book formats.

We are continually introducing new formats based upon research and reader preferences. Visit our web-site to see all of our formats and learn how you can Personalize our books for yourself or as gifts. Sign up to Become A (RHYW) Registered Reader.

www.readhowyouwant.com

CPSIA information can be obtained
at www.ICGtesting.com
Printed in the USA
BVHW050906300820
587367BV00003B/33